Surveillance Futures

From birth to adulthood, children now find themselves navigating a network of surveillance devices that attempt to identify, quantify, sort and track their thoughts, movements and actions. This book is the first collection to focus exclusively on technological surveillance and young people. Organised around three key spheres of children's day-to-day life: schooling, the self and social lives, this book chronicles the increasing surveillance which children, of all ages, are subject to. Numerous surveillance apparatus and tools are examined, including, but not limited to: mobile phones, surveillance cameras, online monitoring, GPS and RFID tracking and big data analytics. In addition to chronicling the steady rise of such surveillance practices, the chapters in this volume identify and problematise the consequences of technological surveillance from a range of multidisciplinary perspectives. Bringing together leading scholars working across diverse fields – including sociology, education, health, criminology, anthropology, philosophy, media and information technology – the collection highlights the significant socio-political and ethical implications of technological surveillance throughout childhood and youth.

Emmeline Taylor is a Senior Lecturer at the Australian National University and has been researching the exponential growth of surveillance technologies in schools and the increasing monitoring of young people for over a decade. She is the author of Surveillance Schools: Security, Discipline and Control in Contemporary Education (Palgrave Macmillan, 2013).

Tonya Rooney is a Lecturer in the Faculty of Education and Arts at the Australian Catholic University and has published widely on children and surveillance technologies.

Emerging Technologies, Ethics and International Affairs

Series Editors: Steven Barela, Jai C. Galliott, Avery Plaw and Katina Michael

This series examines the crucial ethical, legal and public policy questions arising from or exacerbated by the design, development and eventual adoption of new technologies across all related fields, from education and engineering to medicine and military affairs. The books revolve around two key themes:

- Moral issues in research, engineering and design; and
- Ethical, legal and political/policy issues in the use and regulation of technology.

This series encourages submission of cutting-edge research monographs and edited collections with a particular focus on forward-looking ideas concerning innovative or as yet undeveloped technologies. Whilst there is an expectation that authors will be well grounded in philosophy, law or political science, consideration will be given to future-orientated works that cross these disciplinary boundaries. The interdisciplinary nature of the series editorial team offers the best possible examination of works that address the 'ethical, legal and social' implications of emerging technologies.

Most recent titles

1. Social Robots: Boundaries, Potential, Challenges
   Marco Nørskov
2. Legitimacy and Drones: Investigating the Legality, Morality and Efficacy of UCAVs
   Steven J. Barela
3. Super Soldiers: The Ethical, Legal and Social Implications
   Jai Galliott and Mianna Lotz
4. Commercial Space Exploration: Ethics, Policy and Governance
   Jai Galliott
5. Healthcare Robots: Ethics, Design and Implementation
   Aimee van Wynsberghe

Surveillance Futures

Social and ethical implications of new technologies for children and young people

Edited by
Emmeline Taylor and Tonya Rooney

LONDON AND NEW YORK

First published 2017 by Routledge

2 Park Square, Milton Park, Abingdon, Oxfordshire OX14 4RN
52 Vanderbilt Avenue, New York, NY 10017

Routledge is an imprint of the Taylor & Francis Group, an informa business

First issued in paperback 2019

British Library Cataloguing-in-Publication Data
A catalogue record for this book is available from the British Library

Library of Congress Cataloging-in-Publication Data
Names: Taylor, Emmeline (Convenor of criminology), editor. | Rooney, Tonya.
Title: Surveillance Futures/ edited by Emmeline Taylor and Tonya Rooney.
Description: Abingdon, Oxon ; New York, NY : Routledge, 2016. | Includes bibliographical references.
Identifiers: LCCN 2016008652| ISBN 9781472455635 (hardback) | ISBN 9781315611402 (ebook)
Subjects: LCSH: Electronic monitoring of youth. | Electronic monitoring of children. | Electronic monitoring of students. | Electronic surveillance. | Schools—Safety measures. | Parent and child. | Technology and youth—Social aspects.
Classification: LCC HQ799.2.E54 S87 2016 | DDC 303.48/30835—dc23
LC record available at https://lccn.loc.gov/2016008652

ISBN: 978-1-4724-5563-5 (hbk)
ISBN: 978-0-367-28163-2 (pbk)

Typeset in Times New Roman PS
by diacriTech, Chennai

An important collection that addresses the place of children as vital targets of new (as well as longstanding) surveillance practices. Contributors raise important questions about transformations in power, privacy and identity, accentuating how concern for the wellbeing of children can often culminate in forms of coercion and control.

Kevin D. Haggerty, University of Alberta, Canada

Youth today are exposed to an overwhelming and diverse array of surveillance applications. Creepy spy toys, drug tests, GPS location tracking, mobile phone monitoring, extractive games, and social media sites represent just some of the many controlling mechanisms that shape kids' lives. This book offers a remarkable multi-disciplinary investigation into this understudied but hugely important area.

Torin Monahan, The University of North Carolina, United States

This timely volume advances our understanding of how it is to grow up in the surveillance age. It documents how surveillance technologies and practices saturate the years from early childhood to adolescence and beyond. The collection provides an outstanding contribution to literature on the changing nature of surveillance in the 21st century.

Heidi Mork Lomell, University of Oslo, Norway

Contents

Acknowledgements

We are indebted to many people, both professionally and personally, who have helped to make this book a reality. We would particularly like to thank the authors for their generous contributions. Every author was approached because they were known to be an active researcher on the topic of surveillance and young people, and we are grateful for their efforts towards ensuring that the collection offers new, timely and important research.

We drew upon the good will and expertise of several academic colleagues and friends and we'd like to thank them for their very helpful insights and suggestions, in particular Michael Birnhack, Pete Fussey, Kevin Haggerty, Aaron Kupchik, Sandra Leaton-Gray, Ian Loader, Jason Nolen, Anastasia Powell, Priscilla Regan, Peter Rogers, Paul Tranter and Jennifer Whitson.

We would also like to thank the series editors, Jai Galliott, Avery Plaw and Katina Michael, and the publishing team.

Notes on Contributors

Carol Barron is an academic in the School of Nursing and Human Sciences at Dublin City University. Carol holds a PhD in Anthropology. Her research interests focus on children's play, play spaces and mobility. She has also published in the area of participatory research methodologies with children. Carol is the Chairperson of Súgradh, the national Irish organisation, promoting the child's right to play in Ireland. She is currently working with historical archives examining children's play in the early twentieth century.

Thomas Crofts is Professor of Criminal Law and Director of the Sydney Institute of Criminology at the University of Sydney Law School. His research in criminal law, criminology and criminal justice centres on criminalisation and criminal responsibility, particularly the criminal responsibility of and for children, comparative criminal law, and criminal law reform. He is the co-author of *Sexting and Young People* (Palgrave Macmillan 2015), co-editor of *Queering Criminology* (Palgrave, 2016) and *Criminalisation and Criminal Responsibility* (OUP, 2015), and author of *Criminal Responsibility of Children and Young People* (Ashgate, 2002) as well as several criminal law texts.

Jessica Nihlén Fahlquist is a Senior Lecturer at the Centre for Research Ethics and Bioethics at Uppsala University, Sweden. Her research focuses on concepts and notions of moral responsibility and ethical aspects of risks in health, engineering and environment. Her publications include articles in *Public Health Ethics*, *Journal of Agricultural and Environmental Ethics*, *Science and Engineering Ethics* and *Nursing Ethics*.

Michael Gard is Associate Professor of Health, Sport and Physical Education at the University of Queensland. He teaches, researches and writes about how the human body is and has been used, experienced, studied, educated and governed. His published work includes numerous journal articles and book chapters on this theme and the following authored books: *The Obesity Epidemic: Science, Morality and Ideology* with Jan Wright (Routledge, 2005), *Men Who*

Dance: Aesthetics, Athletics and the Art of Masculinity (Peter Lang, 2006), *The End of the Obesity Epidemic,* (Routledge, 2011) and *Schools and Public Health: Past, Present, Future*, with Carolyn Pluim (Lexingham Books, 2014).

Andrew Hope is Associate Professor in the School of Social Sciences at the University of Adelaide where he currently leads the criminology programmes. His research interests include surveillance in late modernity, risk and cultural criminology, Foucault, social control and resistance and critical explorations of educational technology. He has published widely on these topics.

Murray Lee is Professor in Criminology at the University of Sydney Law School and Sydney Institute of Criminology. He has published widely in the areas of representations and perceptions of crime, and crime and technology. He is author *of Inventing Fear of Crime: Criminology and the Politics of Anxiety*, co-author of *Policing and Media: Public Relations, Simulations and Communications*, and *Sexting and Young People*, and co-editor of *Fear of Crime: Critical Voices in an Age of Anxiety*. Murray is also editor of the scholarly journal *Current Issues in Criminal Justice.*

Deborah Lupton is Centenary Research Professor in the News and Media Research Centre, Faculty of Arts and Design, University of Canberra. Her latest books are *Medicine as Culture,* 3rd edition (2012), *Fat* (2013), *Risk*, 2nd edition (2013), *The Social Worlds of the Unborn* (2013), (as editor) *The Unborn Human* (2013), *Digital Sociology* (2015) and *The Quantified Self: A Sociology of Self-Tracking* (forthcoming). Her current research interests are in the social impacts of big data, self-tracking cultures, the digitisation of children, academic work in the digital era and critical digital health studies.

Emma Rich is Senior Lecturer in Sport and Education, Department of Education, University of Bath. Her research engages with the varied expressions of active physicality as they emerge in different sites and practices of contemporary culture, drawing on the disciplines of physical cultural studies and public pedagogy. She has co-authored *The Medicalization of Cyberspace* (2008); *Education, Disordered Eating and Obesity Discourse: Fat Fabrications* (2008) and *Debating Obesity: Critical Perspectives* (2011).

Tonya Rooney is a Lecturer at the Australian Catholic University and has published widely on children and surveillance technologies, engaging in particular with themes of trust, risk and vulnerability. Tonya's research interests focus on the spatial and affective dimensions of children's encounters with the world, drawing on the disciplines of philosophy, childhood studies, science and technology studies and critical geographies.

Valerie Steeves is Associate Professor in the Department of Criminology, University of Ottawa. Her research interests span privacy and surveillance, human rights and technology, media stereotyping and online hate propaganda and pornography. She has published widely on the digital child and young people's online networking and privacy.

Emmeline Taylor is a Senior Lecturer at the Australian National University and has been researching the exponential growth of surveillance technologies in schools and the increasing monitoring of young people for over a decade. She is the author of *Surveillance Schools: Security, Discipline and Control in Contemporary Education* (2013), shortlisted for the British Society of Criminology annual book prize and the *Surveillance and Society Journal* book prize 2014. She is an elected associate member of the Surveillance Studies Network and committee member of the Australian and New Zealand Society of Criminology.

Rosamunde Van Brakel is a researcher and PhD candidate at LSTS – Vrije Universiteit Brussel. Her project, from which her chapter draws, is titled 'Taming the Future? A Rhizomatic Analysis of Preemptive Surveillance of Children and Its Consequences'. In addition to her PhD research, she currently works as a seconded research fellow on the Big Data, Privacy and Security project for the Scientific Council for Government Policy in The Netherlands and is daily coordinator and CFO of the annual international conference Computers, Privacy and Data Protection in Brussels. She is an associate member of the Surveillance Studies Network and executive director of the NGO Privacy Salon vzw.

Jacqueline Ryan Vickery is Assistant Professor in the Department of Media Arts at the University of North Texas. She conducts research on young people's digital media practices as they intersect with issues of equity, identity, privacy, literacy and policy. She approaches research from a qualitative perspective and draws methodologically from ethnography, feminist media theory and discourse analysis. Additionally, she teaches courses on social activism, digital media and youth cultures.

Ben Williamson is a Lecturer in the School of Education at the University of Stirling. He led the Code Acts in Education project to examine the role of software code, algorithms and big data practices in shaping educational spaces, policies and institutions. His published research articles focus on the participation of think tanks, innovation labs and emerging data companies in education and public service reform in the context of current social scientific debates about digital data. He has also researched the formation of the movement around 'learning to code' and 'digital making' and has examined the technological practices and organisations involved in 'educating the smart city'. He is co-author of *Learning Identities in a Digital Age: Rethinking Creativity, Education and Technology* (2013).

1 Digital playgrounds

Growing up in the surveillance age

Emmeline Taylor and Tonya Rooney

Surveillance has always been a feature of childhood. However, recent technological innovations have enabled the monitoring of young people to reach unprecedented levels of intensity and ubiquity. Children now find themselves navigating a network of surveillance devices that attempt to identify, quantify, sort and track their thoughts, movements and actions. This collection explores surveillance practices across multiple spheres of childhood and youth, from birth to adulthood. Numerous surveillance apparatus and tools are examined, including, but not limited to, mobile phones, surveillance cameras, online monitoring and GPS tracking. In addition to chronicling the steady rise of such surveillance practices, the chapters in this volume identify and problematise the consequences of technological surveillance from a range of multidisciplinary perspectives. Bringing together leading scholars working across diverse fields – including health, education, sociology, anthropology, philosophy, criminology, media and information technology – the collection draws together a range of perspectives on the social and ethical impacts of technological surveillance throughout childhood and youth.

Emerging trends in childhood surveillance

Childhood is a relatively new concept (Ariès, 1962) and understandings of this formative period continue to shift and evolve. Children have historically been viewed in conflicting ways. Drawing from Nietzsche, Jenks (2005) identifies two archetypal categories of children in Western culture: the 'Apollonian child', perceived as innocent and pure, and the 'Dionysian child', viewed as uncivilised, immoral and potentially evil. In contemporary society, arguably the former is subjected to surveillance mechanisms to preserve this innocence and protect them from the harms prevalent in the world, whereas the latter group receives routinised monitoring by omnipresent and diverse surveillance mechanisms to contain their perceived incivility. Common idioms, such as 'keeping an eye on the kids', expose the inherent complexities and contradictions harboured by surveillance practices; on the one hand, surveillance can be perceived as a protective measure to stave off exposure to potential dangers; on the other hand, it can refer to assurance that young people do not cause trouble or mischief (Taylor, 2013). There is certainly ambiguity regarding the applications of surveillance. Lyon (2003) suggests that the underlying reasons for surveillance can be situated along a 'continuum from care to control', arguing that 'some element of care and some element of control are nearly always present'. Similarly, Nelson and Garey (2009: 8) view the motivations of care and control 'in a dialectical relationship with each other, and not a simple dichotomous one'.

Complicating things further, surveillance is often viewed as being imposed on reluctant subjects, but this 'fails to recognise that often individuals are complicit in their own surveillance and at times even court the salacious opportunity for exposure that various forms of surveillance provide' (Taylor, 2013: 9). In this sense, children are viewed here as active agents in the emerging forms of subjectivity, creativity, performativity and resistance that arise through the possibilities and challenges of living in the contemporary surveillance society. The relationship between children and technology is (re)configured in a number of ways, ultimately revealing a fluid and emerging notion of subjectivity where children and technologies both shape and are shaped by the world around them (Prout, 2005). A central aim of this collection is to make visible the concealed workings of the multiple surveillance technologies that increasingly permeate the lives of young people and explore the significant social and ethical issues they animate.

Even before birth, surveillance technologies make their presence felt. With developments in pre-natal ultrasound and imaging techniques, the level of information available about the child before he/she is born is expanding, as are the corresponding challenges and pressures on parents to obtain information and make decisions for and about their unborn child. It is no longer unusual for pre-natal scan images of a foetus in utero to be shared via social media (Leaver, 2015; Lupton, 2013a), resulting in the most intimate of realms, the child in the mother's womb, being offered for public consumption. Utilising social media sites, such as Facebook and Instagram, the progress of the child is charted through infancy and beyond. For example, a survey of parents in ten countries revealed that more than 80 per cent of parents with a social media profile had shared images of their child under the age of two years (Holloway *et al.*, 2013). Once parents could playfully tease their children by threatening to show a new girlfriend or boyfriend pictures of them when they were babies, now the images are stored in perpetuity, a potential source of embarrassment for future selves but, more importantly, compromising their right to be forgotten.

Once a baby is born, surveillance of the infant child often begins in the hospital. This includes many measures of health and well-being, but increasingly is augmented with a range of new surveillant technologies. One of the most longstanding applications of radio frequency identification (RFID) is in the paediatric area of hospitals (Baldwin, 2005). Some hospitals place a bracelet around the baby's ankle embedded with an RFID chip that is matched to the mother's. For example, 'Hugs' is an RFID system that can be linked to the hospital's security system so that if the signal between reader and receiver is interrupted, security cameras are activated, electronic doors are locked, elevators cease operating and essentially the ward is placed in 'lockdown' (Wyld, 2009). Furthermore, if the bracelet is cut or tampered with, it will trigger an alarm. Wyld (2009) outlines how the Hugs RFID system was credited with assisting in preventing the abduction of a baby in 2005 from a hospital in North Carolina, which has since secured the system as a 'necessary precaution'. Despite the rarity of newborn abduction (Goodman, cited in Wyld, 2009) and the 'exceedingly small' likelihood of this happening, the use of RFID on newborn infants is steadily becoming the accepted standard in the safeguarding of babies. But it's not just the threat of abduction, the RFID-enabled system also has a complementary component, 'Kisses', which links the child to its mother. Should a baby be 'mismatched' with the wrong parent, an audible alarm sounds (Wyld, 2009), whilst the correct pairing results in a gentle lullaby being played. The use of terms of affection such as 'hugs' and 'kisses' to promote an infant security system is an example of how surveillance marketers can co-opt 'care' discourses in an attempt to personalise what is a highly impersonal, and arguably excessive, response system.

At home, the devices available to parents to watch and monitor their child now extend far beyond baby monitors that transmit sound from the child to apparatus and even clothing that measure a baby's breathing and conditions, such as temperature and humidity and that send alarms or messages to parents if any unusual datum presents itself. Child-monitoring products are often placed in objects that portray a sense of fun or benignity, including the 'My Little Eye' baby monitor fitted with an infrared camera mounted in a large plastic flower with a flexible stem to enable the live streaming of video, and the 'Vtech Sleepy Bear Digital Baby Monitor'. Whether this is for discretion or to reassure parents they are practising care, not surveillance, remains ambiguous. Drawing together multiple developments, the Mimo™ group is developing what they call the 'Smart Nursery', comprised of products that can communicate with one another and are accessible and controllable from a parent's smart device. One such product is what the Mimo™ website describes as the 'world's smartest baby monitor', which is a wearable babygrow fitted with numerous sensors that collect information about the baby's breathing, body position, sleep activity and skin temperature, as well as audio. Data collected by the sensors are transmitted, via Bluetooth, to the cloud and are accessible on any connected smart device. Whilst the website cautions that the Mimo™ Baby Monitor 'is not to be used as a substitute for adult supervision', it declares that: 'It's going to change the way parents think about and learn about their babies'. Indeed, such artefacts of monitoring represent a cultural shift in what it means to be a responsible parent and benchmark expected levels of digitally enhanced care. As Lupton (2013b: 46) articulates:

> The infant's body becomes the focus of the intense, anxious parental gaze in the context of a culture in which parents – and particularly mothers – are held accountable for any harm that may befall their infants or any failure to conform to accepted measures of health, growth and development.

Furthermore, the normativity of these devices quickly overrides other concerns, such as the safety of early and sustained exposure to wireless microwave radiation or the interception of devices. There are numerous reports of connected devices, such as baby monitors and toys, being hacked by outsiders who are then able to view live footage of the child (and family), talk to the infant and even control the camera remotely (Computerworld, 2015; Taylor and Michael, 2015). The digitised swaddle that now surrounds the newborn is supposed to reassure anxious and responsible parents who are eager for objective indicators of the health and well-being of their infant. But, far from soothing worries, the extent to which devices can preoccupy and consume the new parent can itself become a source of anxiety and stress. In a study of parental views on baby monitors, it was noted how these technologies 'make parental anxiety the expected state of parenthood' (Nelson, 2009: 225). It is easy to see how parental doubts regarding their human capability alone can set in when adrift in the sea of gadgets and gismos that can quantify and externalise the inner workings of an otherwise apparently indecipherable tot.

In early childcare centres too, combinations of surveillance practices that are dually cast as mechanisms of care and a source of information to alleviate the concerns of parents are emerging. For example, many early childcare institutions allow parents to view their children via webcams (Jorgensen, 2004). Originally introduced as devices to allow parents to watch over their children's carers, these systems transmit images of the children and have become just as much a vehicle for parents to monitor their child's development and day-to-day activity.

These types of surveillance opportunities and practices challenge notions of parental responsibility. If products, such as wearable sensors rigged to smart devices, become socially normalised, then choosing not to use such devices may be seen as irresponsible, lacking in care, reckless even. In this vein, the infant child is viewed as permanently '"at risk" from harm, unpredictable, never far from the threat of illness or death. It is a body that is culturally primed for intense and continuous surveillance on the part of its anxious parents' (Lupton, 2013b: 45). The surveillance device itself becomes seen as a greater source of knowledge or truth about the child's well-being over and above the multiple ways in which children may be cared for by those around them (Rooney, 2012). The sudden swell of wearable electronics and biosensor devices transform the child's body into a site of scrutiny and measurement: 'bodies are experienced and conceptualized in relation to other bodies, as well as to discourses, practices, spaces, ideas and non-human objects and other living things' (Lupton, 2013b: 39).

Along with the intensification in the biomedical monitoring of infants, there are other ways in which behaviour, movement, thoughts and actions are scrutinised throughout a child's life.

The modern school is a key site of surveillance, but in many ways this is 'nothing new' (Taylor, 2013: 3) since many common aspects of schooling have inherent surveillance properties: 'registration confirms attendance, student reports compound activity, continual examination and assessment monitors progress, the containment of pupils on a bounded campus enables close observation of behavior, and the contravention of rules attracts swift and often visible punishment' (ibid). But, for all the structurally integrated modes of surveillance in the school, the technological sophistication of recent processes and apparatus presents a radical shift in the intensity of surveillance experienced by schoolchildren, which in turn advances new ethical and social implications. New technologies – including, biometrics, digital imaging, fingerprinting and RFID tags – are increasingly deployed to identify, profile and track pupils. Moreover, their sophistication and potency have intensified as high-end military and defence apparatus find use in everyday environments (Casella, 2006; Haggerty and Ericson, 1999), notably the lucrative education market. Schoolchildren have emerged as one of the most heavily surveilled populations in many countries. Such 'surveillance schools' (Taylor, 2012) or 'dataveillance schools' (Williamson, Chapter 4 in this collection) are installing sensor-based and visual-recording devices that continually harvest data about schoolchildren in ever-finer detail.

School can be viewed as part of the socio-cultural landscape of society, a key institution, with considerable flows between it and other institutions, such as the family, community, corporations, government and media. The use and application of surveillance originating in the school often materialises and circulates openly in society, generating claims that schools have become test-beds for new technologies. Conversely, events and behaviours that originate in society can soon influence school practices. Moral panic around youth violence, drug use, obesity and sexting, to name but a few, can import major changes to the school campus. The scope of school surveillance is expanding and there have been many exposés of schools extending their reach beyond the campus walls and into the family home via surveillance technologies. For example, a school in Pennsylvania was sued in 2011 for allegedly activating a school-owned laptop's built-in webcam to watch a student at home and using the information gathered for disciplinary means (Clarke, 2010).

Whilst schools are infused with surveillance practices, when children are at home there are also multifarious ways in which surveillance continues to shape their world. Webcams and surveillance cameras allow parents to remotely view their children over the internet from anywhere, such as from a workplace or while travelling overseas. Security devices can be set up with a variety of alerts that send a message to the parent when their child arrives home from school: for example, devices such as 'Z-Wave Home Monitoring' or 'Total Connect'; the latter allowing parents to automatically receive a video of the child entering the home. In the expanding market of surveillance devices, companies play not only on parents' anxieties about the safety and well-being of their child, but also on their fear of, or guilt about, missing key childhood moments due to other commitments. As one security article promises parents:

> You can watch your children sleep, eat and play … Your home coming will always be a happy event. You can show off that you've never missed a day with your kids because of your hard-working video surveillance. It's like you've been home all the time. (Roberts, 2007)

In this example, the video camera becomes the surrogate parent, observing the child's activity and development, absent yet continually 'present'. Hofer *et al.*

(2009) describes what they term an 'electronic tether', which could itself be considered as a digitised extension of the umbilical cord, and has come to typify relationships between parents and their children, particularly in emerging adulthood. An important avenue for future research will be to explore the impacts of digitised parenting on family dynamics and childhood relations.

Information about children accessed from the sanctity of the family home is now routinely being transmitted to external databases for viewing and analytics by external agencies and corporations. For example, not content with the 'Barbie Video Girl', which has a camera lens disguised as a pendant embedded in the doll's chest, Mattel's latest doll, 'Hello Barbie' is pioneering a new trend in 'smart toys'. The doll uses voice-recognition software, an evolving database of recordings and access to the internet via Bluetooth and Wi-Fi to attempt to engage the child in intelligible and free-flowing conversation by asking and responding to questions. Algorithmic software enables the doll to *learn* about its users over time. Illustrating this, at the New York Toy Fair in 2015, a journalist writing for the *Washington Post* (Halzack, 2015) reported:

> [T]he Mattel representative chatting with Hello Barbie mentioned that she liked being onstage. Later in the conversation, when the Mattel representative asked Hello Barbie what she should be when she grew up, the doll responded, 'Well, you told me you like being onstage. So maybe a dancer? Or a politician? Or how about a dancing politician?'

The Barbie doll is a powerful example of the reach of large corporations into the privacy of the home via ostensibly benign products. Children often do converse with toys, share their innermost thoughts and act out various scenarios; clearly, this is without any knowledge that this information might be accessed, analysed and exploited for commercial gain. Not only can parents choose to receive daily or weekly emails with access to the audio files of their children's conversations with Hello Barbie, all audio recordings from Hello Barbie are uploaded to ToyTalk, which operates the speech processing services for Mattel. A review of their privacy policy reveals that the information recorded could be used in a variety of ways, including being shared with third parties:

> [W]hen we believe in good faith that we are lawfully authorized or required to do so or that doing so is reasonably necessary or appropriate to (a) comply with any law or legal processes or respond to lawful requests or legal authorities, including responding to lawful subpoenas, warrants, or court orders; or (b) protect the rights, property, or safety of ToyTalk, our users, our employees, copyright owners, third parties or the public, to enforce or apply this Policy, our Terms of Use, or our other policies or agreements. (ToyTalk Privacy Policy cited in *The Vigilant Citizen*, 2015: n.p.)

In this manner, and alongside many examples of the blurring of the boundaries between private and public, the family perimeter has become porous and commercial entities are encroaching further into children's lives, using surveillance techniques that are increasingly difficult for children and families to resist. Barbie has become a 'sophisticated surveillance device masquerading as an innocuous child's toy' (Taylor and Michael, 2015, n.p.).

Just as the reach of schools and mass corporations has been shown to extend into the home, the parental gaze is now transported with young people wherever they go. Mobile phones are increasingly being used as surveillance devices by parents, as they enable parents to monitor phone usage, including the content of SMS messages sent and received, identify callers (even when caller ID is withheld), approve or block contacts, as well as a range of other functions. With almost ubiquitous use of mobile phones by teenagers, the proliferation of teen-tracking apps is notable. For example, parents can use an iRecovery Spy Stick to access and download mobile phone web history, emails, photographs and text messages, even the deleted ones retrospectively, or alternatively install 'Mobile Spy', which provides real-time tracking of online activity and geographical location, providing electronic 'breadcrumbs' that reveal where the child has been and when. There are also apps such as 'Teensafe' and 'Family Tracker'. The use of such apps highlights the tensions between safety and trust (Rooney, 2015).

As children get older and move into their teenage years, the marketing of surveillance devices to parents persists. Home drug-testing kits, such as the 'First Check Home Drug Test Kit', is an example of the types of tools offered as 'responsible' practices to parents (Marx and Steeves, 2010; Moore and Haggerty, 2001). Vehicular surveillance devices are also available to parents and use GPS technology or satellite services to monitor driving speed and location, and send an email or SMS to the parent if any of the boundaries, predefined by the parents, are breached. If speeding is detected, it is possible for parents to remotely trigger the car's horn or flash the lights until the driver slows down (for example, see products such as 'Motosafety' or 'SafeDriver'). Some devices monitor smartphone activity while driving (such as the 'Canary' app) and send a message to parents if their child is texting or talking on the phone while driving. In a world where parental monitoring is a growth industry, spying in effect 'becomes an enhanced parenting tool' (Marx and Steeves, 2010: 205). The prevailing messages about parental responsibility become confused; on the one hand, encouraging parents to continuously monitor the whereabouts of their children through electronic devices, whilst, on the other, communicating that parents no longer need to be present or available to discuss with their children where they are, what they are doing and with whom they are hanging out, so long as they are tracking them.

Information and communications technologies (ICTs), and notably social networking, are becoming embedded in the lived experiences of children of all ages, and some commentators now claim that it is increasingly difficult to separate the virtual and non-virtual domains of children's experiences. Marsh (2010: 25), for example, describes this as a 'continuum in which children's online and offline experiences merge'. A survey conducted across 25 European countries indicated that 'one third of 9–12 year olds and three quarters of 13–16 year olds who use the Internet in Europe have their own profile on a social networking site'

(Livingstone *et al.*, 2011). Even though many social networking sites state that account holders must be over the age of 13, the report by Livingstone *et al.* (2011) confirms that nevertheless many users are 'under age', with children simply providing incorrect age information online. Online activity, increasingly viewed as criminogenic, has become a focus of surveillance with internet tracking and what Hope (2008) describes as a 'culture of over-blocking' websites. For example, in England under the Counter-terrorism and Security Act 2015, there is a requirement that schools 'have due regard to the need to prevent pupils being drawn into terrorism'. This has resulted in the emergence of several companies providing anti-radicalisation software products to schools, such as Future Digital, Securus and Impero, to monitor schoolchildren's online activity. The software operates by detecting the use of keywords included in a glossary of terminology that supposedly could indicate radicalisation.

These examples provide only a small snapshot of the proliferation of surveillance devices available to parents, schools, companies, governments and children themselves that are being increasingly used to monitor, observe, calculate and control different aspects of children's lives. Of course, technologies (and indeed non-technological modes of surveillance) evolve, are updated and fall in and out of use. At the same time, there are often shifts in the parameters of what is viewed as acceptable, ethical and desirable in the lives of young people. The overview, however, illustrates the growing complexity of the ways in which children's lives are increasingly caught up in a vast array of surveillance practices that require us to attend more closely to what it means to grow up in a 'surveillance society', including what it means for parents, schools and governments to make decisions that impact on surveillance in young people's lives.

Growing up in a surveillance society: social and ethical implications

Surveillance brings with it numerous profound changes. Amongst these are the significant socio-political and ethical implications raised by the increasing use of surveillance to monitor the young lives of the next generation. This book navigates the tensions between the positive aspects of surveillance processes whilst cautioning, where applicable, about the dangers and risks that are often embedded in their uncritical appropriation. Importantly, whilst several authors highlight the potential negative ethical and societal impacts of unfettered surveillance, contributors are keen to highlight that not all aspects of surveillance are inherently bad. Indeed, they bring many benefits and conveniences. For example, location-based services (LBS), such as GPS and RFID, provide the convenience of route-finders, locating lost items, assisting with emergency responses and safeguarding vulnerable people. Along with these benefits, however, multiple issues are raised relating to autonomy, location privacy, trust, freedom of movement and expression of identity. These issues are not insignificant. As Dobson argues, 'human-tracking devices pose the greatest threat to personal freedom ever faced in human history' since they have the potential to 'alter social relationships … more dramatically than any other product emerging from the information revolution' (2006: 187). Similarly, Arnold (2010: n.p.) argues that children can be 'denied personhood by being reduced to digits traversing the virtual spaces found in Google Maps and similar geospatial services'. Of these issues, the brief analysis below focuses on the tensions surrounding the experience of privacy and trust as examples of the inherent complexities in the relationship between children, technologies and surveillance practices.

Surveillance and privacy are often presented as being in opposition – 'a tug of war between two social forces' (Taylor, 2013: 62). Many argue that sacrificing some privacy is necessary for the security benefits that surveillance provides. The trouble with presenting the surveillance/privacy debate in this way is that it obscures the more complex motivations and workings that underpin surveillance practices, such as how they interrelate with ideology and inequality, and whether surveillance practices are actually effective solutions to the problem (Fussey, 2008).

There are salient reasons why the concept of a 'right to privacy' is far from straightforward. It is 'an extremely slippery virtue – intangible, hard to define and harder still to measure' (Madgwick and Smythe, 1974: 9) and perhaps one of 'the most equivocal of all human rights in terms of definition and circumscription' (Taylor, 2010: 383). Some have even gone so far as to say that privacy 'is beyond the scope of the law' (Hixson, 1987: 98). When applied to children, the issue is even more complex. In many legal and policy contexts, children are often deemed too young to be afforded a sense of privacy in their own right, despite the UN Convention (1989) that simultaneously enshrines the child's right to privacy and acknowledges that children also need special safeguards, care and legal protection. Exploring the complexities of children's need for and understanding of what it means to have some sense of privacy provides insight into some of the broader intricacies of privacy/surveillance discourses.

As noted by Rooney (Chapter 11 in this collection), children's sense of and need for privacy are more acute than is often acknowledged. Children, from an early age, are aware of the presence of a surveillance gaze; they play differently, for example, when being watched by others. However, with the rise of new forms of exposure and self-revelation, particularly prominent on social networking sites, it has been contended that we are witnessing 'the end of privacy', that we are now living in a 'participatory panopticon' or a state of 'total surveillance' (Whitaker, 1999: 139) in which we are all complicit. The nature of the way teenagers engage online, for example, to some, demonstrates that young people no longer care for their privacy, particularly given the increasing evidence that 'teens flock to the Internet to share their intimate thoughts' (Barnes, 2006). In parallel, teens also 'develop intricate strategies to achieve privacy goals', which often 'challenges the ways in which privacy is currently conceptualized, discussed, and regulated' (boyd and Marwick, 2011: n.p.). For example, according to boyd (2012), they often rely on 'in-jokes' and 'encoded messages', which can limit access to the meaning of the information, even if not the content itself.

Clearly, the boundaries between private and public spheres have become increasingly blurred, raising challenges for children and young people who want to have 'private lives' (for example, from their parents or teachers) in these new spaces. The complexity of understanding what it means to have 'privacy' in these new contexts and the type of choices children and others will face within a multi-layered surveillance network requires more nuanced attention beyond public/private and privacy/security distinctions. Young people often lack the resources required to effectively express their desire and need for privacy, as well as the ability to negotiate with those who seek to control it. This becomes particularly problematic when the dominant discourse tramples on the complex and subtle ways that young people construct privacy. Corporations are particularly conversant in peddling the view that young people voluntarily relinquish all semblances of privacy (Steeves, 2012; Taylor, 2013). In a context where the right to privacy is not just under threat, but becoming more difficult to articulate and define, the chapters in this collection highlight how the experience of children and youth can shed light on the inherent tensions and need for new directions in thinking about privacy in the digital age.

In addition to challenging privacy, surveillance has the potential to bring ambiguity to established means of developing trust. It has been claimed that surveillance practices 'embody a mistrust that corrodes personhood' and are often 'an electronic substitute for the trust and risk-sharing that we might see as fundamental to family life' (Arnold, cited in the *Canberra Times*, 2011: n.p.). Supporting this view, empirical research exploring the impact of CCTV found that schoolchildren perceived visual surveillance to be 'equated with mistrust', since 'to demonstrate trust is not to surveil' (Taylor, 2013: 52; see also Chapter 2). Trust is bound up with responsibility; the more children are trusted, the more they learn to be responsible for themselves and those around them. An additional complexity is that messages about trust are often difficult to interpret, as 'the ambiguity of the surveillance gaze makes it unclear who in the population cannot be trusted' (Rooney, 2010: 352).

While, on the one hand, children find the minutiae of their day-to-day lives controlled to a level of detail that has previously not been possible, on the other hand, somewhat paradoxically surveillance technologies can provide more freedom. A parent anxious about the safety of their child riding their bike with friends might feel reassured by the use of GPS tracking (Chapter 9) or concern about allowing a child unsupervised internet access might be alleviated by the use of software apps that monitor activity while blocking sites deemed inappropriate. These examples highlight how the notion of 'trust' can become a point of negotiation in deciding how much freedom of movement or association a child is afforded. If a parent trusts a child to go out on the condition he/she take a mobile phone with a GPS tracking system enabled, then although the child may have more freedom, it is nonetheless a conditional freedom where that condition is enacted through a surveillance device. This tension serves to highlight the complicated relationship between trust and surveillance. Despite the opportunities for freedom that tracking devices may present, for children, it may not always be clear whether they are not trusted or whether a surveillance device is there to protect them – yet another representation of the shifting and ambiguous boundaries between care and control mentioned earlier.

Seen but not heard? The absence of children's voices in the study of surveillance

Despite the overall sensitisation to the concerns of subjects of surveillance, children and young people have historically been 'hidden'. Highlighting the need to understand how, why and to what effect young people are subjected to an intensification of surveillance, a study of CCTV in a British city found that teenagers were targeted by camera operators 'for no apparent reason', whereas in contrast, 'those over thirty years old are rarely the subject of surveillance' (Norris and Armstrong, 1999: 9). As the surveillance of young people intensifies, it is paramount to privilege accounts of the impacts and effects on their lives. Just as childhood voices have at times been '"muted" within the social sciences' (Christensen and James, 2003: 1), it has been claimed that until recently, the child's body has similarly been 'an absent presence' in the new social studies of childhood (Colls and Horschelmann, 2009; Lupton, 2013b; Woodyer, 2008). Several chapters in this collection draw upon empirical research conducted with young people to provide an avenue for them to voice their own views and opinions regarding surveillance practices and the impact on their worlds. Other chapters grapple with the conceptual ethical and social implications for future generations growing up in a surveillance society, raising a number of significant questions regarding how we envisage childhoods of the future and what this means for regulatory and policy frameworks that are designed to protect, educate and govern young people.

Structure of the book

The book is organised around three key spheres of children's day-to-day life: schooling, the self and social lives. Of course, these zones are inextricably intertwined, and the structure is not intended to impose any superficial parameters around different aspects of children's being, but to recognise substantial flows between them. The parts, taken as a whole, highlight the extent to which surveillance now pervades every aspect of a child's life as he/she moves between different institutions, places and spaces. The aim is to provide analyses of some of the multiple ways in which contemporary modes of surveillance are being shaped by and are, in turn, shaping what it means to be young and living in a surveillance society.

Schooling and education

The chapters in Part I, 'Schooling and education', focus on institutional-level technological surveillance that children experience in contemporary schooling. In Chapter 2, Emmeline Taylor explores CCTV, the most common method of electronic visual surveillance in schools. Drawing on media analysis and empirical research in schools, the chapter highlights how the media representation of CCTV in schools presents it as largely unproblematic, in contrast to the impact it has on students. Taylor argues that the use of CCTV, particularly in classrooms and student toilets, can radically change the school environment with important ramifications for the growth and development of young people. In Chapter 3, Deborah Lupton and Michael Gard chart the close historical connection between health and education, arguing that 'it is difficult to think of a public health matter, large or small, which has not at one time been given to schools to solve'. They pay special attention to the 'algorithmic authority' projected on digitised children in educational contexts and the potential socio-political, material and health implications this gives rise to. Ben Williamson in Chapter 4 focuses on two components of what he terms 'dataveillance schools': learning analytics (which capture data from children's educational activities) and personal analytics (which track, monitor and assess schoolchildren's bodies and functions). Like Lupton and Gard, Williamson highlights the ways in which 'algorithmic power' is shaping children's lives, providing a critically informed account of the implications for schoolchildren. The final chapter in Part 1, 'Teaching us to be "smart"', draws on the example of RFID tracking in schools to examine how weaving new technologies 'into the institutional fabric of the school' can serve to normalise them. Taylor describes schools as 'institutional incubators' for new surveillance technologies and practices and, furthermore, environments within which the ostensible neutrality of surveillance technologies can be constructed before they are circulated in society. The chapter outlines how schoolchildren are also tracked beyond the school premises, sometimes overtly as part of initiatives designed to encourage cycling or walking to school or whilst travelling on school buses, but sometimes unwittingly as a result of the reach of the transmitter, raising issues of safety, privacy and ethics.

Self, body and movement

Part II focuses on the ways in which the child's body is made readable, rankable and regulatable through surveillance practices. This section seeks to outline how the body has become a site on which surveillance is enacted. This raises important questions regarding the digitisation of the self and how this potentially and profoundly influences understanding of the self, identity and body. In the opening chapter of this section, Murray Lee and Thomas Crofts examine the regulation of childhood sexuality using the phenomenon of 'sexting' as an example. They seek to bring to the fore the pejorative policing of sexting and intimate the body as a new site on which control can be exerted. Following on, Jacqueline Vickery examines the media discourses that surround mobile phone technology and how they serve to normalise surveillance in domestic spaces in the United States. Drawing on empirical qualitative data, Vickery argues that rather than being passive subjects of surveillance, teen girls can resist aspects of the parental gaze using their mobile phones. Carol Barron in the next chapter takes an anthropological approach to the ways in which mobile phones are increasingly used by parents in a bid to monitor and control their children. Rejecting dominant perceptions that subjects of surveillance are passive and powerless, Barron emphasises that children are able to successfully negotiate and resist parental surveillance via this means. Jessica Nihlén Fahlquist explores the moral implications of GPS tracking young people in Chapter 9. Describing GPS as 'part of a parent's tool box', she explores some of its uses before considering what some of the impacts might be, particularly for a child's development of a sense of responsibility. 'Children need to become autonomous individuals, able to take care of themselves and others', she argues, and the use of GPS tracking could potentially stunt 'their progress towards self-sufficiency'. Charting the growth of mHealth technologies in Chapter 10, Emma Rich attends to the child's body as a site of regulation on which various cultural normativities are played out. Rich identifies a trend towards digitised health and physical education (HPE) or what Gard (2014) has termed 'eHPE', and uses the 'health crisis' that is childhood obesity to discuss the ways in which childhood bodies are scrutinised through a range of different health apps and technologies.

Social lives and virtual worlds

The third and final part turns to children's social and playful encounters. As Whitson and Simon (2014: 309) remind us, 'there is something primordial about the relationship between surveillance and games'. Opening this section, Tonya Rooney explores the importance of play and childhood games as spaces in which children can learn about and 'grapple with issues such as power, exposure, secrecy and deception'. Of salience to surveillance studies, Rooney observes that private spaces are often a prerequisite for experimental and creative play, cautioning against the erosion of these spaces through 'increasing forms of control, supervision and surveillance'. In Chapter 12, 'World of Spycraft', Andrew Hope considers the variant ways in which online gaming domains have become sites of surveillance by government agencies, as well as the game corporations themselves. Hope argues that 'children's use of gamified devices and video games have increasingly become embroiled in practices of almost relentless monitoring', which opens up discussion of the notions of responsibilisation, desensitisation and marketisation of online spaces frequented by young people. In Chapter 13, Valerie Steeves draws upon her research involving 5,436 young people in Canada. The chapter outlines the surveillance of the top fifty sites most frequented by the young people in her sample. While Steeves notes that 'the commercialisation of young people's online environment has been taking place for some time', she highlights the ways in which the 'major players', including Google and Facebook, operate increasingly integrated information-collection systems, sharing personal information and data between the various sites that they own. Far from being willing participants in the commercialisation of online space, Steeves highlights how young people are unhappy about their personal data being accessed and used, raising issues with the current regulatory framework. In the final chapter, drawing on a case study from the RYOGENS (Reducing Youth Offending Generic Electronic National Solution) database, Rosamunde Van Brakel examines the advent of pre-emptive surveillance practices. The database was developed to improve communication and co-ordination between partner agencies in order to identify children who were at risk of harm or of engaging in criminal activity. While conceived out of a genuine desire to improve service delivery, this 'pre-emptive turn' has important social and ethical consequences, which Van Brakel documents. She uncovers the implications of the ways that surveillance technologies are used not only to control, monitor or care for children, but also, arguably, to pre-define the possibilities for selfhood in ways that may limit or restrain a child's future potential.

The intensity with which surveillance practices and technologies have begun to saturate the years from early childhood to adolescence and beyond raises numerous ethical and social concerns. As a whole, the chapters in this collection provide important conceptual foundations for future theoretical and empirical research, inviting us to find new ways to question the often taken-for-granted surveillance creeping into children's lives. The volume will contribute to the broader debates on emerging surveillance practices, while at the same time bringing into focus the implications for children and young people. After all, it is the young people of today who will shape the surveillance scape of the future. The chapters in this collection offer a vital opportunity to consider the intricate and dynamic workings of surveillance in society and provide an important stepping stone towards new discussions and future directions for research in this field.

References

Ariès, P. (1962) *Centuries of childhood: a social history of family life*. New York: Vintage Books.

Arnold, B. (2010) 'Digital handcuffs or electronic nannies: children, privacy and emerging surveillance technologies', paper presented at the Children, Young People and Privacy Conference, Melbourne, 21 May.

Baldwin, G. (2005) 'Emerging technology: hospitals turn to RFID', *SnapsFlow Healthcare News*. Available at http://snapsflowhealthcarenews.blogspot.com/2005/08/emerging-technology-hospitals-turn-to.html (accessed 20.07.2015).

Barnes, S. (2006) 'A privacy paradox: social networking in the United States', *First Monday* 11(9). Available online at http://firstmonday.org/issues/issue11_9/barnes/index.html (accessed 22.03.2016).

boyd, d. (2012) 'Networked privacy', *Surveillance and Society*, 10(3): 348–50.

boyd, d. and A. Marwick (2011) Social steganography: privacy in networked publics, paper presented at ICA, Boston, MA, 28 May.

Canberra Times (2011) 'Helping, handcuffs or both?', 16 Jan.

Casella, R. (2006) *Selling us the fortress*. London: Routledge.

Christensen, P. and A. James (2003) 'Researching children and childhood: cultures of communication', in P. Christensen and A. James (eds), *Research with children: perspectives and practices*. London: Falmer Press.

Clarke, S. (2010) 'Pa. school faces FBI probe, lawsuit, for using webcams on laptops to watch students at home', ABC News. Available online at http://abcnews.go.com (accessed 20.07.2015).

Colls, R. and K. Horschelmann (2009) 'The geographies of children's and young people's bodies', *Children's Geographies* 7 (1): 1–6.

Computerworld (2015) '2 more wireless baby monitors hacked: hackers remotely spied on babies and parents'. Available online at www.computerworld.com/article/2913356/cybercrime-hacking/2-more-wireless-baby-monitors-hacked-hackers-remotely-spied-on-babies-and-parents.html (accessed 21.07.2015).

Dobson, J. E. (2006) 'Geoslavery', in B. Warf (ed.), *Encyclopedia of human geography*. London: Sage, pp. 186–8.

Fussey, P. (2008) 'Beyond liberty, beyond security: the politics of public surveillance', *British Politics*, 3(1): 120–35.

Gard, M. (2014) 'eHPE: A history of the future', *Sport, Education and Society*, 19(6): 827–45.

Haggerty, K. and R. Ericson (1999) 'The militarization of policing in the information age', *Journal of Political and Military Sociology*, 27(2): 233–45.

Halzack, S. (2015) 'Privacy advocates try to keep "creepy," "eavesdropping" Hello Barbie from hitting shelves', *Washington Post*. Available oneline at www.washingtonpost.com/blogs/the-switch/wp/2015/03/11/privacy-advocates-try-to-keep-creepy-eavesdropping-hello-barbie-from-hitting-shelves/?tid=sm_tw (accessed 21.07.2015).

Hixson, R. (1987) *Privacy in a public society: human rights in conflict*. New York: Oxford University Press.

Hofer, B. K., C. Souder, E. K. Kennedy, N. Fullman, and K. Hurd (2009) 'The electronic tether: communication and parental monitoring during the college years', in M. K. Nelson and A. I. Garey (eds), *Who's watching? Daily practices of surveillance among contemporary families*. Nashville: Vanderbilt University Press, pp. 277–94.

Holloway, D., L. Green, and S. Livingstone (2013) 'Zero to eight: young children and their internet use', EU Kids Online: LSE. Available online at http://eprints.lse.ac.uk/52630/1/Zero_to_eight.pdf (accessed 22.03.2016).

Hope, A. (2008) 'Internet pollution discourses, exclusionary practices and the "culture of over-blocking" within UK schools', *Technology, Pedagogy and Education*, 17: 103–13.

Jenks, C. (2005) *Childhood*, 2nd ed. London: Routledge.

Jorgensen, V. (2004) 'The apple of the eye: parents' use of webcams in a Danish day nursery', *Surveillance and Society*, 2: 446–63.

Leaver, T. (2015) 'Researching the ends of identity: birth and death on social media', *Social Media + Society* (Apr–June): 1–2.

Livingstone, S., K. Olafsson, and E. Staksrud (2011) 'Social networking, age and privacy', LSE Research Online Report. Available online at http://eprints.lse.ac.uk/35849/1/Social%20networking%2C%20age%20and%20privacy%20%28LSERO.pdf (accessed 22.03.2016).

Lupton, D. (2013a) *The social worlds of the unborn*. Basingstoke, UK: Palgrave Macmillan.

Lupton, D. (2013b) 'Infant embodiment and inter-embodiment: a review of sociocultural perspectives', *Childhood*, 20(1): 37–50.

Lyon, D. (2003) *Surveillance as social sorting: privacy, risk and digital discrimination*. London and New York: Routledge.

Madgwick, D. and T. Smythe (1974) *The invasion of privacy*. Pitman: Oxford.

Marsh J. (2010) 'Young children's play in online virtual worlds', *Journal of Early Childhood Research*, 8: 23–39.

Marx, G. and V. Steeves. (2010) 'From the beginning: children as subjects and agents of surveillance', *Surveillance and Society*, 7(3): 6–45.

Moore, D. and K. Haggerty (2001) 'Bring it on home: home drug testing and the relocation of the war on drugs', *Social and Legal Studies*, 10(3): 377–95.

Nelson, M. K. (2009) 'Watching children: describing the use of baby monitors on Epinions.com', in M. K. Nelson and A. I. Garey (eds), *Who's watching? daily practices of surveillance among contemporary families*, pp. 219–38. Nashville: Vanderbilt University Press.

Nelson, M. K. and A. I. Garey (2009) 'Who's watching? An introductory essay', in M. K. Nelson and A. I. Garey (eds), *Who's watching? Daily practices of surveillance among contemporary families*, pp. 1–16. Nashville: Vanderbilt University Press,

Norris, C. and G. Armstrong (1999) *The maximum surveillance society: the rise of CCTV*. Oxford: Berg.

Prout, A. (2005) *The future of childhood: towards the interdisciplinary study of children*, London: Falmer Press.

Roberts, N. (2007) 'Don't shortchange your family: get video surveillance'. Available online at http://ezinearticles.com/?id=798152 (accessed 31.07.2015).

Rooney, T. (2010) 'Trusting children: how do surveillance technologies alter a child's experience of trust, risk and responsibility?', *Surveillance and Society*, 7(3/4): 344–55.

Rooney, T. (2012) 'Childhood spaces in a changing world: exploring the intersection between children and new surveillance technologies', *Global Studies of Childhood*, 2(4): 311–42.

Rooney, T. (2015) 'Spying on your kid's phone with Teensafe will only undermine trust', *The Conversation*, 29 Apr. Available at online at https://theconversation.com/spying-on-your-kids-phone-with-teensafe-will-only-undermine-trust-40385 (accessed 22.03.2016).

Steeves, V. (2012) 'Hide and seek: surveillance of young people on the internet', in K. Ball, K. D. Haggerty and D. Lyon (eds), *Handbook of surveillance studies*, pp. 352–60. London: Routledge.

Taylor, E. (2010) 'I spy with my little eye: the use of CCTV in schools and the impact on privacy', *Sociological Review*, 58(3): 381–405.

Taylor, E. (2012) 'The rise of the surveillance school', in K. Ball, K. D. Haggerty and D. Lyon (eds.), *Handbook of surveillance studies*. London: Routledge.

Taylor, E. (2013) *Surveillance schools: security, discipline and control in contemporary education*. Basingstoke, UK: Palgrave Macmillan.

Taylor, E. and K. Michael (2015) 'Hello Barbie, hello hackers: accessing your data will be child's play', *The conversation*. Available online at https://theconversation.com/hello-barbie-hello-hackers-accessing-personal-data-will-be-childs-play-52082 (accessed 06.01.2016).

The Vigilant Citizen (2015) 'Hello Barbie: the creepy doll that spies on kids … and their parents'. Available online at http://vigilantcitizen.com/latestnews/hello-barbie-the-creepy-doll-that-spies-on-kids-and-their-parents/ (accessed 24.07.2015).

UN General Assembly, Convention on the Rights of the Child, 20 November 1989, United Nations, Treaty Series, vol. 1577, p. 3. Available online at www.refworld.org/docid/3ae6b38f0.html (accessed 31.07.2015).

Whitaker, R. (1999) *The end of privacy: how total surveillance is becoming a reality*. New York: New Press.

Whitson, J. and B. Simon (2014) 'Game studies meets surveillance studies at the edge of digital culture: an introduction to a special issue on surveillance, games and play', *Surveillance and Society*, 12(3): 309–19.

Woodyer, T. (2008) 'The body as research tool: embodied practice and children's geographies', *Children's Geographies*, 6(4): 349–62.

Wyld, D. (2009) 'Preventing the worst case scenario: an analysis of RFID technology and infant protection in hospitals', *Internet Journal of Healthcare Administration*, 7(1): 1–7.

Part I

Schooling and education

2 'If I wanted to be on Big Brother, I would've auditioned for it'

Examining the media representation of CCTV in schools and the impact of visual surveillance on schoolchildren

Emmeline Taylor

Elsewhere I have provided detailed accounts of the prevalence, use and objectives of the manifold surveillance technologies now used in schools (Taylor, 2010a, 2010b, 2012, 2013), exploring how practices converge and coalesce to form the Surveillance School. My focus is primarily on visual surveillance in the form of Closed Circuit Television (CCTV), as the most common method of electronic visual surveillance found in schools.

Two key sources of empirical data are drawn upon in this chapter. First, the findings from a content analysis of media coverage of the use of CCTV in schools in Australia provide an example of representation in one country, informing us about the dominant cultural narrative pertaining to visual surveillance in education. The media depiction of CCTV in schools largely presents it as unproblematic and a necessary, normative and value-neutral development. CCTV denotes progress in security and a risk-ready approach to student and staff safety, a view encapsulated in the Australian Government's *Schools Security Programme*, which provides funding to enhance school security, typically by installing CCTV. The chapter also draws upon empirical evidence from three schools in England to counter the media portrayal of CCTV in schools as neutral and benign. I elucidate the impacts that visual surveillance can have on students and, in particular, how continuous monitoring by delegated technologies is challenging and transforming a range of societal values, such as privacy and trust. I explore the capacity for surveillance cameras to rescript cultural conventions and produce novel kinds of behaviours while repressing other modes of conduct. I argue that contrary to media discourse, visual technological surveillance in schools, in the form of CCTV and webcams, is transforming young people's expectations about personal freedoms, such as privacy, trust and anonymity, and is ultimately teaching new lessons about democratic participation in the surveillance age.

Theorising surveillance: the Panopticon and beyond

There has been some pivotal research on school surveillance that requires discussion, and works that offer some useful conceptual tools for understanding the phenomenon and impact of school surveillance. It cannot, for example, be ignored that a major strand of the sociological discourse on surveillance and, in particular, CCTV, has been based on the Panopticon. Indeed, it has become one of 'the most powerful metaphors' (Norris, 2003: 249) for explicating the theoretical and social significance of surveillance in contemporary society. Scholars routinely draw upon panopticonism as a theoretical framework, or what Glaser terms a 'pet code' (1978: 73), through which analysis is filtered. Whilst schools can appear to be 'disturbingly panoptic' (Gallagher, 2010: 264) upon first inspection, emblematic panopticonism has reached such hyperbolic proportions in surveillance studies that some now describe it as 'oppressive' (Haggerty, 2011: 23). It has been suggested that the Panopticon has, somewhat ironically, come to exert an imperious influence on surveillance studies. Despite continued pleas to 'tear down the walls' and 'demolish the panopticon' (Haggerty, 2011: 23), it continues to overshadow alternative analyses of surveillance, with such critiques only materialising sometime after Foucault's (2007) own rejection of the pervasive nature of panopticism. While it retains some value, it should be recognised that it co-exists with other registers of power and that there are multiple readings of surveillance.

Science and technology studies (STS) provides some useful analytical tools, not least the recognition that technologies, or non-humans, can have agency and exert an influence upon actors who interact with them and the environment within which they are located. Proponents reject what has been seen as a tendency to 'discriminate between the human and inhuman' (Latour, 1988: 303), proposing that all entities and enterprises are part of a network of forces in which none is privileged with ontological superiority. Surveillance is complex and messy, and there is certainly no one theoretical framework that articulates and accounts for all the materiality and experiential antagonisms that it summons. The analysis in this chapter draws upon this approach to further understand the ways in which surveillant apparatuses are shaped by and, in turn, shape the environment in which they are located and the subjectivities and movements of those that interact with them.

According to Latour, objects, while inscribed with subjective meaning, 'script' actors, 'prescribe' conduct and exert influence over the environment in which they are located. For example, CCTV alters conduct by inhibiting behaviours that might be perceived as incriminating, unconventional or embarrassing, while inviting transgressions that cannot be seen on a camera, or by displacing certain activities to a different space that is not monitored. However, while technologies are social entities that can exert their own agency, this should not overshadow the ways in which power can 'act at a distance' (Amin, 2002) through the technologies created, implemented and advocated. Objects are entwined with ideology, power, institutional objectives and social inequalities and can be used to shape interactions while obscuring the exercise of disciplinary forces and governance through their ostensible neutrality.

This chapter is divided into four main sections, beginning with an overview of the methodologies. The second section briefly presents findings from a media analysis of newspaper coverage of CCTV in schools to highlight that the dominant message broadcast to the public is that CCTV is a natural development and one that is instigated to care for and protect school premises, property, teachers and schoolchildren. By examining the media representation of CCTV in school, it becomes apparent that it is overwhelmingly portrayed as a crime-control technology that operates in a value-neutral and benign way. This leads into an overview of the reasons, justifications and objectives that have been expounded to explain the intensifying use of CCTV in schools. This section seeks to critique the dominant discourse that presents CCTV as simply securing and protecting people and property, while being devoid of negative impacts, by outlining some of the more nefarious and trivial uses it has been put to. Finally, the data from empirical research on the impact of CCTV schools is presented to illustrate that, far from being benign, visual surveillance impacts and disrupts a number of important societal attributes and qualities such as privacy, trust, and creativity. The analysis explores the effects and affects of CCTV in different locations around the school (such as the classroom, corridors, and student toilet areas) to illustrate its bearing upon behaviours aside from those of a criminal nature.

Methodology

The chapter draws upon data from two empirical studies: a content analysis of Australian media coverage of CCTV use in schools; and qualitative research exploring the experience and perception of CCTV among schoolchildren in England. Newspaper articles relating to surveillance technologies in Australian schools published during the period 1 August 2010 to 31 July 2015 were accessed using the online database Factiva, a current international news database of national, international and regional newspapers from over 200 countries. Key search terms were employed to identify and extract the news stories. After excluding those less than 100 words, those from non-mainstream outlets (such as industry websites), those not relating to surveillance in schools, and removing duplicates (most newspapers are syndicated across several states), 265 relevant articles remained, two-thirds of which (n=176) focused on CCTV in schools. A coding instrument was developed to capture key features of each story. This included: the specific surveillance technology discussed (CCTV, GPS, RFID, and so on), key concepts (for example, privacy and civil liberties), the explicit objective of the technology (improving attendance, crime control, health, etc.), which stakeholders were consulted as part of the story and how the story was framed.

The second study drawn upon in this chapter aimed to provide much-needed empirical insight into how CCTV shapes everyday interactions. Research on CCTV has tended to focus on evaluating its effectiveness as a crime-control technology (for example, see Welsh and Farrington's [2002, 2008] systematic reviews of CCTV evaluations), and the few studies that have explored the impact on the experiences and behaviours of non-criminal populations have almost exclusively focused on how CCTV affects feelings of safety among the general public (Ditton, 2000; Spriggs *et al.*, 2005). Hence, the empirical findings presented in this chapter offer valuable insight into how CCTV can radically alter the subjectivities and lived experiences of those who routinely fall beneath its gaze. Three schools, located in the north of England, took part in the research. Site visits were made to each school and focus groups with pupils were held, with a total of 21 pupils across four groups. In addition, semi-structured interviews were conducted with eight teachers and two site managers. The schools have been given pseudonyms: 'Single Sex Comprehensive' (SSC), 'City Comprehensive' (CC) and 'Urban High' (UH), as have all participants. The interviews and focus groups were recorded and fully transcribed. A more detailed description of the methodology, research process and rationale can be found in Taylor (2014).

Media representation of CCTV in schools

Greenberg and Hier (2009: 462) identify that 'empirical analyses of how news media frame surveillance practices and technologies are surprisingly limited'. Supporting this contention, there have been no prior studies that explore the media depiction and framing of surveillance technologies in schools. Hier *et al.* (2007: 733) highlight how the media can influence public opinion about CCTV by constructing and presenting the 'symbols, myths and images that embody and represent social problems' in tandem with moralising discourses that serve to legitimise surveillance.

Of the 176 stories relating to the use of CCTV in or around schools, 53 (30 per cent) were reporting on an incident relating to a school in which footage had been captured. The stories stated that police were investigating CCTV footage, that footage had been released (for example, 'Can you identify this man?', *Queensland Times*, 2 Aug. 2012) or reported that an individual or group had been identified by using CCTV footage ('Two teens caught after alleged school arson', *Bunbury Mail*, 15 Aug. 2012). Vandalism (n=15), violence both actual and threatened (n=10), unlawful entry (n=8) and arson (n=8) were the main incidents that CCTV was used to investigate. Animal abuse (n=7), usually in the form of violent attacks on school pets (including alpacas and chickens), was also covered, although some of these stories related to the same event. Although these stories didn't present any particular angle regarding the use of CCTV, its use as a technology to assist in crime control is clearly implied and could, thus, provide a latent function in cementing the perception that CCTV is effective in aiding investigations. There were no stories, for example, stating that CCTV did not capture the footage or that it was unable to gain a clear image of assailants. This finding supports suggestions that the perceived role of CCTV has shifted from deterring crime to an 'after the event forensic tool to aid investigations' (Taylor and Gill, 2014).

CCTV was depicted as largely being implemented to protect school premises and property from theft, vandalism, graffiti and arson. In terms of human-centric monitoring, the discourse of protection continued; CCTV was installed to protect teachers from intruders, teachers from parents, students from intruders, teachers from teachers and students from students. There was an explicit sentiment throughout that CCTV could instill good behaviour and introduce polite, well-mannered conduct among those who otherwise were exhibiting problematic behaviour. For example, CCTV was being used by some schools to enforce parking restrictions and ensure that parents behaved appropriately on the school run; others were calling for CCTV to protect teaching staff from abusive and violent parents. Here CCTV was presumed to have a disciplining effect.

Instilling the view that CCTV is primarily a frontline security technology, in 2007 the Australian *Schools Security Programme* was launched to provide 'non-recurrent funding for security infrastructure, such as closed-circuit television (CCTV) systems, lighting and fences, and for the cost of employing security guards'. By 2015, it had provided $35 million for security measures in 126 projects at 76 government and non-government schools and preschools. The allocation of funding prioritised government and non-government schools 'assessed as being at risk of attack, harassment or violence stemming from racial or religious intolerance' (Attorney-General's Department, 2015). The 2014–15 scheme, providing $18 million of funding to eligible schools, generated numerous news stories. Although 'security fencing and CCTV cameras' were cited as key investments, 'none of the schools gave specific details' about how the money would be used (Patterson, 2015). However, there was a clear presumption in all publications following the announcement that CCTV was the de facto security mechanism; it was not apparent exactly how CCTV would safeguard against racially motivated violent attacks. Monahan (2006) pointed out that despite CCTV surveillance failing to prevent violent attacks in schools – for instance, the Columbine High School massacre – these events are still drawn upon to justify increased surveillance and security in schools.

Aside from the focus on crime and security, there were 12 CCTV stories that related to bullying. The views were mixed: some perceived it to be 'an effective weapon against bullies', others rejected its use since CCTV would 'only capture incidents of overt physical aggression, not the causation: the exclusion, teasing, gossip, etc which is often unrelenting' ('Bullying Unresolved', *The Advertiser*, 15 November 2010). Often, CCTV is installed as a panacea for a range of issues without considering how its capabilities could meet intended objectives (Taylor, 2011a). Interestingly, proponents of deploying CCTV to assist in tackling bullying referred to 'anti-bullying cameras', thus removing any connotations of surveillance, monitoring or control. The Director of the South Australian Association of State School Organisations asserted 'the State Government has installed cameras in schools to stop vandalism and theft, to protect property, so why not to protect the children?' (cited in Williams, 2014). Reflecting the 'surveillance creep' that often accompanies technologies, such as CCTV, following the Schools Security Programme, there was a perceptible shift in the use of CCTV. As one story outlined, 'They had criminals, vandals and terrorists in their sights – but surveillance cameras at schools have actually stopped playground bullies in their tracks.' Although the cameras were 'meant to protect school property after hours', the schools were now 'using video footage to root out troublemakers, thieves and thugs among their students' (McDougall and Danks, 2012). This function creep was not problematised in the article; rather, CCTV was presented as delivering numerous supplementary benefits – a technology that could remedy a spectrum of societal problems, ranging from terrorism to bullying.

It should be recognised that the reasons offered to justify or explain the implementation of CCTV do not always tally with how it is then operated in reality. Despite a pervasive presumption that school CCTV is solely implemented to prevent crime, as found in the media analysis, as well as other studies (Taylor, 2011a), it has found many non-crime-related applications, such as the invigilation of exams (BBC News, 2008), monitoring teaching performance (BBC News, 2009a), curtailing general 'horseplay' and even tackling the 'misuse of paper towels and soap' in pupils' toilets (BBC News 2009b). A survey by the Association of Teachers and Lecturers (ATL) found that although 98 per cent of teachers claimed CCTV was installed for security purposes, 50 per cent reported it being used in other ways, such as to monitor pupil behaviour.

News stories largely presented an overarching positive stance towards the desirability and effectiveness of CCTV in schools, praising its ability to detect and deter undesirable behaviours. Just ten stories were coded as having an overall negative depiction of CCTV. Interestingly, they related to CCTV being proposed to tackle 'aggro mums' and angry parents, a rejection that CCTV could be a 'quick fix' to school bullying and a general lamentation that schools were becoming like 'Fort Knox'. One article, for example, was written by a former head teacher who bemoaned the 'fortress-like mentality' that schools were increasingly adopting. But overall, the analysis demonstrated that the media depiction of CCTV in schools between 2012 and 2015 painted it as a useful and effective development. For example, one head teacher, who was cited across numerous stories, declared following the introduction of 59 CCTV cameras in the school that he worked: 'there is no vandalism in this school any more, there is no graffiti in this school any more' (cited in McClellan, 2012). CCTV was largely uncritically portrayed as a technology capable of resolving numerous school-related problems, such as bullying and aggressive behaviour, as well as easing broader societal issues, such as racial tensions and even terrorism. The following section examines some of the myriad impacts, effects and affects that the use of CCTV in schools provokes. The purpose is to illuminate that even when intended purposes are benign and neutral, the reality is that CCTV can radically alter the dynamics of the school environment.

Exploring the experiences and impact of CCTV in schools

Just as the media play a major role in selecting and framing societal issues, schools are important sites of socio-political and cultural filtration. They play a key part in cultural and social reproduction, broadcasting messages about identity, personhood and citizenship. Essentially, they are the means by which children learn how to interact with humans and non-humans and, thus, reassemble the social (Callon, 1986; Latour, 1988). Vander Schee (2009: 558) asserts that surveillance technologies and apparatus transmit particular 'knowledges and truths about the ways in which individuals should conduct their lives for the betterment of self and society'. In this respect, it is important to ascertain the way in which the presence of CCTV scripts children to modify their behaviour in certain ways, privileges certain ways of being and transmits messages about the expectations of a range of societal values.

The CCTV camera, an article comprised of plastic, metal and glass, could be regarded as inanimate and trivial. However, it is argued that it is invested with immensely powerful symbolism and meaning. It encodes the teaching environment with messages that, when translated by those falling within its field of vision, can radically alter classroom dynamics. It is also important to note the way in which artefacts of surveillance, and particularly CCTV, are normalised through exposure and ubiquity, becoming 'an *almost* unnoticed aspect of everyday life' (Ellis *et al*., 2013, emphasis in original). CCTV cameras can be at once visible and invisible, 'simultaneously present yet absent' (ibid.), unnoticed due to their 'utter familiarity', yet invested with the power to 'structure how we write the world' (Thrift, 2004: 585). The following section draws on the empirical research in schools in England to examine the effect and affect of surveillance cameras in schools.

Awareness of CCTV in the school

It was apparent from the media analysis that in Australia at least, there is little awareness among parents and the public about the use of CCTV in schools. For example, some parents reported being 'shocked' and 'scared' by revelations that the school their child attends had been using CCTV in the classroom, often for several years prior (Domjen, 2012). In the study of three English schools, teachers and students varied in the extent to which they were mindful of the presence of CCTV cameras at their school. Essentially, the teachers indicated that they were not particularly cognisant of the cameras and had become accustomed to their presence over time, with one teacher at City Comprehensive explaining:

> I don't really take heed of them [cameras] now … I think I was more aware of them when I first started [working here] but you just get used to them. I don't notice now, but now that I've spoken to you I'll probably get all paranoid again [laughs].

This teacher reported initially being more wary of, even 'paranoid' about, the cameras but that this feeling subsided as the cameras became embedded into the school environment, at which point they registered 'on the margins of consciousness'

(Ellis *et al.*, 2013). However, the teachers did not perceive themselves to be the true objects of observation, and so for them, it was 'easy to forget' that the cameras were there.

In contrast, pupils were far more aware of the use of CCTV cameras in their school and many claimed to know the exact positioning of the majority of cameras. Following some deliberation, in one focus group, the consensus was that pupils knew where they were located and, equally as important, where there was no camera coverage:

> [Steven, UH] … if I was walking around [the school] now I could say where they [the cameras] were. I couldn't sit here and list all the places … well, probably most of them actually. I'm saying you know when there is one coming up. If I'm walking down the corridor, I know the places where they are. I know where to look for them.
>
> [Simon, UH] Yeah, that's true. I know the places where there aren't any. Like I know that there aren't any on the stairs and I know that there aren't any where everyone goes and smokes.

Even if the pupils were unable to identify and recall the exact positioning of the CCTV cameras, they could quickly identify the areas that were not covered. Another pupil stated that although an individual may not be aware of the exact location of all the cameras in the school, they would always check to see if there was one in the vicinity before engaging in any deviant behaviour:

> Sometimes you might not know exactly where they all are but if you were gonna do something then you'd have a look about and check. What I'm saying is: you don't need to know exactly where they are cos you can just look up to check. (Ajay, SSC)

This awareness implies that although pupils may not be fully conscious of the cameras at all times, they have internalised their presence to the extent that they would remember to look for them.

Use of CCTV in schools: Delegation and purpose

Rather than protecting them from crime, students perceived the CCTV at their school was used to 'keep an eye' on them and to ensure they weren't 'getting into trouble or breaking the law' (Rowan, SSC). Supporting this perception, it became apparent through observation and the interviews with teachers that CCTV was being used as part of the disciplinary apparatus aimed at ensuring compliance and good behaviour from students, rather than to detect, prevent or control criminal activities (for further findings regarding the perceived purposes of CCTV in schools, see Taylor, 2011b). The Association of Teachers and Lecturers survey (2008) similarly found that CCTV was often used for 'pupil behaviour monitoring' and 'pupil behaviour control'.

Further contradicting the crime and security discourse surrounding CCTV, the case studies revealed that the technology could actually instil a false sense of security. Teachers and staff reported being less inclined to directly intervene in school incidents, such as fall-outs among pupils or acts of vandalism, because they presumed the 'camera will capture it'. A 'diffusion of responsibility' materialised following the installation of the cameras, whereby staff deferred duty to the cameras. The CCTV camera in this example became what Latour (1992: 157) describes as a 'delegated nonhuman character', invested with the role of documenter, and charged with instilling discipline and control in some instances. On a more macro level, discipline, safety and security in schools are increasingly delegated to the technological apparatus and personnel of a range of external providers. Some schools voluntarily relinquish discipline and rule enforcement to other agencies, such as police and security officers; in some locales, the transfer has become enshrined in law. For example, the NYC Board of Education, alongside many US states, voted to transfer responsibility for school safety to the police. This process can augment the blurring between school discipline and criminal justice and encourages flows of power between the two.

CCTV and privacy in school

Empirical research on the impact of CCTV often encompasses, not surprisingly, a focus on privacy (McCahill and Finn, 2010; Taylor, 2010a). Westin (1967) has defined privacy as 'the claim of individuals, groups or institutions to determine for themselves when, how, and to what extent information about them is communicated to others.' Although the articulation of privacy might be highly subjective, the need for some form of privacy has been claimed to be nearly universal (Michael, 1994). In this study, CCTV's ability to transgress student expectations of privacy relied upon a number of factors, such as location of the cameras, the rationale underpinning usage and the level of monitoring. The pupils were particularly expressive about their need for (relative) privacy in the school environment and attributed a number of values to it, such as the ability to express emotions that they did not want to be publicly observed. Importantly, the majority of students felt that a balance could be struck between visual surveillance and privacy in the school, but most did not feel this had been achieved. Discussion of privacy was dominated by the presence of CCTV cameras in the pupils' toilet area at City Comprehensive and Urban High. It was stressed that cameras at both schools were positioned so as not to be able to see into cubicles when the doors were closed. Despite these reassurances, the pupils were unanimous that it was a huge invasion of their privacy, and many described feeling uncomfortable and upset by the presence of cameras:

> I really don't like the cameras in the toilets. When I first saw them I freaked. Me and Michelle were just like 'argh, what are we gonna do?' I've seen them

at train stations and I get that, but in a school? Like what's gonna happen? (Sarah, UH)

I try to spend as little time as possible in there now. You can't help but wonder if they are watching you. It's not just about going to the loo, it's blowing your nose, yeah, you know, putting your make up on and that. If girls are upset they run to the toilets so no one sees them. That's why you do things like that in the toilets in the first place. (Lisa, UH)

The bathroom represented a private domain for pupils, particularly for female students, where they can discard their public performance and reside 'backstage' (Goffman, 1959). It was considered to be a private sanctuary, where intimate and emotional acts, such as crying or behaviours deemed unfit for public display, could be conducted. Sometimes, students, like everyone, need 'time out' and the ability to withdraw from pressured social interactions and the trials and tribulations of adolescence played out publicly in the school. The toilets provided schoolchildren with 'a chance to lay their masks aside' (Westin, 1967: 35), but the introduction of CCTV defeats the ability of students to successfully accomplish their impression management. Even those pupils who perceived that the CCTV cameras have some positive attributes felt that their use in the student toilet area was excessive:

I agree with there being some cameras. My mum is a teacher at another school and her school is always getting vandalized. She wants more cameras to stop the school from being damaged and things being stolen … I think that is fair enough … I don't like them being in the toilets … There are just some places that are private – and the toilet is one of them. (James, CC)

Overall, pupils at City Comprehensive and Urban High felt that the use of cameras in the toilet area was an unjustifiable invasion of their privacy and disproportionate to any risk. Demonstrating its powerful agentic impact, the mere presence of CCTV cameras can be enough for students to attempt to repress bodily functional urges by not using the bathrooms, even refusing to attend school. Similarly, some parents have removed their children from the school based on what they considered to be an 'outrageous invasion of privacy' (BBC News, 2009b). CCTV, in this respect, is considered to be so abhorrent in a location as quintessentially private as the bathroom that it eclipses all other considerations about the school and education.

(Mis)trust and CCTV

Privacy, surveillance and (mis)trust are all inextricably linked. Ericson and Haggerty (1997: 117) claim that 'privacy can expand only with trust, but trust can expand only with surveillance', thus creating an irredeemable paradox.

As surveillance technology is increasingly relied upon, it can only ever produce a veneer of trust or a 'thin trust' (Crawford, 2000: 209), which ultimately results in a need to verify and confirm. The atmospheres of mistrust and suspicion created by surveillance can undermine 'social cohesion and solidarity' and ultimately result in a 'slow social suicide' (Wood *et al.*, 2006). Giroux (2003: 554) claims that a 'deep distrust' has enveloped interactions with children. Supporting this, the empirical research illustrated how students correlate the increased use of surveillance at their schools with diminishing trust. Surveillance practices take on particular symbolic meanings in the school environment, conveying messages to young people about how they are viewed in society. Pupils described how the use of CCTV at their school was symptomatic of an underlying mistrust of them:

> If you want pupils to act responsibly then you need to show them that they are trusted. You need to treat them … with a little bit of respect. For some it becomes a self-fulfilling prophecy. If you are always expecting them to be up to no good then they might decide that they might as well misbehave. …
> (Sarah, UH)

Mistrust was perceived to breed misbehaviour and the students believed that they were perceived as inherently deviant and required control to curtail their inevitable misbehaviour. This can create a 'morality of low expectation' (Furedi, 1997) of students and result in a focus on managing pupils rather than engaging them in active learning and critical thought. CCTV was the very embodiment of suspicion, and the presence of the cameras was regarded as a symbol of mistrust and enough to galvanise 'a self-fulfilling prophecy'. The agency of CCTV in altering behaviour is further demonstrated by its ability to impact on interactions in the school.

Traditional patterns of sociation can be interrupted as CCTV displaces 'face-to-face' interaction with parents, teachers and peers, replacing it with a privileging of electronically verified versions. In the case studies, CCTV was viewed as a 'guardian of truth', an impartial medium that could be called upon to verify events, elicit truthful responses from students and provide evidence. It provided an 'all-seeing eye' that could verify or disprove a pupil's version of events; simply referring to possible CCTV footage was enough to elicit confessions from some pupils. Illustrating this, McCahill and Finn (2010) found that there was diminishing opportunity for dialogue or negotiation with teachers for issues such as late arrival. Nolan *et al.* (2011: 26) note that using surveillance in this way 'can shift children from developing autonomous relationships that reciprocally respect others to relationships based on avoidance, secrecy, and denial'. Piaget (1932) highlighted the problematic thinking and underdeveloped moral reasoning that can flourish when children are taught in a culture of heteronomy. He draws upon the example of children's perception of telling lies: heteronomous children generally believed that telling lies was only bad if they were discovered and punished, and acceptable if they were not. The case studies discovered a similar heteronomous approach to activities, such as playing truant and smoking:

> [Becky, UH] … I know that there aren't any [cameras] where everyone goes and smokes.
>
> [Ryan, UH] That's true. Why don't they put them there – everyone knows that's where people go to smoke and to wag it [play truant], so surely they'd be better off there than in the middle of the corridor where no-one is gonna do anything anyway?
>
> [Becky, UH] But that's why people go to smoke there – cos they are not there. If you put them there, then they'd just go and smoke somewhere else.
>
> [Ryan, UH] I guess so, but then they'd be off the school premises, so in a way it wouldn't matter.

The pupils perceived deviant activities as location-specific rather than intrinsically wrong, and of little relevance once they had moved beyond the school gates. The extract supports the assertion that CCTV displaces deviant activities, rather than preventing them in their entirety. Spatial displacement is when a crime is shifted from one location to another, typically because of 'target hardening' (referring to the increased security mechanisms applied to vulnerable locations or items). An individual may decide not to commit a criminal act in an area covered by CCTV, but rather than being fully deterred, they simply move beyond the cameras' field of vision. Evidence of displacement has been found in most CCTV evaluations (Welsh and Farrington, 2008). As these examples illustrate, the presence of CCTV encourages heteronomous decision-making, whereby rule breaking is an outcome of perceived rewards or punishments rather than critical thinking and evaluation (Nolan *et al.*, 2011).

CCTV and the 'chilling effect' on interaction and mobility

A familiar Foucault-inspired argument within surveillance studies is that over time, surveillance practices encourage the self-regulation of behaviour; an automatic functioning of power materialises as those believing themselves to be under observation concede to anticipatory conformity. This is particularly pertinent in the school, where creativity, intellectual exploration and expression are central to education. McCahill and Finn (2010: 283) found that students are 'acutely aware' when their behaviour and actions (and conversations in some schools) are being monitored by visual surveillance, such as CCTV. The result was that some students would even modify their 'legitimate' behaviour 'due to a concern that their actions could be misinterpreted' by the watchers (ibid.). Similarly, the present empirical study found that CCTV cameras in the classroom subdued interactions, whether they were mischievously inclined or not, and stultified creativity.

If surveillance does indeed impact even on legitimate behaviours, schoolchildren could be self-regulating in order to avoid presenting a particular reading of their character and interests. Just as Hudson (2014) claims that the absence of CCTV encourages experimentation, the presence of CCTV in the classroom can close off opportunities for free creative, innovative and expressive thought and action. Furthermore, students described how they would alter their movements around the school campus in a bid to avoid the cameras, taking alternative routes where possible or congregating in areas where there was no camera coverage. Far from being an inanimate and benign object, the camera, invested with the symbolism of discipline and control, had a tangible impact on the ways in which students acted and interacted.

Resistance and democratic participation

Pupils were resigned to the fact that within the school environment, they had very little power to object to or question the surveillance which they were subjected to. Some pupils articulated their discontent with the use of extensive CCTV at their school by likening it to the Big Brother television show. Alyssa (CC) remarked, 'if I wanted to be on Big Brother I would've auditioned for it', encapsulating the resentment felt by some pupils at the use of CCTV in their school, as well as signifying their lack of power to object to its use.

Resistance in the three schools largely took the form of avoiding or interfering with CCTV cameras and was largely interpreted as harmless and humorous subversive actions. Weiss (2008: 595) asserts, 'everyday surveillance is matched by everyday resistance' and so perhaps these minor acts of defiance become routinised among those who feel subordinated, enabling them to furnish a sense of self beyond institutional controls. Beneath the surface of ostensible compliance, there existed an undercurrent of minor, ritualised, ideological resistance. There have, however, been more overt attempts to challenge the use of CCTV in schools. Weiss (2011) draws upon one of the largest recorded protests in response to surveillance practices in schools to explore the role of resistance.

In the autumn of 2005, 1,500 students at a large comprehensive school in the Bronx, New York, staged a walkout in protest against the implementation of metal detectors and security cameras at their school. The students marched three miles under police escort to demand a meeting with the region's superintendent and other Department of Education officials. Despite generating a huge amount of public and media interest, the protest was not effective in reversing the decision to install CCTV and other techno-security measures. In fact, Weiss reports, it actually increased them. Following the walkout in the Bronx, the students developed alternative means to avoid and evade surveillance, including the 'tactical avoidance' of interaction with security officers. In this way, resistance became 'masked in a kind of complicity' (Weiss, 2008: 9), since it would not be easily observable from the outside but still represented a challenge to those in authority. Students might lack the power needed to change policy but they retain the ability to 'cope with, negotiate, and respond to these practices and injustices' (Weiss, 2011: 595).

As the students in the Bronx discovered, direct action doesn't always result in young people being heard, and resistance is not without consequence. For example, in 2012 in Brazil, 107 students were suspended from school after they protested about the installation of cameras, which they claimed had been introduced with a lack of dialogue between school administrators and the pupils. Compliance with surveillance is, therefore, often based on coercion and students who assert that their rights are confronted with an arsenal of disciplinary mechanisms deployed to stifle dissent. This is of particular salience in the school environment where future citizens are socialised (Morrill *et al.*, 2010). It is precisely at the time that students are developing their rights consciousness that their rights are being denied, which could have profound effects on future expectations of democracy. A cross-national analysis of the surveillance of young people found that the current generation is growing up with a profound mistrust of the state, a diminished belief in democracy, 'cynical views about a broad-based "common good"' and 'little memory of or imagination for a public sphere for the public' (Ruck *et al.*, 2008: 15–6). The full impact of surveillance on young people's development is yet to be discovered, but there are indicators that in an educational environment, it can stifle creativity, teach young people that the only means of trust is through technological means, and erode privacy.

Conclusion

Technological surveillance apparatus can have implications and impacts that were not anticipated since 'objects too have agency' (Latour, 2005) and, therefore, cannot be presumed to be neutral equivalents to what preceded them. Although dominant discourses often represent CCTV as solely a crime and security technology, protecting schoolchildren and schools, there are often unintended consequences – the by-products of prolonged exposure to technological surveillance mechanisms. As Winner (1997) asserts: 'technical innovations of any substantial extent involve a reweaving of the fabric of society, a reshaping of some of the roles, rules, and relationships that comprise our ways of living together'. It is important to recognise the ways in which objects, such as CCTV, can be operated as 'delegates', invested with certain prerogatives and ideologies. Ragnedda (2010: 356) argues:

> surveillance is much more than simply monitoring, watching and recording individuals and their data. … Surveillance is an interaction of power that creates and advances relations of domination. In practice, surveillance is a mode of governance, one that controls access and opportunities.

Power is translated through delegated technologies to exercise certain wishes and compel particular actions. Such delegation to technological surveillance apparatus makes visible and privileges some behaviours and ways of being, while precluding or dismissing others within the school. Just as school league tables and the standardised test 'valorizes some kinds of knowledge skills and renders other kinds invisible' (Bowker and Star, 1999: 6), each surveillant apparatus casts its own inference about desirable and appropriate behaviour and action. Accounts that seek to objectivise or make benign the influence of technology ignore the subjectivities, biases and partialities that permeate the design, application and impact of such technological apparatus.

Given the discordance between media representations of CCTV in schools, on the one hand, and the empirical evidence that speaks to its transformative power when used to monitor schoolchildren, on the other hand, there is clearly a need for greater transparency regarding the everyday uses of CCTV and for public debate about the appropriateness of its use in education facilities. News stories focus overwhelmingly on the use of CCTV as a crime control technology, whilst ignoring other impacts and effects. Although a handful of stories questioned the desirability of CCTV in schools, these were in the minority and most stories presented a positive outlook on CCTV as an effective and neutral technology, enhancing safety and reducing criminal activity in and around the school. It is little wonder that the uptake of CCTV in schools continues apace, as rarely is its usage beyond crime control ever raised, and dissenting and critical voices are seldomly given a platform.

References

Advertiser, The (2010) 'Bullying Unresolved'. *The Advertiser*, 15 November.

Amin A. (2002) 'Spatialities of globalisation', *Environment and Planning A*, 34: 385–99.

Association of Teachers and Lecturers (2008) '85% of teachers have CCTV in their schools and nearly 25% worry about hidden cameras'. Available online at www.atl.org.uk/media-office/media-archive/CCTV-in-schools.asp (accessed: 04.04.2015).

Attorney-General's Department (2015) *Schools security programme: programme guidelines, 2014–15 to 2016–17*. Available online at www.ag.gov.au (accessed 04.11.2015).

BBC News (2008) 'CCTV could be used in exam rooms'. Available online at http://news.bbc.co.uk/2/hi/uk_news/education/7342432.stm (accessed 06.01.2016).

BBC News (2009a) 'Teachers watched on CCTV cameras'. Available online at http://news.bbc.co.uk/2/hi/uk_news/england/manchester/7923731.stm (accessed 06.01.2016).

BBC News (2009b) 'School head defends toilets CCTV'. Available online at http://news.bbc.co.uk/2/hi/uk_news/wales/mid_/7851282.stm (accesed 06.01.2016).

Bowker, G. C. and S. L. Star (1999) *Sorting things out: classification and its consequences*. London: MIT Press.

Callon, M. (1986). 'Some elements of a sociology of translation: domestication of the scallops and the fishermen of St Brieuc Bay', in J. Law (ed.), *Power, action and belief: a new sociology of knowledge?*, pp. 196–223. London: Routledge.

Crawford, A. (2000) 'Situational crime prevention, urban governance and trust relations', in A. Von Hirsch, D. Garland and A. Wakefield (eds), *Ethical and social perspectives on situational crime prevention*. Oxford: Hart Publishing.

Ditton, J. (2000) 'Crime and the city: public attitudes towards open-street CCTV in Glasgow', *British Journal of Criminology*, 40: 692–709.

Domjen, B. (2012) 'Class cameras row', *Sunday Telegraph*, 21 October 2012.

Ellis, D., I. Tucker, and D. Harper (2013) 'The affective atmospheres of surveillance', *Theory and Psychology*, 23(6): 716–31.

Ericson, R. and K. Haggerty (1997) *Policing the risk society*. Toronto: University of Toronto Press.

Foucault, M. (2007) *Security, territory, population*. Basingstoke, UK: Palgrave Macmillan.

Furedi, F. (1997) *Culture of fear: risk taking and the morality of low expectation*. London: Cassell.

Gallagher, M. (2010) 'Are schools panoptic?', *Surveillance and Society*, 7(3/4): 262–72.

Giroux, H. A. (2003) 'Racial injustice and disposable youth in the age of zero tolerance', *International Journal of Qualitative Studies in Education*, 16(4): 553–65.

Glaser, B.G. (1978) *Theoretical sensitivity: advances in the methodology of grounded theory*. Mill Valley, CA: Sociology Press.

Goffman, E. (1959) *The presentation of the self in everyday life*. London: Penguin.

Greenberg, J. and S. Hier (2009) 'CCTV surveillance and the poverty of media discourse: a content analysis of Canadian newspaper coverage', *Canadian Journal of Communication*, 34(3): 461–86.

Haggerty, K. D. (2011) 'Tear down the walls: on demolishing the panopticon', in D. Lyon (ed.), *Theorizing surveillance: the panopticon and beyond*. London: Routledge.

Hier, S. P., J. Greenberg, K. Walby, and D. Lett (2007) 'Media, communication and the establishment of public camera surveillance programmes in Canada', *Media, Culture & Society*, 29(5), 727–51.

Hudson, J. (2014) 'The affordances and potentialities of derelict urban spaces', in B. Olsen and Þ. Petursdottir (Eds.) *Ruin memories: materialities, aesthetics and the archeology of the recent past*. Oxon: Routledge.

Latour, B. (1988) 'Mixing humans and nonhumans together: the sociology of the door closer', *Social Problems*, 35(3): 298–310.

Latour, B. (1992) 'Where are the missing masses? The sociology of a few mundane artefacts', in W. E. Bijker and J. Law (eds), *Shaping technology/building society: studies in sociotechnical change*. Cambridge, MA: MIT Press.

Latour, B. (2005) *Reassembling the social; an introduction to actor-network-theory*. Oxford: Oxford University Press.

Leonard, A. (2012) 'Two teens caught after alleged school arson'. *The Bunbury Mail*, 15 August.

McCahill, M. and R. Finn (2010) 'The social impact of surveillance in three UK schools: "angels", "devils" and "teen mums"', *Surveillance and Society*, 7(3/4): 273–89.

McClellan, B. (2012) 'The principal with 59 eyes: crime falls thanks to CCTV', *Blacktown Advocate*, 7 March 2012.

McDougall, B. and K. Danks (2012) 'School security CCTV puts bullies on pause', *Daily Telegraph*, 28 March 2012.

Michael, J. (1994) *Privacy and human rights*. Dartmouth: UNESCO.

Monahan, T. (2006) 'The surveillance curriculum: risk management and social control in the neoliberal school', in T. Monahan (ed.), *Surveillance and security: technological politics and power in everyday life*. New York: Routledge.

Morrill, C., L. B. Edelman, K. Tyson, and R. Arum (2010) 'Legal mobilization in schools: the paradox of rights and race among youth', *Law and Society Review*, 44(3/4): 651–94.

Nolan, J., K. Raynes-Goldie, and M. McBride (2011) 'The stranger danger: exploring surveillance, autonomy, and privacy in children's use of social media', *Canadian Children Journal*, 36(2): 24–32.

Norris, C. (2003) 'From the personal to the digital: CCTV, the panopticon, and the technological mediation of suspicion and social control', in D. Lyon (ed.), *Surveillance as social sorting: privacy, risk and digital discrimination*, pp. 249–81. London/New York: Routledge.

Patterson, R. (2015) '$1.5m makes schools safer', *Wentworth Courier*, 11 March 2015.
Piaget, J. (1932) *The moral judgment of the child*. London: Kegan, Paul, Trench, Trubner & Co.
Queensland Times, The (2012) 'Can you identify this man?'. *The Queensland Times*, 2 August.
Ragnedda, M. (2010) 'Review of Monahan and Torres (eds.) *Schools under Surveillance*', *Surveillance and Society*, 7(3/4): 356–7.
Ruck, M., A. Harris, M. Fine, and N. Freudenberg (2008) 'Youth experiences of surveillance: a cross-national analysis', in M. Flynn and D. C. Brotherton (eds.), *Globalizing the streets: cross-cultural perspectives on youth, social control, and empowerment*, pp. 15–30. New York: Columbia University Press.
Spriggs, A., M. Gill, J. Argomaniz, and J. Bryan (2005) 'Public attitudes towards CCTV: results from the pre-intervention public attitude survey carried out on areas implementing CCTV', Home Office Online Report. London: Home Office.
Taylor, E. (2010a) 'I spy with my little eye: the use of CCTV in schools and the impact on privacy', *Sociological Review*, 58(3): 381–405.
Taylor, E. (2010b) 'From finger-painting to fingerprinting: the use of biometric technology in schools', *Education Law Journal*, 4: 276–88.
Taylor, E. (2011a) 'UK schools, CCTV and the Data Protection Act 1998', *Journal of Education Policy*, 26(1): 1–15.
Taylor, E. (2011b) 'Awareness, understanding and experiences of CCTV amongst teachers and pupils in three UK schools', *Information Polity: An International Journal of Government and Democracy in the Information Age*, 16(4): 303–18.
Taylor, E. (2012) 'The rise of the surveillance school', in K. Ball, K. D. Haggerty, and D. Lyon (eds.), *Handbook of surveillance studies*. London: Routledge.
Taylor, E. (2013) *Surveillance schools: security, discipline and control in contemporary education*. Basingstoke, UK: Palgrave Macmillan.
Taylor, E. (2014) 'Easy as A, B, CCTV? Using semi-structured interviews and focus groups in a case study on surveillance technologies in schools', *Sage Research Methods*. Available online at http://dx.doi.org/10.4135/978144627305013514657 (accessed 23rd May 2016).
Taylor, E. and M. Gill (2014) 'CCTV: Reflections on its use, abuse and effectiveness', in M. Gill (ed.), *The handbook of security*. Basingstoke, UK: Palgrave Macmillan.
Thrift, N. (2004) 'Movement-space: the changing domain of thinking resulting from the development of new kinds of spatial awareness', *Economy and Society*, 33(4): 582–604.
Vander Schee, C. (2009) 'Fruit, vegetables, fatness, and Foucault: governing students and their families through school health policy', *Journal of Education Policy*, 24: 557–74.
Weiss, J. (2008) 'Under the radar: school surveillance and youth resistance', PhD thesis, City University of New York.
Weiss, J. (2011) 'Valuing youth resistance before and after public protest', *International Journal of Qualitative Studies in Education*, 24(5): 595–9.
Welsh, B. C. and D. P. Farrington (2008) *Effects of closed circuit television surveillance on crime*. London: The Campbell Collaboration.
Welsh, B. C. and D. P. Farrington (2002) *Crime prevention effects of closed circuit television: a systematic review*. Home Office Research Study 252. London: Home Office Research, Development and Statistics Directorate.
Westin, A. (1967) *Privacy and freedom*. New York: Atheneum.
Williams, T. (2014) 'Cameras to stop bullying', *The Advertiser*, 22 December 2014.
Winner L. (1997) 'Technology today: utopia or dystopia?', *Social Research*, 64(3): 990–1.
Wood, D. M., K. Ball, D. Lyon, C. Norris, and C. Raab (eds) (2006) *A report on the surveillance society*. Wilmslow: Office of the Information Commissioner/Surveillance Studies Network.

3 Digital health goes to school

Implications of digitising children's bodies

Michael Gard and Deborah Lupton

All public health policies and interventions are an expression of competing narratives about the past, present and future. They all say something about the causes of ill health and pass explicit or implicit judgement on previous attempts to solve particular health problems. They are shaped by contemporary socio-political conditions and prioritise specific areas of concern over others. Perhaps above all else, they attempt to describe a world that is better than the one we currently live in and the path that should be followed to get there. In sum, they are never simply disinterested, evidence-driven forms of action. Much the same can be said about any educational endeavour, and particularly those that sit at the intersection between schools and public health, which is our subject in this chapter. In fact, school-based public health initiatives are worthy of scholarly attention, we will argue, precisely because of the tensions that lie behind what might seem their common-sense appeal.

As a field of study and practical intervention, school health is difficult to define for two related reasons: the conceptual elasticity of 'health'; and the tendency for almost everything that schools do to be seen as having health implications. Nonetheless, it is possible to outline pragmatically a set of school-based practices that have been and are currently justified on physical and mental health grounds. The curriculum area of physical education is perhaps the most familiar and long-standing of these, but we could also include drug, alcohol and tobacco education, the provision of food, anti-bullying initiatives and mental health programmes. For the sake of brevity, we will group all of these under the term 'school health'.

School health is in the early stages of its engagement with digital technology. For this reason, the developments that we write about in this chapter are relatively new and have not yet been the subject of extensive scholarship. Still, two guiding insights drawn from history are likely to be relevant to school health's digital future. First, despite the idealistic rhetoric that tends to frame it, school health interventions are never solely concerned with the health of students. The sale of food in schools, for example, is in many countries a lucrative commercial enterprise (Levine, 2008), whereas sex education, regardless of what form it takes, is unavoidably a form of moral instruction (Di Mauro and Joffe, 2007). Second, while important exceptions exist, the amount of time, energy and resources that has been devoted to school health initiatives far exceed their measurable effect, a point that explains the long list of scholars who have questioned the worth of school health initiatives (including Cuban, 1986; Tupper, 2008) and cautioned against unrealistic hopes for their impact on the health of students (St Leger, 2004).

For both of these reasons – that school health is never just what it purports to be and doubts about its efficacy, interest in a digital approach to school health is growing. In what follows, we contextualise this enthusiasm against a broader set of educational, medical, economic and technological developments. We then go on to discuss one concrete example – the US-developed school students' physical fitness programme 'Fitnessgram' – that, at least to our eyes, exemplifies why digital school health needs to be the subject of more penetrating critical reflection than has yet been the case (see Chapter 4).

Educational politics of school health

From their inception, educational systems in Western countries have always been premised, at least in part, on public health grounds. Many educational reformers of the eighteenth, nineteenth and early twentieth centuries, for example, saw schools as a way of producing a physically and psychologically robust population (Urban and Wagoner, 2000). Both eugenic and imperial concerns with racial purity and vigour were fundamental motivating forces for the bodily inspection programmes that sprang up in English-speaking schools in the first half of the twentieth century (Martineau, 1996). Likewise, Cold War tensions and growing anxiety about the physical capacities of American children led directly to the US government creating a series of school-based fitness interventions (McElroy, 2008).

Against this backdrop of enduring belief in their public health mission, schools have proven to be a remarkably flexible discursive tool in the hands of health advocates, social reformers, politicians and ideologues of virtually any persuasion. In fact, it is difficult to think of a public health matter, large or small, which has not at one time been given to schools to solve; skeletal posture, infectious disease, non-infectious disease, mental health, under-nutrition, over-nutrition, social cohesion, sexual behaviour, moral rectitude, alcohol and drug use, road safety and the perceived perils of urban living are among the most long-standing and best known, but are by no means an exhaustive list (Gard and Pluim, 2014). In each case, however, school health interventions have been the culmination of professional and political struggles and compromises. To take just one example, the introduction of subsidised school lunches in American public schools immediately following World War II was presented to the electorate as a public health measure to feed under- or malnourished children. But as Levine (2008) has demonstrated, the programme was originally developed as an economic measure to support the incomes of struggling American farmers and, perhaps more importantly, as a product of the suspicions, antipathies and deal-making that have long characterised the North–South divide in US party politics.

This essentially symbolic dimension of school health is captured in the shifting classroom practice of physical education since its emergence in the late nineteenth century and the various arguments that have been mobilised by its advocates. At various points in history, physical education's purpose was variously seen as readying working-class children for factory work, preparing young men for war, liberating children's innate corporeal and artistic creativity, inculcating self-control and a love of play, promoting social cohesion and producing future sporting champions (Kirk, 1992, 1998). From the 1950s onwards, however, a more bio-medical mission emerged. In fact, given growing concerns about overweight, obesity and chronic disease in recent years, physical education's public health role has grown steadily into a moral obligation in the eyes of many within the profession itself (Himberg, 2005). This is interesting because evidence for a physical education 'effect' on health has proven to be extremely elusive, despite the efforts of many researchers to demonstrate it (Green, 2014). But as Wright (1996) and Kirk (2000) have pointed out, the reorientation of physical education towards a more scientific and bio-medical outlook is less a matter of evidence and more the product of the struggles between different knowledge traditions for resources and institutional prestige, particularly within universities.

While the insights we might draw from this history are potentially numerous, for our purposes, what matters is the enduring power of the *idea* of schools as an instrument of public health policy. Although their motivations have been hugely varied, it has suited a broad cross-section of interests to believe in (or at least to claim to believe in) the ameliorative potential of schools. This convergence of interests helps to explain why this belief has proven to be impervious to the steady flow of contrary evidence.

In some respects, trying to prioritise public health outcomes cuts against schools' primary mission to educate children, a point which partly explains why so many school health initiatives are unsuccessful or prove unsustainable. This is especially true given the growing tendency for Western educational authorities to devote time and resources to improving student performance on standardised high-stakes numeracy and literacy tests. Looked at from a more broadly sociological perspective, however, there are reasons to suspect that a *digitised* school health movement might be well placed to ride the waves of global educational change.

We will have space here only to summarise what has been described by scholars, mostly pejoratively, as the global educational reform movement, referred to by its acronym, GERM (Macdonald, 2014). Scholars have characterised this as the reconfiguring of educational processes and outcomes according to neoliberal principles of market forces, consumer choice and accountability (Ball, 2003). In particular, the focus on accountability partly explains why regimes of standardised and (allegedly) internationally comparable testing have emerged so rapidly in recent years. It also explains the re-emergence of performance pay schemes for teachers in some parts of the world. But, as many researchers have argued, systems of this kind are designed to measure and reward things that can be measured, leading, they suggest, to both a narrowing and vulgarising of educational aspirations (Rizvi and Lingard, 2009).

The champions of educational reform emphasise what they claim will be the energising effect of free market forces on education, leading to both innovation and efficiency. Two factors are fundamental to this vision: first, increased involvement of the private sector in the supply of educational resources and the delivery of educational services; and second, the role of digital technology. As a result, educational systems worldwide are now experimenting with various kinds of partnerships with a range of edu-businesses, including the global giant Pearson Education and News Corporation's educational subsidiary Amplify (Ball, 2013). In this version of educational reform, the synergy of capital and technology is fundamental; virtual schools, computer-generated learning plans for individual students and wearable digital technology are already a feature of the educational landscape. These changes are happening for many reasons, including the potential for digitally delivered educational services to turn a profit and generate large amounts of data about children, teachers, schools and entire educational systems. Thus, the exploitation of large digital data sets, or 'big data', is held up as yet another reason why private investment and digital technology will lead to superior education outcomes.

If we combine an appreciation of the broader global educational landscape, the aspirations of school health's many advocates, and the increasing sophistication of mobile and pervasive computing technologies, a formidable field of possibilities for digital school health presents itself. At the relatively low-tech end, there are already examples of businesses, like the Coca-Cola company, delivering online health education instruction to schools (Powell, 2014). However, our focus in the remainder of this chapter considers a more hi-tech future for school health, based on the collection, analysis and dissemination of digital data.

Digital data and education

It is important to recognise the broader sociocultural, political and material context in which school health is moving towards digitisation. When we use the term 'material', we are referring to the physicality of digital technologies and the ways in which they are entangled with human and other non-human actors to form dynamic assemblages (Gillespie *et al.*, 2014). This perspective draws on sociomaterialism (Fenwick and Edwards, 2011) and the new materialism (Coole and Frost, 2010) in emphasising the embodied interactions of people with objects: in this case, such objects as wearable self-tracking devices, mobile or desktop computers, software and algorithms and the digital data on people's behaviours, emotions and thoughts that are generated from these interactions.

A growing body of literature is beginning to examine the implications of digital software and hardware on people's concepts of embodiment, selfhood and social relations. Writers have pointed to the ways in which knowledge has become digitised and is increasingly controlled by the internet empires – Google, Apple,

Amazon, Facebook and Twitter – and other digital corporations (Franklin, 2013; Fuchs, 2014; Lash, 2007; Van Dijck, 2013). Digital scholars have emphasised the ways in which computer software and hardware are sociocultural artefacts, the products of human decision-making and political as well as commercial agendas (Manovich, 2013). The structuring role played by algorithms, or 'algorithmic authority', has also attracted critical attention. Scholars writing on this topic have noted that software algorithms are increasingly playing a part in shaping knowledge and information and determining futures (Cheney-Lippold, 2011; Mackenzie and Vurdubakis, 2011; Totaro and Ninno, 2014).

The notion of lively data (Lupton, 2016) also requires attention as part of recognising the materiality of digital technologies. Digital data are ceaselessly collected on the users of digital technologies, from their search engine encounters to their online shopping habits and social media status updates. Qualculation (quantitative calculation) (Thrift, 2004) underpins concepts concerning how digital data should be gathered and acted upon. Qualculation has been intensified by digital technologies that are able to monitor and record continuously minute details of people's bodies and behaviours (Thrift, 2004), including the generation of personal and big digital data sets. According to Thrift (2004: 584), these forms of qualculation are generating new ways of understanding and experiencing space and embodiment, changing what he describes as the 'human sensorium', or humans' embodied and sensual experiences of their world. Instead of fixed numerical values being configured, the flow of data that is afforded by digital technologies generates new values incessantly, involving endless calculations and recalculations, which we are required to assess and act upon. People come to view themselves not only as the subjects of continual measurement and quantification but also as interpreters and actors upon these forms of information who are moving around in environments in which they are data-emitting objects feeding into the digital data economy.

The questions of how data are understood and represented and the recursive effects they have on human cognition, embodiment and social relations in these new conditions of digitised qualculation remain to be explored in any great depth. In the context of school health, it may be argued that such technologies configure qualculated assemblages, in which digital data are represented as vital to both generating detailed information on students' bodies and as motivating students by allowing them to 'see' what they have achieved via what are considered to be the neutral, objective insights of digitised quantified data. These ideals are routinely expounded in the devices, discourses and practices related to self-tracking or 'quantifying the self' (Lupton, 2013a, 2013b, 2014a).

In the digital knowledge economy, such data have become valuable commodities, viewed as producing important insights into human behaviours. They also contribute to people's attempts to optimise themselves: to be self-entrepreneurs. In discourses on using personal data for improving health, well-being and productivity, algorithmic authority often plays an important role. The digital data that are collected on individuals, either on their own behalf or by other actors and agencies, such as social media sites, customer loyalty programmes or search engines, are represented as providing important information that people can employ to engage in work on themselves as part of the project of selfhood (Lupton, 2013a, 2016). In the case of children, parents and teachers employ monitoring and surveillance technologies in the interests of optimising children and maximising their health, well-being, learning and life skills. This is, therefore, a form of imposed or even coercive self-tracking, in which external actors or agencies seek to persuade or force people to collect data on themselves. When these data are employed principally for the benefit of others (for commercial, managerial or research use) rather than those who have generated the data, they contribute to the mode of exploited self-tracking (Lupton, 2016).

In recent years, the domain of school education more generally has been increasingly digitised; yet, the perspectives on digital technologies that we have outlined above are only beginning to be incorporated into the sociology of education, much less the more specific sociology of school health. This is partly because this field has not traditionally devoted much attention to a theoretically informed analysis of digital technology, tending to view such objects as useful or even revolutionary tools (or what Selwyn (2012) refers to as the 'ed-tech bubble' perspective) rather than as sociocultural artefacts worthy of sustained critical attention (Edwards, 2015; Selwyn, 2012, 2015).

In countries such as the UK and USA, the spaces of the classroom and playground, and even changing rooms and lavatories in many schools, are monitored by CCTV cameras. Some schools require students to wear RFID chips in badges or incorporated into clothing to monitor their movements, and use biometric technologies, such as fingerprint recognition devices, to identify them (Taylor, 2013). Students' use of digital technologies in school is frequently monitored as part of ensuring that they are not accessing inappropriate websites or engaging in cyberbullying. Such surveillance technologies are often justified in the name of improving security and reducing the risks to which students may be exposed. However, digital technologies in schools are expanding well beyond security devices. A number of monitoring devices are beginning to focus on students' learning achievements, using software algorithms to closely track progress and predict future learning (learning and predictive analytics) (Edwards, 2015; Selwyn, 2013; Williamson, 2013, 2015a).

In the context of schools, algorithmic decision-making comes to bear on the ways in which student behaviour is monitored and measured and the predictions that are made about future behaviour. The development of the 'smart school' (Williamson, 2015b) or 'sentient school' (Lupton, 2015a) has configured a space in which tracking software and sensor-based and visual-recording technologies are able to track students in ever-finer detail, continually generating various forms of data sets about them. Given the increasing prevalence of digital technologies in schools, it has been contended that software and hardware should be viewed as elements of the 'hidden curriculum' of education that require identification and critical analysis (Edwards, 2015). The commercial elements of these technologies, as we noted earlier, require attention. Not only are digital companies and entrepreneurs profiting from selling software and hardware to schools in the name of innovation, security and better learning and teaching, but the digital data that are generated from students' use of these technologies are also highly valuable in the digital knowledge economy and for government policy development.

The health and physical education curriculum is also moving towards the use of digital devices for student surveillance. We see here a merging of pedagogical with surveillance rationales. Student learning objectives are represented as accomplished via the instructional attributes of quantifiable data. To view one's data, it is assumed, is to achieve greater knowledge about one's body and its functions and sporting performance. The use of digital technologies in school health is just one iteration of a number of developments in the digitising of health, fitness and sporting practices. The apparatus of digital health incorporates such technologies as patient monitoring and self-care devices, telemedicine (remote clinical care), diagnostic, risk management and decision-making tools for healthcare workers and managers, digital devices for administering medicine or regulating body functions, digital imaging and 3D printing, digitised medical education, health promotion using digital technologies (for example, text messages, apps and wearable self-tracking devices), online platforms, blogs and other social media for the sharing of information and experiences by patients and healthcare workers, digital epidemiology, 'smart' healthy cities initiatives, electronic patient records and healthcare management software, 'smart homes' designed to support assisted living initiatives for the elderly and digital games for sport and fitness (Lupton, 2014b, 2015b).

Sporting and fitness activities are now frequently monitored by digital devices. These include technologies that are able to film physical motion and apply algorithms to analyse the movement, and wearable devices that track a range of bodily functions and activities and generate digital data. A form of applied computer science, often referred to as sport/s informatics, has developed, which capitalises on the plethora of digital monitoring and sensor-based devices and software available for athletes and sportspeople at all levels to analyse performance (Sykora *et al.*, 2015). As in many other domains in which digital data are used, these data are viewed as offering new insights by virtue of their volume and apparent accuracy and opportunity to generate fine-grained, continuous information on active bodies.

Health and physical education teachers are beginning to see the potential of using these technologies as part of measuring their students' physical fitness and sporting prowess and engaging students' interest in the curriculum. The concept of 'gamification' is central to recent initiatives in school health. Gamification, or the rendering of aspects of using digital technologies and self-tracking as games, is an important dimension of new approaches to self-tracking. The principles of gamification have entered many social domains, including education, the home and the workplace. Gamification is viewed as a motivating factor in inspiring people to compete with others, achieve their own goals or simply have fun while engaging in mundane, difficult or repetitive tasks and activities (Jagoda, 2013;

McCormick, 2013; O'Donnell, 2014). In the context of schools, digital game technologies (sometimes referred to as 'exergames'), such as Wii Fit, Xbox Kinect, and a multitude of apps, have been advocated to address a range of 'problems', including children's lack of physical activity, body weight, mental health, diet, smoking and skin cancer prevention, physical rehabilitation and co-ordination and asthma and diabetes self-management (Öhman *et al.*, 2014; Reddy, 2014).

The digital gamification of school health has a number of potential consequences. One is the rendering of external surveillance objectives into internalised desires to monitor and measure one's physical activities and capacities. By making an act of surveillance playful and voluntary, it becomes far more acceptable compared to those acts of surveillance that are perceived to be imposed on oneself by others. Another consequence is rendering activities that might otherwise be viewed and experienced purely as ludic into the apparatus of self-management and bodily regulation for the sake of good health and physical fitness. Fun becomes subject to various forms of monitoring and measuring as part of achieving standard approved outcomes in the interests of good health.

Case study: Fitnessgram

Finally, we turn to a more detailed example of the digitisation of school health. The programme known today as Fitnessgram, began as a computer-generated fitness report card system in a group of Texas schools in the late 1970s. The system's creator, Charles L. Sterling, later joined the Dallas-based Cooper Institute, founded in 1970 by the so-called 'father of aerobics', Ken Cooper. With the support of the Cooper Institute, Sterling spent the following decades developing, refining and promoting Fitnessgram (Plowman *et al.*, 2006). According to publicity material, Fitnessgram is now used in tens of thousands of American schools and, like its predecessors, is exported around the world (Cooper Institute, 2014a).

Fitnessgram's advocates have been at pains to describe it as 'driven by data', while also tapping into the growing prestige of and interest in digital technology. For example, while there has been little change over time in the fitness-testing protocols used, each new version of Fitnessgram has invariably been distinguishable by increasingly sophisticated software systems for recording and disseminating data and their ability to integrate with other digital platforms. The recent release of version 10.0 is particularly interesting in this respect. While earlier versions had simply instructed teachers in how to conduct fitness tests and communicate the results, version 10.0 now includes systems for capturing data about what children eat and the amount of physical activity they do, additions the Cooper Institute calls 'Nutrigram' and 'Activitygram'. As an integrated surveillance system, Fitnessgram 10.0 is now being advertised as a way to 'complete the equation for good health' by focusing on the 'whole child' (Cooper Institute, 2014a). In the case of Nutrigram, children are required to take periodical surveys that then generate reports about their nutritional knowledge and behaviour. For Activitygram, a three-day survey period is recommended, in which children log their physical activity in 30-minute increments.

In short, Fitnessgram is steadily evolving into physical education's equivalent of the high-stakes literacy and numeracy testing that we described earlier in this chapter. A number of US states have already passed legislation making Fitnessgram testing compulsory in government-funded schools, and others are preparing to follow suit. Enacting legislation, in most cases, requires data to be analysed at the school, district and state level and then reported to state legislatures on a yearly basis. Fitnessgram 10.0 appears to have been developed precisely with the collection, aggregation and reporting of large amounts of data in mind.

Whether or not these developments are to be welcomed is something people might legitimately disagree about – and perhaps somewhat beside the point, given this volume's focus on surveillance. We will suggest here only that the philosophy repeatedly articulated by Fitnessgram's advocates – that data and information drive behavioural change – is very much at odds with mainstream health education thinking. In fact, Fitnessgram's explicitly deficit-model approach – that we need to understand where children are going wrong so that we can then fix them – has been the subject of sustained and explicit critique by health educators for some time (Antonovsky, 1996; Morgan and Ziglio, 2007). With respect to surveillance, however, two points are worth making.

First, it is generally argued by researchers that self-reported measures of both eating and physical activity are unreliable, particularly when data is supplied by children (Tremblay, 2004). This is important because, as we described above, research into ever more sophisticated and physically unobtrusive biometric surveillance systems is now underway. In this light, the published leadership groups of the Cooper Institute are instructive. For example, alongside politicians, banking, oil, finance and retail CEOs, owners and chairmen of professional baseball and football teams, motivational speakers and medical researchers and clinicians, the Cooper Institute's Board of Trustees and advisory committees are populated by leaders from large data management (such as Digital Equipment Corporation) and computing hard- and software (such as Electronic Data Systems) corporations (Cooper Institute, 2014b).

It is surely not overly conspiratorial to assume that future versions of Fitnessgram will be designed primarily to interface with increasingly sophisticated digital devices that capture and analyse biometric data. Fitnessgraph apps are already available for both children and teachers. The app for children encourages them to take tests to assess their health and fitness 'literacy' and monitor their physical activity and sedentary levels before, during and after school. It also produces 'personalised reports' for each user based on these data. The teachers' app facilitates the testing and measurement of students on mobile devices, allowing data entry in a diverse range of locations. While the Fitnessgram platform does not yet include self-tracking devices for automatic monitoring of students' physical activity levels, it is no doubt only a matter of time, given the gradual spread of these devices into domains such as the workplace, customer loyalty programmes, health and life insurance and in other health and fitness initiatives in schools (Gard, 2014; Lupton, 2015a, 2016). There also appears to be no reason why these data will be limited to physical fitness, food and physical activity. Given Fitnessgram's recent rhetorical shift towards the 'whole child', there is obvious scope for it to branch out into a wide range of other health-related areas, such as drug use, sexual behaviour and mental health.

Second, while the Cooper Institute is officially a non-profit organisation, Fitnessgram is not. This perhaps explains why the Cooper Institute appears to put so much energy into cultivating relationships with political and business leaders and, by extension, why it has been so successful in marketing and selling Fitnessgram across the USA. For example, Fitnessgram was recently endorsed as the recommended school fitness-testing system by the federally funded Presidential Youth Fitness Program. In fact, it is now an apparently successful and important commercial entity in its own right. For example, the publishing house Human Kinetics sells and distributes Fitnessgram materials globally. In the USA, the commercially and culturally powerful National Football League (NFL) recently partnered with Fitnessgram, so that many Fitnessgram products now carry the NFL logo. The Cooper Institute has also begun to expand its product range by rebranding Fitnessgram for sale to the military, ambulance and fire services. In each case, the formula is the same: a simple – we might even say crude – set of physical fitness tests supported by a rapidly developing set of digital paraphernalia. So, while Fitnessgram looks very much like a case of the Quantified Self movement being transplanted from the wider culture to schools, there are some signs that the flow of surveillance technologies might also stream in the other direction.

With money to be made, elections to be won, a war on obesity to be waged and neoliberal accountability regimes to be implemented in public education systems, Fitnessgram has an obvious list of potential and actual allies. Perhaps most surprising, though, is that few ethical or educational concerns have been raised. In fact, press reports of children and parents refusing to comply with particular aspects of Fitnessgram, most notably body weighing, suggest that resistance will come from those with the least to gain from it (Svokos, 2014).

We referred above to the hidden curriculum promulgated by digital technologies in schools. In the case of digitised school health technologies, certain tacit assumptions, beliefs and practices are represented and reproduced. Those devices and technologies that are directed at qualculative rationales render the human body – and in the case of digitised school HPE, children's bodies – into a narrowly defined set of attributes. These include the notions that physical fitness is essential for good health, that good or poor health status can be assessed via levels of physical fitness and even knowledge about exercise (as in 'physical literacy'), that physical fitness and health can be readily discerned by using measurements that can be compared against norms, and that certain set standards are evidence of either a lack of fitness or a high enough level of physical activity or appropriate fitness and activity levels. As the Fitnessgram website puts it, their assessments are designed to measure not skill or agility but 'health-related fitness'. Students are 'not compared to each other, but rather criterion-based Healthy Fitness Zone standards, carefully established for each age and gender, that indicate good health'. Such a position on the inextricable relationship between health status and physical fitness (as well as body weight: body mass index is one of the criteria) suggests that it is well nigh impossible for children to be healthy if they are not physically fit, as determined by the standards that are set by the programme. More broadly, these technologies both support and reproduce the discourses of techno-utopianism, data-centricism and technological solutionism that are evident in popular perspectives on digital health and educational technologies.

Conclusion

As school health curricula and practice become increasingly influenced by digitisation, there are significant consequences for the ways in which both children and teaching staff are monitored, measured and evaluated. The introduction of online assessments and sensor-based tracking technologies into school health, often by commercial developers seeking to profit both from selling their software and devices and the digital data that are generated by users, has afforded continuous and detailed surveillance of students and teachers. Critical analyses of the implications and consequences of the digitisation of school health need to reach beyond the standard theoretical perspectives that have traditionally been adopted in the sociology of education to embrace sociocultural investigations into the power and structuring role played by software and code, algorithms, hardware devices and big data in contemporary social life and social relations. There is also a pressing need to connect the somewhat insular academic field of school health with the broader sociology of the body literature, in order to trouble naive assumptions about the impact of and motivations for digital school health interventions.

The emotional repercussions of digitising children's bodies require attention as well. While educational and other data on children's bodies are typically represented as neutral fonts of information, they can have significant affective effects, not only for the children themselves but also for their teachers and parents (Sellar, 2014). Like other social institutions, schools have become code/space assemblages (Kitchin and Dodge, 2011), in which computer software and hardware are entangled not only in pedagogies and curricula but in the very ways in which students' bodies are represented, investigated, monitored and understood. As we have shown in this chapter, in the case of digitised school health, older forms of the privileging of health and physical fitness and notions of ideal bodies, as well as the acceptance of the entry of commercial entities into schools, are taken up and interpreted via the discourses and practices of informatics, the quantified self and big data.

References

Antonovsky, A. (1996) 'The salutogenic model as a theory to guide health promotion', *Health Promotion International*, 11(1): 11–18.

Ball, S. J. (2003) 'The teacher's soul and the terrors of performativity', *Journal of Education Policy*, 18(2): 215–28.

Ball, S. J. (2013) *Global policy networks, social enterprise and edu-business*. London: Routledge.

Cheney-Lippold, J. (2011) 'A new algorithmic identity: soft biopolitics and the modulation of control', *Theory, Culture and Society*, 28(6): 164–81.

Coole, D. H. and S. Frost (2010) *New materialisms: ontology, agency, and politics*. Durham, NC: Duke University Press.

Cooper Institute (2014a) Fitnessgram. Available online at www.cooperinstitute.org/youth/fitnessgram (accessed 10.12.2015).

Cooper Institute (2014b) Board of Trustees. Available online at www.cooperinstitute.org/board/ (accessed 10.12.2015).

Cuban, L. (1986) 'Sex and school reform', *Phi Delta Kappan*, 68(4): 319–21.

Di Mauro, D. and C. Joffe (2007) 'The religious right and the reshaping of sexual policy: an examination of reproductive rights and sexuality education', *Sexuality Research and Social Policy*, 4(1): 67–92.

Edwards, R. (2015) 'Software and the hidden curriculum in digital education', *Pedagogy, Culture & Society*, 23(2): 265–79.

Fenwick, T. and R. Edwards (2011) 'Considering materiality in educational policy: messy objects and multiple reals', *Educational Theory*, 61(6): 709–26.

Franklin, M. (2013) *Digital dilemmas: power, resistance, and the internet*. Oxford: Oxford University Press.

Fuchs, C. (2014) *Social media: a critical introduction*. London: Sage.

Gard, M. (2014) 'eHPE: a history of the future', *Sport, Education and Society*, 19(6): 827–45.

Gard, M. and C. Pluim (2014) *Schools and public health: past, present, future*. Lanham, MD: Lexington Books.

Gillespie, T., P. J. Boczkowski, and K. A. Foot (2014) 'Introduction', in T. Gillespie, P. J. Boczkowski and K. A. Foot (eds), *Media technologies: essays on communication, materiality, and society*, pp. 1–19. Cambridge, MA: MIT Press.

Green, K. (2014) 'Mission impossible? Reflecting upon the relationship between physical education, youth sport and lifelong participation', *Sport, Education and Society*, 19(4): 357–75.

Himberg, C. (2005) 'The great challenge for physical education', *Teachers College Record* (11873). Available online at www.tcrecord.org/PrintContent.asp?ContentID=11873 (accessed 05.12.2015).

Jagoda, P. (2013) 'Gamification and other forms of play', *boundary 2: An International Journal of Literature and Culture*, 40(2): 113–44.

Kirk, D. (1992) *Defining physical education: the social construction of a school subject in postwar Britain*. London: Falmer Press.

Kirk, D. (1998) *Schooling bodies: school practice and public discourse 1880–1950*. London: Leicester University Press.

Kirk, D. (2000) 'The reconfiguration of the physical activity field in Australian higher education, 1970–1986', *Sporting Traditions*, 16(2): 17–38.

Kitchin, R. and M. Dodge (2011) *Code/space: software and everyday life*. Cambridge, MA: MIT Press.

Lash, S. (2007) 'Power after hegemony: cultural studies in mutation?', *Theory, Culture and Society*, 24(3): 55–78.

Levine, S. (2008) *School lunch politics: the surprising history of America's favorite welfare program*. Princeton: Princeton University Press.

Lupton, D. (2013a) 'Understanding the human machine', *IEEE Technology and Society Magazine*, 32(4): 25–30.

Lupton, D. (2013b) 'Quantifying the body: monitoring and measuring health in the age of mhealth technologies', *Critical Public Health*, 23(4): 393–403.

Lupton, D. (2014a) 'Self-tracking cultures: towards a sociology of personal informatics', paper presented to the Australian Conference on Human-Computer Interaction (OzCHI), Sydney.

Lupton, D. (2014b) 'Critical perspectives on digital health technologies', *Sociology Compass*, 8(12): 1344–59.

Lupton, D. (2015a) 'Data assemblages, sentient schools and digitised health and physical education (response to Gard)', *Sport, Education and Society*, 20(1): 122–32.

Lupton, D. (2015b) 'Health promotion in the digital era: a critical commentary', *Health Promotion International*, 30(1): 174–83.

Lupton, D. (2016) *The quantified self: self-tracking cultures*. Cambridge: Polity Press.

McCormick, T. (2013) 'Gamification: anthropology of an idea', *Foreign Policy*, 201(Jul./Aug.): 26–7.

Macdonald, D. (2014) 'Is global neo-liberalism shaping the future of physical education?', *Physical Education and Sport Pedagogy*, 19(5): 494–9.

Mackenzie, A. and T. Vurdubakis (2011) 'Codes and codings in crisis: signification, performativity and excess', *Theory, Culture and Society*, 28(6): 3–23.

Manovich, L. (2013) *Software takes command*. London: Bloomsbury Publishing.

Martineau, S. (1996) 'Dangerous liaison: the eugenics movement and the educational state', in J. Ross Epp and A. Watkinson (eds), *Systemic violence: how schools hurt children*. London: Routledge Falmer.

McElroy, M. (2008) 'A sociohistorial analysis of U.S. youth physical activity and sedentary behavior', in A. L. Smith and S. H. Biddle (eds), *Youth physical activity and sedentary behavior: challenges and solutions*. Champaign, IL: Human Kinetics.

Morgan, A. and E. Ziglio (2007) 'Revitalising the evidence base for public health: an assets model', *Promotion and Education*, 14(2 suppl): 17–22.

O'Donnell, C. (2014) 'Getting played: gamification, bullshit, and the rise of algorithmic surveillance', *Surveillance and Society*, 12(3): 349–59.

Öhman, M., J. Almqvist, J. Meckbach, and M. Quennerstedt (2014) 'Competing for ideal bodies: a study of exergames used as teaching aids in schools', *Critical Public Health*, 24(2): 196–209.

Plowman, S. A., C. L. Sterling, C. B. Corbin, M. D. Meredith, G. J. Welk, and J. R. Morrow (2006) 'The history of FITNESSGRAM®', *Journal of Physical Activity and Health*, 3(Suppl. 2): S5–S20.

Powell, D. (2014) 'The corporatization of health education curricula: "part of the solution" to childhood obesity?' in K. Fitzpatrick and R. Tinning (eds), *Health education: critical perspectives*, pp. 142–56. London: Routledge.

Reddy, S. G. (2014) 'How gamification improves health and health education outcomes in children', *Nuviun*. Available online at http://nuviun.com/content/series/how-gamification-improves-health-and-health-education-outcomes-in-children (accessed 24.11.2014).

Rizvi, F. and B. Lingard (2009) *Globalizing education policy*. London: Routledge.

St Leger, L. (2004) 'What's the place of schools in promoting health? Are we too optimistic?', *Health Promotion International*, 19(4): 405–8.

Sellar, S. (2014) 'A feel for numbers: affect, data and education policy', *Critical Studies in Education*, 56(1): 131–46.

Selwyn, N. (2012) 'Bursting out of the "ed-tech" bubble', *Learning, Media and Technology*, 37(4): 331–4.

Selwyn, N. (2013) *Education in a digital world: global perspectives on technology and education*. New York: Routledge.

Selwyn, N. (2015) 'Data entry: towards the critical study of digital data and education', *Learning, Media and Technology*, 40(1): 64–82.

Svokos, A. (2014) 'Student sent to principal's office after refusing to be weighed', *Huffington Post Australia*, 10 Nov. Available online at www.huffingtonpost.com.au/2014/11/18/refusing-bmi-school-test_n_6180892.html?ir=Australia (accessed 05.12.2015).

Sykora, M., P. W. H. Chung, J. P. Folland, B. J. Halkon, and E. A. Edirisinghe (2015) 'Advances in sports informatics research', in S. Phon-Amnuaisuk and T. Wan Au (eds), *Computational intelligence in information systems*, pp. 265–74. Zurich: Springer.

Taylor, E. (2013) *Surveillance schools: security, discipline and control in contemporary education*. Houndmills, UK: Palgrave Macmillan.

Thrift, N. (2004) 'Movement-space: the changing domain of thinking resulting from the development of new kinds of spatial awareness', *Economy and Society*, 33(4): 582–604.

Totaro, P. and D. Ninno (2014) 'The concept of algorithm as an interpretative key of modern rationality', *Theory, Culture and Society*, 31(4): 29–49.

Tremblay, M. (2004) 'The need for directly measured health data in Canada', *Canadian Journal of Public Health*, 95(3): 165–6.

Tupper, K. W. (2008) 'Drugs, discourses and education: a critical discourse analysis of a high school drug education text', *Discourse: Studies in the Cultural Politics of Education*, 29(2): 223–38.

Urban, W. J. and J. L. Wagoner (2000) *American education: a history* (2nd ed.). New York: Routledge.

Van Dijck, J. (2013) *The culture of connectivity: a critical history of social media*. Oxford: Oxford University Press.

Williamson, B. (2013) 'The future of the curriculum: school knowledge in the digital age', in *The John D. and Catherine T. MacArthur Foundation reports on digital media and learning*. Cambridge, MA: MacArthur Foundation.

Williamson, B. (2015a) 'Governing software: networks, databases and algorithmic power in the digital governance of public education', *Learning, Media and Technology*, 40(1): 83–105.

Williamson, B. (2015b) 'Algorithmic skin: health-tracking technologies, personal analytics and the biopedagogies of digitized health and physical education', *Sport, Education and Society*, 20(1): 133–51.

Wright, J. (1996) 'Mapping the discourses of physical education: articulating a female tradition', *Journal of Curriculum Studies*, 28(3): 331–51

4 Calculating children in the dataveillance school

Personal and learning analytics

Ben Williamson

New forms of digitally enhanced surveillance are emerging in educational settings. Increasingly automated and enabled by sophisticated software and analytics, they are routinising the collection and analysis of children's data. Focusing on two areas of such 'dataveillance' techniques in schools – 'learning analytics' (which capture data from children's educational activities) and 'personal analytics' (which track, monitor and assess schoolchildren's bodies and functions) – this chapter provides a critically informed account of the emergence of 'dataveillance schools' and their implications for children. First, I survey theoretical concepts that have developed to explain surveillance, in order to locate 'dataveillance' in a broader context. Then, I argue that schools are becoming increasingly active and adaptive through digital interaction with schoolchildren and that dataveillance is a key means by which children are calculated and surveilled.

Like Taylor (2013) in *Surveillance Schools*, I want to avoid the rush to judgement that often accompanies critical accounts of surveillance. Techniques of dataveillance in schools could provide some benefits for children and the school itself, but also raise concerns regarding privacy, trust, personal freedom and the potential for passive acquiescence to surveillance mechanisms. In addition, it is important to recognise the role of schools in society and avoid compartmentalising them since, as Taylor (2013) argues, 'their unique position in society bestows upon them the ability to determine how future generations will understand, perceive and experience surveillance'. I argue here that dataveillance schools are being formed as prototypes and laboratory sites for emerging modes of governance and control, ready to be rolled out in other sectors of the state.

Panopticon, oligopticon, graphopticon

This section provides an analytical framework for considering emerging strategies of 'dataveillance' in schools, in particular by tracing shifts from 'panoptic' to 'oligoptic' and 'graphoptic' forms of surveillance. Foucault (1977) provided an influential conception of a generalised version of surveillance in the model of the Panopticon. Originally conceived by the English political philosopher Jeremy Bentham in the 1780s, the Panopticon was an institutional structure with a 'supervisor' in a central tower and its 'captives' arranged in cells around the periphery in a state of 'conscious and permanent visibility that assures the automatic functioning of power' (Foucault, 1977: 200–1). For Foucault, however, the promise of the Panopticon was not merely in prison design but as a more generalised technology of societal control. Rather than a blueprint for a particular building, Foucault (1977: 205) argued that the Panopticon is:

> the diagram of a mechanism of power reduced to its ideal form ... it is in fact a figure of political technology that may and must be detached from any specific use ... Whenever one is dealing with a multiplicity of individuals on whom a task or a particular form of behaviour must be imposed, the panoptic schema may be used.

The Panopticon is a kind of 'seeing machine' that has 'become a transparent building in which the exercise of power may be supervised by society as a whole' (Foucault, 1977: 207). Panoptical regimes of surveillance could be detected not just in designs for prisons but in the organisational arrangements of hospitals, factories, the family and schools. Panopticism has exerted considerable influence on surveillance studies, particularly as a theoretical framework for those studying visual surveillance, such as CCTV. However, its usefulness as a conceptual device has been questioned with the rise of 'big data'– digital datasets that are huge in volume, highly varied, collected at extraordinary velocity and that allow people to be surveilled in new ways (Kitchin, 2014). Digital big data has led some commentators to argue that 'post-panoptic' forms of control (Gane, 2014) are now more relevant, based on the claim that people are surveilled through partial, 'oligoptic', vantage points provided by multiple different datasets. The shift from panoptic to post-panoptic techniques of surveillance is part of a broader shift from Foucault's disciplinary society to 'societies of control', originally conceptualised by Deleuze (1992). Whereas panoptical disciplinary societies concentrated power through institutional confinements, such as the school, factory and family, for Deleuze 'control societies' are characterised by the dissolution of social structures and institutions and they were replaced by mobile, free-floating and flexible forms of power. Control operates through computerised information and communication technologies, datasets and codes that are able to identify, tag and track people and objects at any given time. In turn, access to resources, spaces and knowledge becomes increasingly regulated, often without those subject to such control systems being aware of these processes.

Importantly, in this context, Grosser (2014) has coined the term 'graphopticon' to refer to the ways in which 'the many watch the many' in contemporary regimes of 'social surveillance'. He particularly highlights database techniques, such as the production of a 'social graph', a mapping system of the connections, interactions and relationships between people and their various interests and attributes. As Lyon (2014: 8) has argued, database mechanisms like the social graph are employed in governmental security systems to enable the identification and visualisation of emergent data patterns (see also Chapter 13, for discussion of the surveillance of young people's favourite websites). In addition, the idea of the graphopticon registers the increase of the graphical visualisation of data in social media. In other words, instead of the central watchtower of the state, oligoptic and graphoptical dataveillance is characterised by a proliferation of sites and spaces of watching what people do and whom they interact with through visualisations of their data.

In their influential paper drawing on the Deleuzian approach, Haggerty and Ericson (2000) suggest that the convergence of computers and graphoptical techniques now renders surveillance far more intensive and far-reaching than ever before. Rather than the figure of the prisoner seen in the Panopticon, the subject of oligoptic and graphoptic surveillance is assembled out of diverse component parts, captured from different data sources, linked and recombined 'in the hope of developing strategies of governance, commerce and control' (Haggerty and Ericson, 2000: 613). Computer technologies are essential to the linking, reassembling and visualisation of disparate sources of information. Likewise, Kitchin and Dodge (2011: 86) argue that software is important in the creation of societies of control 'as it makes possible a fundamental shift in how information is gathered, by whom, for what purposes, and how it is applied to anticipate individuals' future lives.'

Algorithmic power and machine learning

The link between software and control is encapsulated by the term 'algorithmic power', the exercise of power through computationally coded algorithms:

> The point here is that rather than [power] operating outside and above, instead the social and cultural structures of the day, exemplified by Web 2.0 applications, organize themselves through the self-organizing and predictive powers of the software with which we live … enabling the data to 'find us' … Rather than power at a distance, this is power up close. (Beer, 2009: 993)

In contemporary societies of control where computational processes and algorithms are increasingly powerful in social organisation, we encounter not the central tower of the Panopticon but a post-panoptic swarm of code, constantly interacting with individuals by extracting their personal data, connecting it up in massive relational datasets, and then self-organising automated recommendations and suggestions. The disciplinary gaze from above has given way to modulated control, as we interact with software, leave data trails of our every interactions and transactions and experience the power of algorithms that have been trained to 'learn' about us through tracing and analysing our every move. Commenting on Deleuze's control paper in the context of big data and algorithmic power 20 years on, Gane (2014) argues that 'ever more surveillance technologies are emerging that extend such a system of control … to an extent that has previously been unimaginable.'

Aside from the collection of big data, perhaps the more significant developments are the emerging data analytic techniques used to process it. The processing and analysis of such abundant, varied, exhaustive and messy data has become possible only due to high-powered computational techniques, particularly 'machine learning'. Machine learning refers to 'intelligent' software systems featuring adaptive algorithms that can be taught to anticipate and predict how people act. By being 'trained' with past data, machine learning produces 'taught algorithms' that can interact with both people and other machines and adapt in response. These taught algorithms enable the digital environment to 'learn' from and about users, and to 'talk back' in the shape of feedback and recommendations for future actions. Machine learning and predictive analytics software are, therefore, part of a world in which 'probabilistic outcomes' and predictions about the future now prevail, with significant implications for how individuals think about and anticipate their own futures (Mackenzie, 2013). The capture and processing of big data through the taught algorithms of machine-learning systems are now routinely used in consumer businesses, financial industries, governmental database services and the media. In concert, big data capture and predictive machine-learning systems have made the systems of control into a routine surveillant reality, making everyday lives the subject of constant data collection, graphical visualisation and automated forms of analysis, prediction and feedback (see Chapter 14).

Dataveillance

The merging of surveillance techniques with the everyday realities of big data capture, analysis and visualisation performed by machine-learning algorithms has led to the emergence of what is termed 'dataveillance' (Gitelman, 2013; Kitchin, 2014). Dataveillance refers to a process through which individuals are captured through the data trails of their everyday activities and then processed and analysed using algorithms constructed by programmers (Raley, 2013). For instance, van Dijck (2014) describes the 'datafication' of surveillance regimes as techniques of 'life mining' that have been mobilised to make people's behaviours, sentiments, thoughts and feelings seemingly intelligible by being continuously tracked. Such techniques treat online services, such as Twitter and Facebook, as 'sensors' and 'detectors' of real-time events, consumer behaviours, political predilections and social dynamics.

Dataveillance differs from other forms of purposeful surveillance in that it 'entails the continuous tracking of (meta)data for unstated present purposes' and 'goes well beyond the proposition of scrutinizing individuals as it penetrates every fibre of the social fabric' (van Dijck, 2014: 205). Yet, dataveillance also rests on the assumption that digital data can provide a neutral and unbiased window into human behaviours, moods and sociality, as if the technological mediation of the data through its modes of collection, connection and calculation were irrelevant. This assumption glosses over not just the technical fact of how data-processing technologies structure and organise data but also the work of the 'human hands' that go into programming them, its processes of algorithm design and the formalisation of social phenomena into computational models that can then be automated (Gillespie, 2014).

Dataveillance does not merely involve real-time tracking and monitoring but also the construction of computational models and classifications of social activities that can then be used to predict and intervene before particular behaviours have taken place and facilitate 'social sorting' and pre-emptive practices, such as 'predictive policing' (Lyon, 2014) (see also Chapter 14). In this context, Amoore (2009: 49) refers to 'the glossy techno-science of algorithmic calculation', whereby algorithmic computing applications, biometrics, risk management systems and other new surveillance technologies have been authorised in everything from traffic-management systems to border control to national security systems, and thus brought 'the logic of pre-emption into the most mundane and prosaic spaces'. Machine learning is key to dataveillance because its algorithms appear to make it possible to translate probable associations between people or objects into actionable decisions, and thus by 'connecting the dots of probabilistic associations, the algorithm becomes a means of foreseeing or anticipating a course of events yet to take place' (Amoore, 2009: 52).

Of course, utilising calculative and algorithmic techniques to pre-empt possible futures is not itself novel to big data or dataveillance. Hacking (1990) memorably described the 'taming of chance' as a form of 'risk-thinking' intended to bring the future into the present in order to make it calculable, and thus actionable – in other words, the ability to act in the present to forestall undesirable events predicted in the future. In this sense, dataveillance can be seen as a style of risk-thinking: a way of thinking about, assessing, evaluating and acting upon the world in terms of its apparent risks through diverse techniques of expert management. Lupton (2014a) has more recently argued that we are now seeing the emergence of new kinds of 'digitised risk' through techniques associated with big data and dataveillance:

> Different types of datasets and digital data objects can be joined up to configure risk calculations based on inferences that seek to uncover relationships rather than direct causal connections. … These digital risk assemblages then become targeted for various forms of intervention: managerial, governmental or commercial. … Computer codes, software and algorithms offer a late modernist promise of exerting control over messy, undisciplined scenarios, including the efficient identification and management of risk.

The predictive and pre-emptive techniques of dataveillance represent a form of 'taming chance' through the accelerated modes of technological enactment. For example, Kitchin and Dodge (2011: 109) describe 'automated management' systems in which 'software algorithms work automatically and autonomously' without human intervention or authorisation.

Dataveillance is not, then, about the visual apparatus of the Panopticon that allows continuous real-time surveillance but refers to a new post-panoptic control system that fuses together a complex socio-technical 'surveillant assemblage' (Haggerty and Ericson, 2000) of human and non-human tasks, including future-tense risk-thinking, algorithmic calculation, machine-learning predictivity and automated pre-emption, as a means to 'knowing' and managing social behaviour. The 'knowing' system articulated here, however, is no all-powerful state surveillance system operating by new means, but rather a 'stitching together' of the mundane calculations of business, the security decisions of the state and the prosaic actions of the public (Amoore, 2009). As Ruppert (2012: 118) argues, far from there being an 'all-knowing state, what we have instead is a plethora of partial projects and initiatives that are seeking to harness ICTs in the service of better knowing and governing individuals and populations.' Instead of the universal Panopticon monitoring at all times in all places, dataveillance consists of 'overlapping oligopticons', partial viewpoints from fixed positions, covering more and more aspects of everyday life (Kitchin and Dodge, 2011), as well as graphoptical devices that enable the activities, relations and interactions between people to be visualised and observed through the patchworks of their data (Grosser, 2014).

Dataveillance schools

In education, emerging technologies of dataveillance are now enabling children to be monitored and tracked through their data in the school. There is a shift from what Taylor (2013) described as 'surveillance schools', rigged up with CCTV, metal detectors and pupil-identification systems, to 'dataveillance schools'. Education has fast become a massively data-mineable sector where the data being mined appears to hold the promise of improving everything from national governance of the education system to the administrative processes of the school and the pedagogic apparatus of the classroom. As Selwyn (2015: 72) argues, education is increasingly treated as a 'computational' project characterised by:

> the 'modelling' of education through digital data ... [and] algorithmically driven 'systems thinking' – where complex (and unsolvable) social problems associated with education can be seen as complex (but solvable) statistical problems. Thus, digital data are accompanied by a heightened sense of 'solutionism.' This leads to a recursive state where data analysis begins to produce educational settings, as much as educational settings producing data.

In this context of dataveillance in schools, children are situated as cybernetic collections of 'data points' that can be subjected to algorithmic calculation, with the results then feeding back into pedagogic, pastoral and administrative intervention. Dataveillance functions in schools by capturing children's quantifiable, encodable and machine-readable characteristics, which enable them to be identified, classified, ordered or sorted through data-processing algorithms. These processes are perhaps most significant in relation to the identification of particular children at risk of some kind, and the subsequent shaping of children's lives through automated modes of pre-emption. Dataveillance generates a kind of statistical knowledge about children that can be translated into 'meaningful' graphical and numerical displays and then used as the basis for making decisions about their differential treatment. These automated decision-making systems hold considerable algorithmic power in the shaping of children's lives in an increasingly oligoptic and graphoptic society of control.

The next sections detail how dataveillance has been woven into schooling through the introduction of predictive 'learning analytics' platforms and wearable 'personal analytics' devices. These educational technologies of dataveillance make the child into a machine-readable, enumerable, calculable and therefore actionable object of analysis.

Learning analytics in the dataveillance school

The surveillance of schools through their data has a long history, one rooted in the spectacular exhibitionary practices of the nineteenth century Great Expositions, where educational data were routinely displayed as topographical maps, tables of illustrative statistics and exemplars of students' work for the inspection of visitors (Sobe, 2013). More recently, with the rise of globally standardised testing, such as the Program for International Student Assessment (PISA), schools and education systems have found themselves ranked in league tables and displayed in graphs as a form of public spectacle, a situation exacerbated by the increasing use of data visualisation to make education publicly visible and observable to policymakers, parents and the media (Williamson, 2015a).

The surveillance of schools is now, however, shifting towards techniques of dataveillance, which allow individual students to be monitored and tracked through their production of digital data, in ways that can even be used to predict their future behaviours. In education, new dataveillant techniques of prediction are represented by the burgeoning field of learning analytics, defined as 'the measurement, collection, analysis and reporting of data about learners and their contexts, for purposes of understanding and optimizing learning and the environments in which it occurs' (LAK, 2011). Mayer-Schönberger and Cukier (2014) have detailed some of the major applications of learning analytics, including adaptive learning systems that enable materials to be tailored to each student's individual needs through automated real-time analysis; new forms of data analytics that are able to harvest data from students' actions, learn from them and generate predictions of individual students' probable future performances; and automated personal tutoring software that monitors students passively and gives constant real-time support and shapes the pedagogic experience.

The field of learning analytics, or 'educational data science', is concerned with developing an evolving 'learner model' that would incorporate data beyond those that measure cognitive abilities, including psychometric profiles, indicators of student interactions during learning activities, student mindset, learning media genre preference, and perseverance and persistence not only to identify early warning indicators but also to create predictive learner models (Pea, 2014). In ways that are far more pervasive and invasive than standardised testing, learning analytics platforms can track and assess students' data over time, link them to behavioural models and then combine those data into graphic visualisations that project likely future progress, actions and outcomes. The global learning analytics provider Knewton, for example, collects a variety of different educational attainment data to combine with psychometric information and social media traces, producing a kind of 'cloud' of data on each individual, a cloud that can then be visualised for the inspection of both teachers and children and can also be used as a quantitative record for data mining. Its chief executive has claimed that the Knewton system is able to routinely capture millions of data points on millions of students, amassing one of the world's most extensive data reservoirs –big educational data that can then be mined and analysed for insights on learning processes (Ferreira, 2013).

Significantly, from a post-panoptic dataveillance perspective, learning analytics achieves a constant and seamless collection of millions of data points from students and translates them into statistical models without their direct awareness. The learner represented by learning analytics is disembodied as graphical displays of assessment data, psychometric profiles, social network maps and 'data dashboards'. On this basis, the child is to be rendered and visualised through temporarily aggregated 'flecks of identity' (Raley, 2013). Haggerty and Ericson (2000: 606) argue that post-panoptic surveillance 'operates by abstracting human bodies from their territorial settings and separating them into a series of discrete flows. These flows are then reassembled into distinct "data doubles" which can be scrutinized and targeted for intervention.' The term 'data double' signifies how individuals can be identified and classified by the scattered bits of information they leave that are distributed across various digital systems. From the surveillance studies perspective, Lyon (2014: 7) describes how the data double:

> then acts back on those with whom the data are associated, informing us who we are, what we should desire or hope for, including who we should become. The algorithms grip us even as they follow us … [T]he price of our freedom in both political and consumer contexts is our shaping or conditioning by algorithms.

Likewise, in the educational context, these data doubles, Hope (2014: 11) argued, act as 'simulacra constructed from an individual's data set, which effectively serves to restrict (or permit) certain activities', even 'inhibit educational opportunities'.

More significantly, learning analytics platforms are programmed with the capacity to anticipate or predict pupils' probable future progress. As outlined earlier, learning analytics is the product of 'machine-learning' developments. Machine learning relies on adaptive algorithms and statistical models that can be 'fed training data'; these are, crudely speaking, 'taught algorithms' that learn from being taught with example data (Gillespie, 2014). Customised search engine results, social media suggestions and online consumer recommendations are all examples of machine learning at work. Powered by machine learning, learning analytics platforms, thus, have the capacity to provide detailed predictions of students' future progress. This kind of predictive profiling provides institutions with actionable intelligence that can be used for various statistical determinations and decision-making and can automatically produce personalised and pre-emptive pedagogic interventions to optimise outcomes. Learning analytics platforms act as new kinds of 'artificially intelligent' anticipatory devices that are embedded within the pedagogical apparatus of the classroom. The predictive and prescriptive analytics on which they are based have the potential to shape students' possibilities for action – they create 'actionable insights', as it says on the Knewton website.

A clear example of how such analytics capacities may be embedded in schools is provided by the IBM Smarter Education initiative. The IBM 'smarter classroom' is a 'classroom that will learn you' through 'cognitive-based learning systems' and through the mobilisation of both predictive and prescriptive analytics (IBM, 2014). Predictive tools, IBM claims, can answer the question: based on what's already happened, what's going to happen next? And prescriptive analytics then answer: In light of what we believe is going to happen, what is the best response? Such practices embed anticipatory forms of dataveillance in everyday schooling, including 'pre-emptive' kinds of prediction and 'future-tense' anticipation based on 'human-algorithm relations' where there is 'a deliberate intention to reduce someone's range of options' through 'future-oriented preventative measures' (Lyon, 2014: 5). As Mayer-Schönberger and Cukier (2014) note, the 'robotic algorithms' of learning analytics platforms are able to access spreadsheets of learner data, calculate odds and make probabilistic predictions, and automate decisions about pedagogical intervention in a few milliseconds, with 'the risk that our predictions may, in the guise of tailoring education to individual learning, actually narrow a person's educational opportunities to those predetermined by some algorithm.' In this sense, learning analytics function as pedagogic graphoptical devices, constantly making visible students' progress as enumerations and visualisations, and prescribing preventative interventions to pre-empt any identified risks. Learning analytics enables the child to be algorithmically surveilled and anticipated in terms of academic attainment and progress, but other developments in educational dataveillance also permit greater observation, tracking and monitoring of the body and emotions of the child.

Personal analytics in the dataveillance school

Personal analytics refers to wearable electronics and biosensor devices that are designed to allow users to track, collect and analyse data on their own activities and health – sometimes called technologies of the 'quantified self' or the practice of 'wearing the self' (Evans, 2014). Personal analytics devices incite users to adopt practices of self-surveillance as they collect biophysical data on their own activities and then view and analyse visualisations of them. As Lupton (2015) details, these technologies of the quantified self allow users to keep track of their physical exertion, caloric intake, sleep, mood, sex life, and more.

Such devices are now being targeted towards the schools. For example, Sqord is designed for physical education in schools and consists of a wearable data logger, an online social media environment and a personalisable onscreen avatar called a PowerMe. Sqord is marketed as 'one part social media, one part game platform, and one part fitness tracker'. Extensively piloted and tested in schools in the USA:

> Sqord gives you an administrative reporting tool with quantifiable metrics on the physical activity, levels, and participation of each of your players.

> No more guesswork or gray areas in measuring physical activity. Sqord puts the numbers in plain view, and allows your teachers and coaches to see exactly what's what in real-time. (Sqord, 2014)

Sqord users can compete with one another on an online leaderboard through everyday physical challenges, as measured by their activity trackers, and are able to win medals and. 'sqoins' as rewards for completion of goals, which can be used to purchase upgrades and personalised features. The Sqord social media environment promotes peer competition as a motivational technique. Sqord also provides an administrative reporting tool for educators to access metrics and data visualisations on the physical activity levels and participation of each child player. It makes the child visible in numbers for the inspection of the teacher and school administrator, as well as for the underlying analytics.

Another product targeted at children's physical education is Zamzee, whose strapline is 'Motivate. Measure. Manage' (Zamzee, 2014). According to its website, Zamzee combines state of the art 'accelerometry' technologies, game design and 'motivation science'. Similar to Sqord, it consists of a wearable 'meter' device to 'measure the intensity and duration' of physical activity; an online 'motivational website' featuring challenges and lesson plans; and sophisticated 'group analytics' to enable educators and school administrators to 'track individual and group progress with real-time data'. Importantly, Zamzee has considerable partnerships with major commercial investors, healthcare organisations and philanthropic foundations.

While products like Sqord and Zamzee are not, to date, in mainstream use in schools, they are part of a broader trend to subject the body of the child to surveillance (see Chapters 3 and 10 for discussion of child health and surveillance). Established products, such as Fitnessgram, for example, have long been mobilised to measure and monitor children's health and fitness levels, demonstrating how fitness testing, pedometers and movement analysis software have already been accepted as surveillant technologies in physical education. Indeed, the widespread acceptance of fitness and activity assessment tools like Fitnessgram suggests that … newer digital forms of personal analytics will be easily accommodated into physical education provision in schools in ways that will extend existing uses of student data for surveillant purposes. As Gard (2014: 833) notes in relation to Fitnessgram:

> there is evidence that schools … are structuring their physical education programmes – and therefore the information they use to instruct children and explain their programmes to the broader public – in ways that prioritise student performance in these data collection exercises. … Fitnessgram is one example – doubtless others will follow – of how HPE might be digitally shoehorned into conformity with the worldwide trend towards measurability, accountability, performativity and standardisation in other areas of the curriculum.

The latest upgrades to Fitnessgram itself also feature data-mining functionality, web-based data collection, mobile apps, and reader-friendly graphical visualisations that demonstrate how new technical developments in mobile activity monitoring and data analytics are feeding back into existing school surveillance products. These are making the collection, accumulation and dissemination of large datasets about children's physical health and fitness easier and more efficient to administer and accomplish. As the Zamzee strapline suggests, if children can be 'motivated' to perform particular physical activities, they can be 'measured' while doing so, and from there 'managed' in terms of their data.

Personal analytics devices, such as Sqord and Zamzee, provide graphoptical visual displays of biophysical data that can be accessed and viewed by children, their peers and their teachers alike, as well as by the commercial organisations that produce the devices and harvest the data from them. But they also embed these graphoptical techniques of dataveillance in more 'playful' practices. Indeed, as with many other forms of digital dataveillance, users of 'quantified self' devices, such as Sqord and Zamzee, submit to being monitored and tracked by surrendering their data (Raley, 2013). Part of the seduction of participatory surveillance through self-quantification, particularly as it is now being marketed to children, is the tactic of designing the technologies along the lines of video games or competitions. Popular features of health-related apps for children include the concept of caring for virtual creatures by fulfilling their dietary and fitness needs, often combined with various gaming and competition elements and online social media environments. With its cute avatars and competition functions, Sqord represents the 'gamification' of digital health among children, that is, the adding of game mechanics, technologies and techniques to non-game activities to make real life more like a game and a form of pleasure (Whitson, 2013). Programmes and devices that promote healthy habits using points, competitive challenges and fitness coaches for game consoles are obvious examples of gamification. These techniques of gamification promise to make everyday tasks more rewarding, fulfilling and fun, using incentivisation and rewards to shape desirable behaviours, such as physical exercise or healthy eating habits.

Whitson (2013) refers to gamification as 'pleasurable surveillance' – a kind of self-monitoring and self-policing done voluntarily and for fun (see Chapter 11). Pleasurable self-surveillance techniques enable data to be collected and analysed and for feedback to be provided on how to better care for one's self. As Whitson (2013: 167) argues, 'quantification is an essential tool of governance, the conduct of conduct' and, through influencing and altering behaviour, in 'how we come to know and master the self'. She points out, however, that the software and algorithms that make gamification possible are not neutral or objective; rather, they are rife with embedded value judgements that reward some activities and not others. Through 'the process of collecting, visualising, sharing and monitoring such data on one's body in a public space, users learn about the body in terms of appropriate forms of maintenance, development and repair' (Rich and Miah, 2014: 305–6). While health tracking may be pleasurable, however, it may not always be voluntary. Lupton (2014b: 9) suggests that the use of digital self-tracking devices and apps in school-based health and physical education is a form of 'imposed self-tracking' and argues that 'some physical education teachers are beginning to require their students to wear such devices as heart-rate monitors to determine whether they are fully participating in set exercise activities and to compare their exertions with other students.'

An emerging development at the nexus of both learning analytics and personal analytics is 'emotional learning analytics'. Emotion analytics include devices, such as wearable sensor bracelets that can detect excitement, stress, fear, engagement, boredom and relaxation through the skin, and facial recognition software and computer vision algorithms that have been designed to measure and monitor children's levels of emotional engagement through eye-tracking and facial expression. The identification and measurement of psychological indicators through 'machine emotional intelligence' systems are emerging expert techniques for mining children's emotions, and 'with increased affordances to continuously measure facial and voice expressions with tablets and smartphones, it might become feasible to monitor learners' emotions on a real-time basis' (Rientes and Rivers, 2014: 15). The possibilities of conducting real-time dataveillance on children's emotions represent an attempt to surveil the affective life of the child, to enable the gaze of the observer to penetrate beneath the skin in order to then nudge and coerce them at the level of their feelings. Such devices rely on surveillance techniques at the level of the sweat gland, the voice, facial musculature and eye movement. These biophysical indicators of emotions are then translated into a format for algorithms to inspect and make human affects into the targets of psychological surveillance.

Products, such as Sqord, Zamzee and other biosensor devices, represent a complex interweaving of algorithmic processes with commercially produced tracking devices and contemporary public health and wellness agendas, and their insertion into school pedagogies is intended to govern and shape the ways young people see and watch over themselves. This repositions the child's growing body as the co-constructed product of biology, psychology, political agendas and algorithms – a body in 'algorithmic skin' that is increasingly augmented and expanded through its interconnection with vast coded and networked systems of sensing, monitoring, tracking and control, which are embedded in political discourses pertaining to the risks of public and emotional health (Williamson, 2015b). Personal and emotion analytics encourage the pursuit of 'tuning' and 'perfecting' the body and emotions with the right algorithms, make visible the 'hidden' risks that reside in the child's body and behaviours and nudge children to optimise their healthiness.

Implications of personal analytics and learning analytics in the dataveillance school

Learning analytics, personal analytics and emotion analytics represent three instantiations of dataveillance in schools. Dataveillance schools are emerging institutions in which the environment itself is increasingly 'watching' children and, owing to advanced computational processes, able to 'learn' about them in order to diagnose their problems, identify their risks by visualising patterns in their data, predict probable outcomes and, increasingly, to automate remedial pedagogic and pastoral intervention to pre-empt those risks.

What are the implications of dataveillance schools for children? Perhaps a provocative way of conceptualising the development of dataveillance schools is that dataveillance turns schools into laboratories where children are treated as experimental specimens from which data may be extracted to be used for a variety of forms of analysis and insight. Through learning analytics, dataveillance makes children's learning processes, attainment and progression into a real-time stream of data for observation and inspection, often performed automatically by algorithms that have been trained to detect patterns. Through personal analytics devices, dataveillance transforms children's bodies and emotions into calculable quantities and graphical displays that can then be used to nudge and coerce children to improve and optimise themselves. In the wider society, such techniques are reflected in the rise of talent analytics in the workplace, social media sentiment analytics, happiness apps and mood-monitoring devices, as well as the quantified self-movement, all of which are becoming parts of a governmental strategy that exhorts people to subject themselves to surveillance in order to improve themselves (Cederstrom and Spicer, 2015). As Davies (2015) has argued in relation to the range of data analytics that are used to monitor people's activities, 'society becomes designed and governed as a vast laboratory, which we inhabit almost constantly in our day-to-day lives.'

In this sense, schools are becoming petri dishes of a dataveillance state, where techniques of dataveillance may be prototyped, trialled and tested by data scientists and the analytics systems they deploy to monitor and predict outcomes, with the intention of creating better systems to manage individuals and populations. Ruppert (2012) has described 'database government' as the various strategies of oligoptic data collection and calculation performed by diverse government authorities and commercial organisations (often in concert), which are intended to both see and then act upon the ways in which citizens conduct themselves. Dataveillance schools, equipped with learning analytics platforms and wearable tracking devices, are prototypical of such a laboratory society. These are emerging spaces in which diverse data-based forms of surveillance are normalised for children, not just as graphoptical devices for visualising the patterns of one's own activities, but as active devices that are designed to nudge children to change their behaviours, alter their conduct, comport their bodies and act to improve themselves in order to maintain the social order.

The emergence of dataveillance schools raises clear implications for children's privacy and rights, as well as ethical questions and concerns. As their data is collected and calculated in databases, children's right to privacy is turned inside-out, so that the minutiae of their lives, emotions and their bodies can become visible for scrutiny and inspection through their data doubles. Many of the datasets collected by learning analytics platforms and personal analytics devices are then stored for analysis within the servers and information-storage systems of major commercial organisations, such as Knewton and IBM, which can use the data to produce 'actionable insights' without the informed consent of children. If learning analytics platforms are designed to use children's data to predict outcomes and prescribe forms of pedagogic intervention that are intended as remedial solutions to calculated risks, then these devices become consequential to how children are treated at the individual level, with the risk that their opportunities may be narrowed by algorithms and their lives tamed of chance. In this sense, the children who are coming to inhabit dataveillance schools are experimental subjects in a vast laboratory of observation and calculation, specimens under the microscope of the gaze of a state that increasingly seeks to see and know its citizens, their bodies, health and emotions, through their data – data often collected on behalf of the state by commercial operators – and through doing so, to derive insights into how they might be better managed and governed.

Conclusion: calculating children in the dataveillance school

The emergence of dataveillance schools translates children into calculable datasets whose data can be analysed in order to anticipate and predict their futures, and then used to prescribe and enact interventions to pre-empt or prevent identified risks. Personal and learning analytics platforms act as graphoptical devices that encourage children to measure and monitor their educational performances in terms of its enumeration and graphical visualisation. They make dataveillance schools into spaces where oligoptic and graphoptical practices of watching and being watched through data and its graphical presentation become everyday activities and where the analytics automatically perform a constant diagnostic assessment of children's problems and risks through enumerations and visualisations of their data. Such processes make the child a 'calculable person', the subject of calculations performed by others or by machines that are able to learn from and adapt to their data doubles in real time, and also a calculating subject 'with a range of ways of thinking about, calculating about, predicting and judging their own activities and those of others' (Rose, 1999: 214). These transform the child through the 'scientific and technical imagination' into an 'object-child', rendered in 'manipulable, coded, materialized, mathematized, two-dimensional traces, which may be utilized in any procedure of calculation' (Rose, 1996: 112). 'Calculating children' refers both to how children are being incited to learn to calculate about themselves and the processes used by those who govern (including algorithm machines) to calculate about children in order to manage their lives.

These developments are part of an emerging phenomenon where schools are becoming increasingly automated environments that, owing to the computational capacity and algorithmic adaptivity of predictive analytics software packages, are becoming able to 'learn' about children and 'talk back' to them in the shape of recommendations for activities and prescriptions for pedagogic intervention. These kinds of dataveillance schools will be rich with data analytics technologies and other diagnostic forms of surveillance. They represent a significant speed-up in the circulations of data in education, making data collection and its feedback into a real-time process but also utilising data analytics as a 'future-tense' surveillant technology of prediction, prevention and pre-emption. The form of control described by Deleuze (1992) is realised through such systems, with children coming to see oligoptic processes of identification, tagging and tracking as part of the normal order of everyday life. If surveillance schools see children through the panoptic eye of the CCTV camera, in dataveillance schools, children are disassembled into an oligoptical array of databases and then are constantly recomposed from their data traces into numericised data doubles and visualisations. The child of the dataveillance school is to be known through constant analytics of their academic progress, as well as through the data transmitted from their physical bodies, their eyes, their faces, their skin. In aggregate, these oligoptic traces can be used to identify the child, build up a predictive profile then mobilised in the design of strategies for better management and control that can be enacted by machines they cannot see and about which they know nothing.

More widely, dataveillance schools are an institutional manifestation of the increasing cooperation of commercial technologies and governmental strategies in the organisation and management of the state. In some respects, dataveillance schools act as prototypes for new modes of governing, where a particular population is intensively surveilled and monitored for the purposes of enhancing techniques of state management. In this context, children are becoming subject to a governmentalisation of data, as they are tracked, monitored and managed at a distance right throughout the course of their lives. The child is 'becoming data', a 'good citizen of the state' who can 'be counted … along numerous dimensions, on demand' (Bowker, 2005: 30). As these countable data on children are then calculated and fed back, they shape possibilities for action – ultimately, reconstituting childhood itself as coproduced through data. Extensively and intensively surveilled and data mined, children are increasingly to be seen and known and to see and know themselves, in terms of their data, thus augmenting or perhaps even displacing their own subjective, embodied and sensorial experience of themselves. The good child of the big-data-based state is a child that can be counted and calculated through participation in dataveillance schools. Dataveillance schools are those sites where techniques of surveillance are being prototyped, trialled and tested as part of a new strategy of governance. In this sense, the school becomes part of the oligoptic strategy of the state, one of myriad sites monitored by the state to formulate better techniques of governance and control. This is not the all-seeing state of panoptical imaginings but a state that sees and knows its citizens and populations through an oligoptic patchwork of data from diverse sources, of which dataveillance schools are a key instrument.

This opens up some critical lines of enquiry for both surveillance and childhood studies. According to recent theoretical research in childhood studies, as Prout (2005) has articulated, childhood cannot be reduced to biology alone nor to social influences or technological determinations; instead, childhood consists of myriad extensions of the human and non-human into one another, and their interweaving in complex and hybrid combinations. Big data is the latest extension to childhood, producing child data doubles that allow them to be identified through digital traces of their activities and then acted upon by those who seek to govern their lives. Just as childhood studies has sought to engage with the complexity of childhood, a new genre of childhood data studies may be required to trace the human and non-human forces now calculating and acting upon children through their data. The child of the dataveillance school is an emergent hybrid species of data-child, one whose possibilities for action are to be shaped through interacting with an increasingly automated, calculative educational environment that can itself 'see' and 'learn', and even act to intervene in how children live their lives.

References

Amoore, L. (2009) 'Algorithmic war: everyday geographies of the war on terror', *Antipode*, 41(1): 49–69.

Beer, D. (2009) 'Power through the algorithm? Participatory web cultures and the technological unconscious', *New Media and Society*, 11: 985–1002.

Bowker, G. C. (2005) *Memory practices in the sciences*. London: MIT Press.

Cederstrom, C. and A. Spicer (2015) *The wellness syndrome*. Cambridge: Polity.

Davies, W. (2015) *The happiness industry: how business and government sold us well-being*. London: Verso.

Deleuze, G. (1992) 'Postscript on the societies of control', *October*, 59: 3–7.

Evans, L. (2014) 'Wearing the self', *The Programmable City*, 2 Sept. Available online at www.maynoothuniversity.ie/progcity/2014/09/wearing-the-self/ (accessed 24.03.2016).

Ferreira, J. (2013) 'Big data in education: the 5 types that matter', Knewton blog, 18 July. Available online at www.knewton.com/blog/ceo-jose-ferreira/big-data-in-education/ (accessed 24.03.2016).

Foucault, M. (1977) *Discipline and punish: the birth of the prison,* trans. A. Sheridan. London: Penguin.

Gane, N. (2014) 'The governmentalities of neoliberalism: panopticism, post-panopticism and beyond', *Sociological Review*, 60: 611–34.

Gard, M. (2014) 'eHPE: a history of the future', *Sport, Education and Society*, 19: 827–45.

Gillespie, T. (2014) 'Algorithm', *Culture Digitally*, 25 June. Available online at http://culturedigitally.org/2014/06/algorithm-draft-digitalkeyword/ (accessed 23.03.2016).

Gitelman, L. (ed.) (2013) *'Raw data' is an oxymoron*. Cambridge, MA: MIT Press.

Grosser, B. (2014) 'What do metrics want? How quantification prescribes social interaction on Facebook', *Computational Culture*. Available online at http://computationalculture.net/article/what-do-metrics-want (accessed 24.03.2016).

Hacking, I. (1990) *The taming of chance*. Cambridge: Cambridge University Press.

Haggerty, K. D. and R. V. Ericson (2000) 'The surveillant assemblage', *British Journal of Sociology*, 51(4): 605–22.

Hope, A. (2014) 'Foucault's toolbox: critical insights for education and technology researchers', *Learning, Media and Technology*, 40(4): 536–49.

IBM (2014) 'The classroom will learn you'. Available online at www.research.ibm.com/cognitive-computing/machine-learning-applications/decision-support-education.shtml (accessed 19.05.2016).

Kitchin, R. (2014) *The data revolution: big data, open data, data infrastructures and their consequences*. London: Sage.

Kitchin, R. and M. Dodge (2011) *Code/space: software and everyday life*. Cambridge, MA: MIT Press.

LAK (Learning Analytics and Knowledge) (2011) 'About LAK '11 website'. Available online at https://tekri.athabascau.ca/analytics/ (accessed 24.03.2016).

Lupton, D. (2014a) 'Digital risk society'. Pre-print chapter available online at www.academia.edu/8845140/Digital_Risk_Society (accessed 24.03.2016).

Lupton, D. (2014b) 'Self-tracking modes: reflexive self-monitoring and data practices', paper presented at the 'Imminent Citizenships: Personhood and Identity Politics in the Informatic Age' Workshop, ANU, Canberra, 27 Aug.

Lupton, D. (2015) 'Lively data, social fitness and biovalue: the intersections of health self-tracking and social media'. Available at SSRN, http://ssrn.com/abstract=2666324 (accessed 24.03.2016).

Lyon, D. (2014) 'Surveillance, Snowden and big data: capacities, consequences, critique', *Big Data and Society*, 1(2). Available online at www.dx.doi.org/10.1177/2053951714541861 (accessed 24.03.2016).

Mackenzie, A. (2013) 'Programming subjects in the regime of anticipation: software studies and subjectivity', *Subjectivity*, 6(4): 391–405.

Mayer-Schönberger, V. and K. Cukier (2014) *Learning from big data: the future of education*. New York: Houghton Mifflin Harcourt Publishing Co.

Pea, R. (2014) *Building the field of learning analytics for personalized learning at scale*. Stanford University, Graduate School of Education. Available online at https://ed.stanford.edu/sites/default/files/law_report_complete_09-02-2014.pdf (accessed 24.03.2016).

Prout, A. (2005) *The future of childhood: towards the interdisciplinary study of children*. London: RoutledgeFalmer.

Raley, R. (2013) 'Dataveillance and counterveillance', in L. Gitelman (ed.), *'Raw data' is an oxymoron*. Cambridge, MA: MIT Press.

Rich, E. and A. Miah (2014) 'Understanding digital health as public pedagogy: a critical framework', *Societies*, 4: 296–315.

Rientes, B. and B. A. Rivers (2014) 'Measuring and understanding learner emotions: evidence and prospects', *Learning Analytics Review* 1. LACE Project, University of Bolton. Available online at www.laceproject.eu/learning-analytics-review/measuring-and-understanding-learner-emotions/ (accessed 24.03.2016).

Rose, N. (1996) *Inventing our selves: psychology, power, and personhood*. Cambridge: Cambridge University Press.

Rose, N. (1999) *Powers of freedom: reframing political thought*. Cambridge: Cambridge University Press.

Ruppert, E. (2012) 'The governmental topologies of database devices', *Theory, Culture and Society*, 29(4–5): 116–36.

Selwyn, N. (2015) 'Data entry: towards the critical study of digital data and education', *Learning, Media and Technology*, 40(1): 64–82.

Sobe, N. (2013) 'Educational data at late nineteenth- and early twentieth-century international expositions: "accomplished results" and "instruments and apparatuses"', in M. Lawn (ed.), *The rise of data in education systems: collection, visualization and use*. Oxford: Symposium.

Sqord (2014) 'About Sqord'. Available online at http://sqord.com/ (accessed 24.03.2016).

Taylor, E. (2013) *Surveillance schools: security, discipline and control in contemporary education*. Basingstoke, UK: Palgrave Macmillan.

van Dijck, J. (2014) 'Datafication, dataism and dataveillance: big data between scientific paradigm and ideology', *Surveillance and Society*, 12(2): 197–208.

Whitson, J.R. (2013) 'Gaming the quantified self', *Surveillance and Society*, 11: 163–76.

Williamson, B. (2015a) 'Digital education governance: data visualization, predictive analytics and "real-time" policy instruments', *Journal of Education Policy*. Availabe online at http://dx.doi.org/10.1080/02680939.2015.1035758 (accessed 24.03.2016).

Williamson, B. (2015b) 'Algorithmic skin: health-tracking technologies, personal analytics and the biopedagogies of digitized health and physical education', *Sport, Education and Society*, 20(1): 133–51.

Zamzee (2014). Available online at www.zamzee.org (accessed 24.03.2016).

5 Teaching us to be 'smart'?

The use of RFID in schools and the habituation of young people to everyday surveillance

Emmeline Taylor

On account of its 'profound societal implications', it has been argued that radio frequency identification (RFID) should never extend to tracking humans (Electronic Frontier Foundation, 2003: 1). Nevertheless, 'chipification' (Michael and Michael, 2006), the digital monitoring and spatial tracking of people through multiple applications, has become increasingly commonplace. This chapter examines the ways in which schools have become institutional incubators propagating the use of sensory tracking. It outlines some of the many ways in which RFID is used to track students, both on and off campus, before exploring some of the potential consequences of the technology for schoolchildren and, more broadly, society. I argue that the use of RFID in educational spheres serves the primary purpose of accustoming young people to its use, as a precursor to the integration of sensory tracking into everyday living. Weaving RFID into the institutional fabric of the school serves to normalise an otherwise invasive technology that has hitherto been met with considerable scepticism and resistance. This is functionally expedient in order to nurture a generation of smart citizens ready to inhabit a globalised, digitised, surveillance age.

Keeping track: a background to RFID in schools

RFID was first patented in the USA in 1973 with an initial application of tracking commercial goods, which quickly became 'commonplace and uncontroversial' (Thumala *et al.*, 2013). Passive and active RFID has since found many applications, tracking livestock, pets, vehicles, pharmaceuticals and employees.[1] Highlighting how widespread and lucrative the global RFID market has become, it was estimated in 2014 to be worth \$8.89 billion and is expected to rise to \$27.31 billion by 2024. An often-overlooked aspect of the technological capacity of RFID is that tags go beyond simply emitting and receiving a signal that enables readers to locate them; they also have the capacity to store an ever-increasing amount of data. This distinguishes the technology from other location trackers, such as the Global Positioning System (GPS), the satellite-based navigation system, which only provides location details (see Chapter 9). Currently, high-capacity RFID tags used in the aviation industry store up to 64 kilobytes (kb) of data. In schools, tags typically currently hold up to 4 kb. This is sufficient capacity, however, to store important personal details and sensitive information, such as name, date of birth, ethnicity, address, medical history, family details, educational attainment, discipline record, religious affiliation, and so on. This facilitates the assemblage of once discrete categories of data into one place, a digitised compendium to the corporeal body.

Whilst causing controversy and polemic debate in many spheres when it has been proposed to track humans, RFID has actually been used to monitor schoolchildren as far back as 2004. It has been trialled in schools in many countries including England and the Philippines, but it is Japan, South America and some states in the USA that have really embraced and sought to mainstream the practice of tracking students. As with the use of CCTV in schools, a key objective of tracking schoolchildren with RFID is presumed to be safeguarding children from harm. However, it has been applied far more broadly to mundane and routine activities and behaviours beyond those associated with crime control. By way of examples: A New Jersey school district uses RFID to track students and staff on its fleet of buses; primary schools in Melbourne use RFID to track pupils as they cycle to school as part of a 'Ride2School' initiative; and schools in the Philippines use RFID tags embedded in school passes for borrowing books from the library, purchasing items from the canteen and to monitor attendance and track pupils around campus.

In Brazil, it is estimated that approximately 20,000 students are wearing so-called 'intelligent uniforms' embedded with locator chips under the school crest with the expressed aim of reducing truancy. The education secretary claimed that the RFID was used to prove truancy levels to disbelieving parents. If a student has not arrived and entered his/her class 20 minutes after the school day has commenced, the parent is alerted with an automated SMS message. Similarly, in the USA, RFID is used in an attempt to curtail truancy. However, the impetus is money rather than safety: US schools receive funding based on the number of pupils in attendance. If pupils just need to be on campus (rather than in class) to 'count', the RFID system provides a way of claiming the revenue even if students are not present for roll call.

RFID is usually framed in terms of enabling or augmenting initiatives to tackle a range of childhood issues, including obesity, healthy eating, truancy and punctuality, and the more problematic social and ethical issues it transports into schools are rarely foregrounded or considered. This has facilitated its slow and steady creep into the lives of young people in various guises with very little public awareness or furore. In many instances, RFID is purported to safeguard young people from multiple dangers, ranging from abduction to accidents. A process of fear cultivation has recast the use of surveillance technologies as a necessary and rational addition to school apparatus (Monahan, 2006; Taylor, 2012, 2013). As some schools introduce tracking devices to supposedly increase efficiencies, safeguard students and respond to issues, such as truancy and obesity, other schools quickly follow suit through fear of otherwise being regarded as negligent of their responsibilities. This symbiotic process results in the perception that all schools 'need' ever more sophisticated technologies. Once these systems are viewed as necessary, then any cost, whether financial or social, becomes worth the trade. It is an ingenious strategy to turn limited public funds into private profits. As Thumala *et al.* (2015: 11) note in relation to the GPS tracking of children:

> What follows is an implication that failing to purchase a locator device is less than fully responsible: old habits and technologies such as accompanying the child, sharing care responsibilities with other people, teaching one's children street-skills, taking kids to trusted areas or learning to live with uncertainty, are no longer sufficient to keep parents at ease or children safe from harm.

Parents and carers are, thus, persuaded that old practices are no longer adequate or sufficient.

Excavating the impacts and affects of RFID in schools

Surveillance practices are neither inherently good nor bad. While much literature on surveillance quickly embarks upon the well-trodden path that ultimately leads to urban dystopia or totalitarian regime, highlighting the negatives of surveillance and denying any potential benefits, this simplifies and ignores the complex and varied applications of surveillance in contemporary society. Surveillance can be positive and enabling, liberating and rewarding, providing reassurance, safety and efficiencies; at the same time, it can be oppressive, controlling, imbued with prejudicial tendencies and serves to rupture well-established values and systems in society. While it is important to remain critically attuned to these 'two faces' (Lyon, 1994: 201) of surveillance, this chapter raises concerns about the ways in which surveillance deprives young people of personal freedom, anonymity and privacy, and normalises unprecedented levels of scrutiny and control.

Given the commercial rhetoric of presumed (but not proven) benefits, I focus particularly on the problematic changes RFID freights into education. It would be naive to uncritically accept new technologies as progressive and presume that they bring benefits uncomplicated by any negative consequences to the educational and social environment. As Haggerty (2006) attests, 'whilst we cannot anticipate all of the positive advantages that might be derived from this technology, the negative prospects are almost too terrifying to contemplate.' He points to numerous international atrocities that RFID would have assisted, to caution against the mainstream chipping, coding and remote monitoring of citizens in such a systematic and routinised way. Norris and Armstrong (1999: 248) similarly warn: 'We should not be seduced by the myth of benevolent government, for while it may be only a cynic who questions the benign intent of their current rulers, it would surely be a fool who believes that such benevolence is assured in the future.' These clearly are valid concerns, as RFID becomes more integrated into the lives of citizens and is made necessary for a range of social participatory actions.

RFID, privacy and security

In 2012, privacy advocacy groups argued that RFID tracking in schools is dehumanising, poses potential health risks due to the frequency of electromagnetic energy and serves to condition young people to intensive monitoring of their behaviour and whereabouts (CASPIAN *et al.*, 2012). Furthermore, they argued, tracking children violates students' rights to free speech, association and freedom of movement because the technology tracks not only an individual's location but also gathers information on who congregates together and where (CASPIAN *et al.*, 2012). Spatial tracking could impede freedom of movement if students are concerned about being associated with certain individuals or attending particular events that might imply persuasions, such as political preference or sexual orientation. Civil liberties groups have raised concerns that geographical tracking could label or stigmatise some students. Furthermore, if surveillance does indeed impact on legitimate behaviours, schoolchildren could self-regulate in order to avoid presenting a particular reading of their character and interests. Surveillance can, thus, have a 'chilling effect' (Bennett and Raab, 2007; Greenwald, 2014) on associational activity, curtailing creativity, innovation and experimental modes of expression. Mobility is symbolically tethered by the use of RFID as the physical body becomes suspended in a network of sensors and data points that systematically attempt to render it readable.

As outlined above, the data-storage capacity of RFID is increasing exponentially, and schools now collect student information that extends deep into the personal, social and family lives of children. The concern is that these two processes in concert will result in much of these data being carried by the child in the form of an RFID tag. Since data-protection promises and assurances about the interoperability of devices are relatively weak, the storage of sensitive data in RFID tags is currently hugely problematic (Chowdhury and Ray, 2012; Rieback *et al.*, 2006). For example, RFID tags are what Chowdhury and Ray (2012: 2) describe as 'promiscuous' in that they are designed to be read by any generic reader device. The ease with which readers can now be purchased means that any data stored on the chip are vulnerable to being exposed, as well as present a location privacy threat to the chip's wearer:

> The technology was originally designed for shipping goods and cattle, not taking roll at school, thus RFID chips make the perfect stalking device. Because the technology is easy to acquire, it is vulnerable to hacking which could allow someone outside the school to monitor a student's off-campus whereabouts if they obtained the student's tracking number. (American Civil Liberties Union's public education director, cited in Johnson, 2013)

Transmissions can easily be 'sniffed' or 'eavesdropped' and so, far from safeguarding young people, RFID could potentially place them at risk, particularly since the capturing of personal information could occur without the knowledge of system owners or those carrying the chip (Chowdhury and Ray, 2012). On the one hand, promoting the use of RFID tags bids to soothe anxieties but, on the other hand, it generates a new set of concerns that the tags themselves could be crime facilitators.

Weinberg (2008) identifies three specific privacy threats generated by the use of RFID, which he categorises as 'surveillance, profiling, and action'. In terms of *surveillance*, RFID has the potential to become what Weinberg terms a 'Panopticon geolocator' by compiling a database of all individuals present in a given space at a given time. Second, RFID enables the data collector to create a *profile* of the target, comprised of personal information, such as age, gender, ethnicity, educational attainment, medical history, as well as any other information that might be considered useful or interesting. Finally, data controllers have the ability to take *action* based on the abstracted profile gleaned from the RFID chip, a process that Lyon refers to as 'social sorting' (2003). This could be, for example, permitting or denying access to a location or service, triggering targeted marketing and advertising or activating enhanced monitoring and surveillance based on a risk profile.

Commodification of student data

A number of authors (Apple, 2001) claim that education has undergone a process of marketisation; Sahlberg (2006) refers to this as the global education reform movement, or 'GERM'. The movement is characterised by the reconfiguring of educational processes and outcomes according to neoliberal principles of market forces, consumer choice and accountability. It is no secret that virtual and partial representations of the self, or 'data doubles' (Haggerty and Ericson, 2000: 610), have become very profitable commodities. Student data are of great value to corporate entities, which often donate technology with seemingly benevolent motivations, yet gain considerable advantage through harvesting and repurposing information. Kupchik and Monahan (2006) point to a school in Arizona that used $350,000 worth of equipment donated by a local security company to implement biometric face scanners. The scheme was not based on any demonstrable need or evidence of efficacy, highlighting that the consumption of surveillance equipment often 'has little to do with actual student safety and everything to do with business' (Lewis, 2003: 350).

Not only do schools represent new lucrative markets, recasting students as 'human capital' (Apple, 1998: 6), but they also provide a convenient test bed for new products before rolling them out to other markets. In reaction, the USA is proposing the introduction of a Student Digital Privacy Act to 'prevent companies from selling student data to third parties for purposes unrelated to the educational mission and from engaging in targeted advertising to students based on data collected in school' (Office of the Press Secretary, White House, 2015: n.p.).

Resistance to RFID in schools

There have been pockets of resistance to the use of RFID in schools, and surveillance more broadly (for example, see King, n.d.). In the USA, perhaps the strongest and most fervent objection has been motivated by religion. The last book of the New Testament predicts:

> And he causeth all, both small and great, rich and poor, free and bond, to receive a mark in their right hand, or in their foreheads.
>
> And that no man might buy or sell, save he that had the mark, or the name of the beast, or the number of his name. (Rev. 13: 16–17)

This has been interpreted by some evangelical Christian groups as relating to the use of RFID in the retail sector (for example, see Albrecht and McIntyre, 2006). They take the 'mark' to be the RFID chip, precluding those who do not have it upon them, or even embedded under their skin, from being able to engage in commercial transactions. More broadly, all applications of RFID, including those in schools, have been interpreted by some Christian groups as embodying the 'mark of the beast'.

The biblical prophesising has resulted in a number of high-profile cases in which students and their families have attempted to challenge the coercive or mandatory use of RFID in schools. When John Jay High School in San Antonio, Texas introduced RFID tags for all students as part of their Student Locator Project in 2012, 15-year-old Andrea Hernandez refused to wear the RFID tag on the grounds that it contravened her religious beliefs. She was promptly suspended for noncompliance with the programme. As a supposed compromise, school representatives proposed that if Andrea and her family would agree to cease criticising the initiative, they would provide her with a chip-less badge. However, her father argued that this would amount to tacit consent for the overall programme, which continued to contravene the family's religious convictions. The case went to court where the judge ruled that Hernandez's refusal to wear the badge without the RFID chip undermined her claim that the school district was violating her religious freedom: 'Plaintiff's objection to wearing the Smart ID badge without a chip is clearly a secular choice, rather than a religious concern'. Furthermore, the judge concluded that the student must either accept the school's compromise and wear the badge without the chip or relocate to a different school, but the Northside Independent School District was planning on rolling out the Student Locator Project to all of its 112 schools, reaching a student population of over 100,000.

The window of opportunity for resisting the use of RFID in schools could be short-lived, as new technological surveillance devices have a demonstrable knack of becoming quickly embedded and normalised – for example, the widespread acceptance of CCTV, GPS tracking of mobile phones, fingerprinting in schools (Taylor, 2010). Using RFID to monitor young people is already commonplace in countries, such as Brazil, where the sociocultural landscape welcomes an additional layer of tracking children to protect against potential threats.

In Australia, RFID has morphed into a 'solution' for concerns about healthy eating and exercise among young people and is used to encourage students to walk or cycle to school (see also Chapter 10 for discussion of health and surveillance). In other countries, however, such as the UK, resistance to the roll-out of RFID has been stronger. Yet, surveillance practices tend to be adapted until they find a suitable and acceptable application; so, arguably, the barriers may well be circumnavigated or eroded.

Surveillance school assemblage

Influenced by Deleuze and Guattari's (1987) concept of assemblages, Haggerty and Ericson (2000) discuss the ways in which once discrete technologies and practices converge and coalesce into functional systems. The surveillant assemblage is rhizomatic; it extends through interconnected roots that 'shoot up' and regenerate in multifarious locations. For Haggerty and Ericson (2000: 610), surveillance 'is driven by the desire to bring systems together, to combine practices and technologies and integrate them into a larger whole'. The assemblage of school surveillance may be seen as comprising a 'multiplicity of heterogeneous objects, whose unity comes solely from the fact that these items function together, that they "work" together as a functional entity' (Patton, 1994: 158). Currently, the 'Surveillance School' (Taylor, 2013) is constituted by numerous disparate technologies and processes that identify, verify, profile, track and 'sort' (Lyon, 2003) students, teachers and even the school itself, systematically, routinely, relentlessly and indiscriminately. A number of chapters in this book detail surveillance techniques, including wearable devices to measure health and fitness (Chapters 3 and 10), GPS to monitor mobility (Chapter 9) and CCTV to visually monitor students and teachers (Chapter 2). But the plethora of distinct surveillant processes and techniques could soon themselves be regarded as clumsy, cumbersome and archaic, therefore replacing them with a single implanted microchip might be perceived as the logical next step.

The following section examines the degree to which young people are actively becoming accustomed to geotracking. The argument presented is that in order to normalise the level of monitoring required in the 'smart city', surveillance equipment and advanced technologies must be made to appear banal and fade into the background. The next generation of citizens must be habituated to new requisite ways of thinking and being that reorient the role, expectation and obligations of citizenship.

Creating smart citizens? Habituating children to the surveillance age

The sophistication of RFID technology is advancing at pace; chips are becoming smaller in size, cheaper per unit and greater in data capacity. 'Initially attached to non-living things' then adapted to be carried by humans, 'it now seems inevitable that the components will become *one* with humans'

(Michael and Michael, 2006: 16). The ability to implant subcutaneous microchips in humans has existed for several years, and there are many examples of living creatures, such as livestock and pets, that have subdermal implants to identify them and monitor their whereabouts. Despite declarations of 'tremendous market resistance to any initiative calling for the implantation of RFID tags in live people' (Weinberg, 2008), many humans have already been chipped. For example, Kevin Warwick, a professor of cybernetics, pioneered the use of silicon implants in 1998 in his Cyborg 1.0 trial. But aside from the applied academic sphere, there are other examples of human implants. Patrons of an exclusive beach club in Barcelona have been opting to have a syringe-injected microchip implanted in their arm. The reward for subscribing is access to VIP lounges and the ability to use it as a debit account to purchase drinks (BBC News, 2004). Similarly, employees working at a high-tech office block in Sweden are being encouraged to have an RFID microchip implanted in their hand that enables access to the building and the use of integrated technologies, such as the photocopier (BBC News, 2015).

What originates as volunteerism, often encouraged by incentivising subscription to the programme, can quickly give way to coercion by denying access to services or inconveniencing those people who do not wish to participate. A similar process was found in relation to the use of Automated Fingerprint Identification Systems (AFIS) in schools, which were initially introduced as ostensibly opt-in initiatives. However, schoolchildren who did not wish to have their biometric details taken found that they were restricted and inconvenienced – they couldn't purchase lunch at the school canteen, couldn't borrow library books, couldn't vote for the homecoming King and Queen, and couldn't even enter certain classrooms (Taylor, 2013).

Haggerty (2006) succinctly argues that 'one generation is all they need' in relation to the normalisation of RFID. Arguably, schools hold a particularly privileged position in their ability to mould the views and actions of future generations, so introducing geotracking to the everyday lives of young people through this vehicle is likely to succeed where other corporate entities would generate resistance. The only remaining barriers to mainstreaming RFID implants (or similar) are cultural, not technological. As such, serving up neoteric surveillance technologies in concert with education accustoms young people to accept increased monitoring and scrutiny whilst simultaneously concealing any pernicious effects. Goold *et al.* (2013: 978) argue that 'when objects – particularly security objects – cease to be noticed, these effects can be significantly heightened'. When peculiarity gives way to familiarity, the opportunity for critical discussion quickly dissipates. As Adams (2006: 390–1) notes, 'all objects invite us to extend or change our relationship to our world. These enhancements or transformations can be minor to profound, but the full spectrum of effects is often unanticipated and unseen until the object is integrated transparently into our lives.'

Recent theorising of surveillance has looked to science and technology studies (STS) to provide theoretical tools to excavate and analyse the ways in which surveillant apparatus are shaped by, and, in turn, shape the environment in which they are located and the subjectivities and movements of those who interact with them.

Goold *et al.* (2013) draw on Latour's (1992) analysis of the door as a useful analogy for thinking about the way in which the artefacts of surveillance, in their case, CCTV, become accepted, expected and routinised. According to Latour (1992), the door has become so familiar to us that we no longer stop to think about its social role; its delegated power to selectively permit access to and exit from structures; the alternative modes of admittance and denial it excludes; or the human activity it has appropriated. Similarly, artefacts of surveillance become invisible, no longer receiving attention as a result of their 'utter familiarity', yet they are invested with the power to 'structure how we write the world' (Thrift, 2004: 585). As RFID becomes increasingly embedded in everyday life – required as a means for employees to enter their places of work or for schoolchildren to borrow books from the library, buy food in the canteen or board the school bus – it will become enmeshed in the fabric of society, increasingly difficult to disentangle.

Globally, urban spaces, systems and infrastructures are undergoing a process of digitisation (Klauser and Albrechtslund, 2014) and, since 'cities only become smart when people are smart' (Batty, 2013: 276), many smart city programmes feature a strong emphasis on creating 'smart citizens' (Williamson, 2014). Smart city design is usually predicated on the ways in which sensors can generate new data streams in real time with precise geopositioning. Smart city rhetoric highlights the potential for urban spaces to be made more efficient, safer, greener, sustainable and more connected; a key element of the discourse aims to promote participatory citizenry through direct democracy and e-government facilitated by widespread digital connectivity.

However, there are lessons that can be taken from the emergence of surveillance schools, or what Lupton (2014) terms 'sentient schools', in terms of equality of access to services. The school as a microcosm of the smart city begins to unveil some of the inequities and societal implications of systematic and relentless monitoring and tracking. Far from encouraging widespread public participation and engagement, the smart city can stifle freedom of expression, creativity and diversity. The loss of anonymity potentially manifests itself in a reluctance to experiment, for fear of judgement or reprisal. Furthermore, commercial and government access to real-time personal information raises questions regarding the control of the data stream, what purposes the data will be used for, and what safeguards will be introduced and enforced, and by whom. There are manifest ambiguities in the smart city and 'a dark side' to developments, particularly in the form of privacy, confidentiality and access to connectivity (Batty, 2013: 277).

Conclusion

The creation of 'a massive human inventory' (Haggerty, 2006) has serious implications for society. Far from being uncontroversial, the use of RFID freights potentially profound changes into schools and thereby into society, normalising tracking among the next generation and crafting the foundations of the 'smart citizen' ready to inhabit the smart city. Thrift argues that 'much of the background of life is "second nature", the artificial equivalent of breathing'

(Thrift, 2004: 584) and as surveillance technologies come to be perceptibly as 'mundane as the blackboard at the front of the classroom' (Taylor, 2013), they provide a background that quietly rescripts thoughts and behaviours, creates new affordances and ways of being. By entwining surveillance with modes of learning and teaching apparatus, the technologies quickly become assimilated into the daily unthinking routine, part of the 'epistemic wallpaper' (Thrift, 2004: 585). The process of being '*made* banal' (Goold *et al.*, 2013: 979, emphasis in original) is well under way and the opportunity for critical discussion is fast disappearing. RFID is not an isolated example; as I have outlined elsewhere (Taylor, 2013), schools are already commonly equipped with CCTV, AFIS and, increasingly, wearable devices, as well as many other surveillance technologies and practices.

RFID provides a good example of the ways in which corporations succeed in smuggling profitable devices into education under the guise of promoting healthier, happier, safer and smarter children. Schools have become surveillance test beds, part of a not-so-hidden surveillance curriculum that, in an age of profitable big data, normalises intense scrutiny, monitoring and data capture. The largely uncritical appropriation of RFID has been propagated by large corporations and supported by governments that see the benefits of creating the next generation of smart citizens who are ready to inhabit a globalised, digitised, surveillance age.

Note

1 Passive tags do not contain their own power source, such as a battery, and are, therefore, smaller with a virtually unlimited life span. They remain dormant until stimulated by a radio signal from an external reader device. Conversely, active tags use a localised power source to transmit and broadcast their data. Passive tags are reported to have a reading range of '100 feet or more', depending on the frequency and power of the system, whereas active tags have a far longer range. Neither system requires the tag to be within the reader's line of sight.

References

Adams, C. (2006) 'PowerPoint, habits of mind, and classroom culture', *Journal of Curriculum Studies*, 38(4): 389–411.

Albrecht, K. and L. McIntyre (2006) *Spychips: how major corporations and government plan to track your every purchase and watch your every move*. Nashville: Thomas Nelson Inc.

Apple, M. W. (1998) 'Knowledge, pedagogy, and the conservative alliance', *Studies in the Literary Imagination*, 31(1): 5–23.

Apple, M. W. (2001) *Educating the 'right' way: markets, standards, God and inequality*. New York: RoutledgeFalmer.

Batty, M. (2013) 'Big data, smart cities and city planning', *Dialogues in Human Geography*, 3(3): 274–9.

BBC News (2004) 'Barcelona clubbers get chipped'. Available online at http://news.bbc.co.uk/1/hi/technology/3697940.stm (accessed 13.05.2015).

BBC News (2015) 'Office puts chips under staff's skin'. Available online at www.bbc.co.uk/news/technology-31042477 (accessed 13.05.2015).

Bennett, C. and C. Raab (2007) 'The privacy paradigm', in S. P. Hier and J. Greenberg (eds), *The surveillance studies reader*. Maidenhead, UK: Open University Press.

CASPIAN, EPIC and the Privacy Rights Clearinghouse (2012) 'Position paper on the use of RFID in schools'. Available online at www.spychips.com/school/RFIDSchool PositionPaper.pdf (accessed 14.05.2013)

Chowdhury, M. U. and B. R. Ray (2012) 'Security risks/vulnerability in a RFID system and possible defenses', in N. C. Karmaker (ed.), *Advanced RFID systems, security and applications*. Hershey, PA: IGI Global.

Deleuze, G. and F. Guattari (1987) *A thousand plateaus: capitalism and schizophrenia*. Minneapolis: University of Minnesota Press.

Electronic Frontier Foundation (2003) 'Position statement on the use of RFID on consumer products'. Available online at https://w2.eff.org/Privacy/Surveillance/RFID/RFID_Position_Statement.pdf (accessed 19.05.2015).

Goold, B., I. Loader and A. Thumala (2013) 'The banality of security: the curious case of surveillance cameras', *British Journal of Criminology*, 53(6): 977–96.

Greenwald, G. (2014) *No place to hide: Edward Snowden, the NSA, and the U.S surveillance state*. New York: Metropolitan Books.

Haggerty, K. (2006) 'A generation is all they need', *Toronto Star*. Available online at www.prisonplanet.com/articles/december2006/101206generation.htm (accessed 13.05.2015).

Haggerty, K. D. and R. V. Ericson (2000) 'The surveillant assemblage', *British Journal of Sociology*, 51(4): 605–22.

Johnson, C. (2013) 'Judge: kids must wear locator chips at Texas school', *HLNtv.com*.

King, P. (n.d.) 'Against RFID in schools'. Available online at http://rfidinschools.com/about-2/ (accessed 19.05.2015).

Klauser, F. R. and A. Albrechtslund (2014) 'From self-tracking to smart urban infrastructures: towards an interdisciplinary research agenda on big data', *Surveillance & Society*, 12(2): 273–86.

Kupchik, A. and T. Monahan (2006) 'The new American school: preparation for post-industrial discipline', *British Journal of Sociology of Education*, 27(5): 617–31.

Latour, B. (1992) 'Where are the missing masses? The sociology of a few mundane artefacts', in W. E. Bijker and J. Law (eds), *Shaping technology/building society: studies in sociotechnical change*. Cambridge, MA: MIT Press.

Lewis, T. (2003) 'The surveillance economy of post-Columbine schools', *Review of Education, Pedagogy, and Cultural Studies*, 25(4): 335–55.

Lupton, D. (2014) 'Self-tracking modes: reflexive self-monitoring and data practices', paper presented at the 'Imminent Citizenships: Personhood and Identity Politics in the Informatic Age' Workshop, ANU, Canberra, 27 Aug.

Lyon, D. (1994) *The electronic eye*. Cambridge: Polity Press.

Lyon, D. (2003) *Surveillance as social sorting*. London: Routledge.

Michael, K. and M. G. Michael (2006) 'Towards chipification: the multifunctional body art of the net generation', in F. Sudweeks, H. Hrachovec and C. Ess (eds), *Cultural attitudes towards technology and communication 2006: proceedings of the Fifth International Conference on Cultural Attitudes towards Technology and Communication, Tartu, Estonia, 28 June–1 July 2006*. Perth, W.A.: Murdoch University.

Monahan, T. (2006) 'Preface', in T. Monahan (ed.), *Surveillance and security: technological politics and power in everyday life*. New York: Routledge.

Norris, C. and G. Armstrong, G. (1999) *The maximum surveillance society: the rise of CCTV*. Oxford: Berg.

Office of the Press Secretary, White House (2015) 'Fact sheet: safeguarding American Consumers and Families'. Available online at www.whitehouse.gov/the-press-office/2015/01/12/fact-sheet-safeguarding-american-consumers-families (accessed 22.05.2015).

Patton, P. (1994) 'Metomorphic logic: bodies and powers in a thousand plateaus', *Journal of the British Society for Phenomenology*, 25(2): 157–69.

Rieback, M. R., P. N. D. Simpson, B. Crispo and A. S. Tanenbaum, A.S. (2006) 'RFID malware: design principles and examples', *Pervasive and Mobile Computing* 2: 405–26.

Sahlberg, P. (2006) 'Education reform for raising economic competitiveness', *Journal of Educational Change*, 7: 259–87.

Taylor, E. (2010) 'From finger-painting to fingerprinting: the use of biometric technology in schools', *Education Law Journal*, 4: 276–88.

Taylor, E. (2012) 'The rise of the surveillance school', in K. Ball, K. Haggerty and D. Lyon (eds), *Handbook of surveillance studies*. London: Routledge.

Taylor, E. (2013) *Surveillance schools: security, discipline and control in education*. Basingstoke, UK: Palgrave Macmillan.

Thrift, N. (2004) 'Movement-space: the changing domain of thinking resulting from the development of new kinds of spatial awareness', *Economy and Society*, 33(4): 582–604.

Thumala, A., B. Goold and I. Loader (2015) 'Tracking devices: on the reception of a novel security good', *Criminology and Criminal Justice*, 15(1): 3–22.

Weinberg, J. (2008) 'Tracking RFID', *Journal of Law and Policy for the Information Society*, 3: 777.

Williamson, B. (2014) 'Smart schools in sentient cities'. Available online at http://*DMLcentral.net/blog/ben-williamson/smart-schools-sentient-cities* (accessed 19.05.2015).

Part II

Self, body and movement

6 Sexting and young people

Surveillance and childhood sexuality

Murray Lee and Thomas Crofts

> I agree that sexting is not in its original sending intentionally child pornography, yet it may be the next time it is transmitted or the time after that. … I would, however, say that it is not healthy behaviour of teenagers to win favour with their friends by sending them fully or partially naked photos, nor is it right for so-called friends to pressure other young persons to have their photo taken and send it to others. How often have we heard of rising actresses who have gotten their big break only to be embarrassed by the emergence of compromising photos taken some years earlier? I think there is a need for some penalties in these cases in order to discourage this unhealthy behaviour. I would, however, say that, given that the intention was not originally to be child pornography, the distinction can be made. (Simpkins, 2010)

This 2010 statement by the Hon. Luke Simpkins, a Federal MP from the seat of Cowan in Western Australia, marked the first mention of sexting by young people in the Australian Federal Parliament. Simpkins, while noting that sexting is not necessarily child pornography, bemoans it as 'unhealthy behaviour'. He considers that it is not right for young people to engage in it and opines that in order to save young people from embarrassment in later life, sexting must be 'discouraged' through 'some penalties'. Sexting, clearly, in his view, is an expression of childhood sexuality that requires some form of suppression and/or regulation.

The term 'sexting', which is a portmanteau first used by the media, comes from a conflation of the phrase 'sexy texts'. While originally used to describe the sending or receiving of sexually explicit text messages (Rosenberg, 2011), the term is now more often used to describe the digital recording of naked, semi-naked, sexually suggestive or explicit images and their distribution via mobile phone messaging, email or social networking sites, such as Facebook, Instagram and YouTube (for example, see Crofts *et al.*, 2015; Joint Select Committee on Cyber-Safety, 2011 [4.47]; Lee *et al.*, 2013). As the Law Reform Committee of Victoria (2013: 15) notes, the term 'sexting' is evolving and 'encompasses a wide range of practices, motivations and behaviours'.

While consensual sexting by adults has generally been construed as a fun and sexy addendum to a normal sex life (Crofts *et al.*, 2015), sexting by young people constitutes perhaps just a more contemporary set of moral concerns about childhood sexuality – and, in this case, the sexualisation and pornification of childhood.

Moreover, concerns about a new technological means of digitising and sharing images and a perception of proliferating raunch in society influencing young people has created a perfect storm.

In this chapter, we discuss the ways in which sexting by young people has become subject to a range of regulatory interventions and how it has helped justify a variety of surveillance interventions in the online lives of young people. We begin by putting concerns about sexting into the context of broader historical concerns about childhood sexuality. We then discuss the legal regulation of sexting by young people and how the regulation of this practice became bound up with laws designed to criminalise the production and distribution of child pornography. Finally, we use our own empirical qualitative and quantitative research to illuminate some of the ways in which the sexual lives of young people have become subject to surveillance on the basis that they may be engaging in sexting-type behaviours.

Regulation of childhood sexuality

The visual, physical and technological surveillance and legal regulation of childhood sexuality have long had a role in modern societies. As Egan and Hawkes (2008) noted, health reformer John Harvey Kellogg in his book *Plain Facts about Sexual Life* (1877: 47) strenuously warned parents of the dangers of precocious sexuality in the life of the child. Children were, he said, highly susceptible to corrupting influences, and exposure to dirty stories by 'evil companions' could lead to sexual thoughts that would cloud their minds and lead to deviant actions. Childhood sexuality was, thus, almost mechanical in nature for Kellogg – once unleashed, it was 'almost impossible to stop' (Egan and Hawkes, 2008: 355).

Nonetheless, such ideas are of the modern world. As Fishman (1982) tells us, prior to 1700, little attention was paid to childhood sexuality even by religious moralists who might have had an interest in doing so. However, in the eighteenth century, theological and then medical moralists began condemning childhood sexual activity as sinful or physically harmful. It became a pathological problem. By the nineteenth century, masturbation in particular was considered a 'social evil and not merely an individual problem, a threat to the polity as a whole requiring harsh measures if necessary to eradicate it' (Fishman, 1982: 270).

While Fishman goes on to note the normalisation of childhood sexuality by the later twentieth century – particularly of masturbation, the suppression of which was seen as abnormal in the post-Freudian world of school-based sex education – it is also clear that some alternative expressions of childhood sexuality came to be seen as harmful, even if masturbation was not. Indeed, while Fishman traces the development and distinct changes in discourse around childhood sexuality, there has also developed a more continuous discourse in parallel to the apparent discontinuities. That is, that the sexual health of children was seen as linked to the health of future generations, and indeed the health of the human race:

> The sexualization of children was accomplished in the form of a campaign of health of the race – precocious sexuality was presented from the eighteenth century to the end of the nineteenth century as an epidemic menace that

risked compromising not only the future health of adults but the future of the entire society and species. (Foucault, 1990: 146)

Egan and Hawkes also note that this regulation of childhood sexuality has produced some paradoxical thinking, with a logic that presumed an asexual child subject, while at the same time creating a range of techniques aimed at controlling or managing sexuality once it was demonstrated.

> Such an understanding makes palatable an acknowledgment of childhood sexuality by demarcating its difference from adulthood and legitimates interventions in the lives of children as necessary for their best interest and protection. When a child's desires and/or behaviors directly contradict adult constructions their manifestation is blamed on 'others' who are deemed to be the cause of such abhorrent incitements. (Egan and Hawkes, 2008: 357)

If anxieties about childhood sexuality are a key driver of the regulation and monitoring of young people and sexting, then this anxiety is only intensified by the technological elements of sexting. Constituting a Beckian-style 'new risk' (Beck, 1992), the seeming ungovernable nature of online cultures where e-crimes are commonplace (Grabosky, 2007) plays into a range of technophobic later-modern fear and anxieties.

There is, of course, a range of risks for young people who engage in sexting-type activities, many of which are likely to be gendered in nature. Key among them are those to do with sexual exploitation through the use of their images (Renold and Ringrose, 2011), humiliation and damage to reputation (Lee and Crofts, 2015), the chance of images finding their way to paedophiles (Crofts *et al.*, 2015; Jewkes, 2011), and the capacity for bullying and blackmail (Ringrose *et al.*, 2013; Keeley *et al.*, 2014). However, as serious as such outcomes can be for individuals, research has indicated that these coercive behaviours and negative outcomes from sexting affect only an extremely small number of those who engage in it. Indeed, as Crofts *et al.* (2015) found in a large-scale Internet survey of over 1,400 respondents, only 6 per cent of those who had ever received a sext had sent one to a third party, and the number of young people indicating that they had been pressured of coerced into sending an image was almost insignificant next to those who were motivated by a wish to be 'fun and flirtatious' or give a 'sexy present' to a boyfriend or girlfriend.

Research also suggests that while it is difficult to estimate the prevalence of negative risks, such as cyber-bullying, the risk does 'not appear to be rising substantially with increasing access to mobile and online technologies, possibly because these technologies pose no additional risk to offline behaviour, or because any risks are offset by a commensurate growth in safety awareness and initiatives' (Livingstone and Smith, 2014: 635). Furthermore, a recent study found that young people considered traditional forms of bullying more hurtful than cyber-bullying (Corby *et al.*, 2015). This is not to downplay the potential dangers of sexting for young people, but to suggest that most young people who do engage in the practice do not experience negative outcomes.

Legal regulation of sexting by young people

The anxieties about the impact that new technologies have had on child pornography have internationally spurred moves to strengthen child pornography laws. There is concern that not only have new technologies fuelled the exploitation of children by increasing the demand for 'ever greater levels of depravity' but also 'through the repeated distribution of the image, or images, through international networks' (Attorney-General's Department, 2009: [245]). As early as 1996, there was agreement at the First World Congress against the Sexual Exploitation of Children held in Stockholm that states should review and where necessary revise 'laws, policies, programs and practices to eliminate the commercial sexual exploitation of children'. In 2000, the UN adopted an Optional Protocol on the Sale of Children, Child Prostitution and Child Pornography, seeking to strengthen child pornography laws by setting an age under which a person is deemed to be a child, expanding the definition of child pornography and creating offences to cover possession alongside existing offences of creation and distribution.

The Optional Protocol employs a definition of 'child pornography' that includes 'any representation … of a child engaged in real or simulated sexual activities or any representation of the sexual parts of a child for primarily sexual purposes' (art 2(c)). This definition is in line with the development of typologies of material that might be sexualised by an adult with a sexual interest. For instance, the Combating Paedophile Information Networks in Europe (COPINE) Project developed a 10-point scale, which ranges from sadism/bestiality at one extreme to indicative non-erotic or sexualised images at the other (Taylor *et al.*, 2001: 101). This index recognises that paedophilic interest in images of children may go beyond images of children directly involved in sexual activity and include images that in other contexts might be relatively innocent but are sexualised by the viewer.

In Australia, child pornography (sometimes called child abuse or exploitation material) offences are variously defined in each jurisdiction, but have broadly followed the Commonwealth Government's lead in amending laws in line with its international obligations (Crofts and Lee, 2013). This means that some jurisdictions have raised the age at which a person is deemed to be a child for child pornography offences and expanded the definition of what amounts to child pornography. It is these changes to child pornography laws that mean such laws can also apply to sexting by young people.

In some jurisdictions, a person is deemed to be a child for the purposes of these offences at a higher age level than the age of consent to sexual activity. This has the paradoxical result that in those jurisdictions, a young person can engage in consensual sexual activity, but commits a crime if he/she records images of that activity.[1] The offences also expand beyond images that show a young person engaged in sexual activity or in a sexual context and criminalise images of a young person's naked genitalia, anal region or, in the case of a female, the breasts in a way that a reasonable person would find offensive. This last requirement is designed to prevent overreach of the law; however, adult concerns about young people's sexuality may feed into assessments of whether images of young people taken by young people are seen as offensive. As Jackson states, '[c]hildren are still not generally treated as sexual beings and the possibility that they might be makes many of us feel uneasy' (1982: 3). Considering adults' uneasiness with young people's sexuality, and especially expressions of that sexuality, it is easy to see why the law targets signs of it (Kimpel, 2010: 313).

While the exact extent to which these laws are used and the basis upon which decisions are made to prosecute young people are unclear, it is apparent that young people have been prosecuted under such laws for sexting-type behaviours (Crofts *et al.*, 2015).[2] Such prosecutions may seem surprising, given that it has been expressly acknowledged that child pornography laws were not designed to apply to young people who engage in sexting (for example, see Law Reform Committee of Victoria, 2013: 73). Despite this, there has been relatively little political impetus to remove young people from the reaches of child pornography laws. While some jurisdictions do have a defence for young people in relation to child pornography offences (Tasmania and Victoria), this is not the case in all jurisdictions.

Indeed, when amendments were being made to the Criminal Code Act 1995 (Attorney-General's Department, 2009), there was some discussion about whether it was appropriate for these offences to apply to young people. It was argued that while generally they should not apply to sexting, exempting young people from these offences could weaken protection for them. Such offences were thought to be appropriate in certain cases, for example where the sending of sexually explicit images of themselves or others is malicious or exploitative (O'Connor, 2010; Explanatory Memorandum to the Crimes Legislation Amendment [Sexual Offences against Children] Bill 2010 [Cth]). Moreover, as noted above, it was felt that there was a need to deter young people from sexting (Simpkins, 2010: 2046). Thus, rather than excluding young people from the offences or developing a defence, it was suggested that the best way of ensuring that the laws are only applied in appropriate cases would be to introduce a requirement that the permission of the Attorney-General be sought before commencing any proceedings against a person under 18 years of age for a child pornography offence.

In Australia, so far, only Victoria has taken steps to provide an alternative mechanism for addressing sexting (whether by an adult or a young person), through the creation of two new offences to cover non-consensual distribution of intimate images or the threat to do so (Summary Offences Act 1966 (Vic), ss 41DA, 41DB; amended by Crimes Amendment (Sexual Offences and Other Matters) Act 2014 (Vic)).

It seems then that the reluctance to remove young people completely from the reaches of child pornography offences for sexting-type behaviours is anchored in a desire to constrain young people's sexuality or a fear that without the ability to use criminal law as a tool of control, young people's sexuality will be untrammelled. This is often expressed in paternalistic terms about the need to protect the young person from future harms that they are too immature to appreciate, as expressed in the opening quote. Kimpel (2010) suggests that visual images are a particularly problematic testament to adolescent sexuality, since photos are culturally associated with the beautification and memorialisation of important and valued subjects. This contrasts with the cultural construction of minors as 'innocents' in ways that enable adults to idealise children's lives (Faulkner, 2011). Prosecutions for 'sexting' may, therefore, be seen as a means of fostering these idealised images of childhood innocence, which challenge the threat posed by 'sexting' and young people's sexuality more generally. This framing of sexting by young people as a risky behaviour deserving criminal intervention has flow-on consequences. It justifies a range of measures to monitor young people's behaviour and keep them safe from these risks.

Monitoring technologies

It is not just through legal means that sexting by young people has been subject to regulation. Indeed, the legal regulation of sexting by young people and the discourses that underpin it legitimate other forms of surveillance – both 'hard' and' soft' (Marx, 2006). Hard surveillance incorporates more traditional models, such as selective monitoring, CCTV and the like. Soft surveillance techniques:

> [i]n criminal justice contexts … involve some or all of the following: persuasion to gain voluntary compliance, universality, or at least increased inclusiveness in the dragnet they cast, and emphasis on the needs of the community relative to the rights of the individual. (Marx, 2006: 37)

In this section, we provide examples of both hard and soft surveillance, deployed in a range of ways that seek to either discover sexting behaviours by young people as they take place or retrospectively uncover such behaviour in a manner that problematises the past of the subject of such surveillance.

Methodology

The interviews below were part of an Australian Criminology Research Grant funded project on sexting and young people. They were conducted in 2013 with eight groups of young respondents between the ages of 18 and 20 years. These focus groups comprised students from two universities and a TAFE in New South Wales to ensure a range of viewpoints. All groups were of mixed genders.[3] The interviews were semi-structured and facilitated by a researcher and assistant (who also took notes). All were recorded, transcribed verbatim and coded using NVivo 10. Two researchers conducted the coding and compared themes to ensure inter-coder reliability. Though not included here in detail, the project also involved a survey of 1,400 young people (mostly between the ages of 13 and 18 years).[4]

Hard surveillance

As we have argued above, sexting by young people has been heavily problematised in connection with the growth in social media and smartphone technology. In the following extracts from our focus group interviews, we highlight some of the ways in which sexting operates as a site for the surveillance and regulation of childhood sexuality. Most incidents of young people sexting come to the attention of authorities through reports by parents or schools. The behaviour is usually detected through adults finding sexual images on mobile phones or computers used by young people:

Female 1: The … school found out … about a different girl who sent a nude photo of herself. The school found out because her parents went to the school about the boy that sent it, then all the police got involved and the boy's school that he went to, their principal got involved and I'm pretty sure he got expelled.

Female 2: I don't get how the school could do anything about it if it had nothing to do with the school.

However, in some cases much more active forms of surveillance are engaged in by the school and the teachers. Indeed, the perceived risks of sexting have motivated teachers to monitor students' social media sites, such as Facebook. The next respondent reveals a concerted, if informal, regime of monitoring students' social media sites legitimated by this perceived risk to the students' well-being:

Female 3: Our school was very dodgy the way they did it. They never talked to us about sexting but we found out afterwards that some of the teachers were monitoring our Facebooks.

Facilitator: Excuse me? The teachers were monitoring your Facebook?

Female 4: They would make fake accounts. The stuff they would do – they wouldn't talk to us about it but in a really sneaky way try to monitor our Facebook. This girl actually, what happened? She got into trouble. She got suspended because she started – I don't know what she posted online. Oh she posted something bad about the school. She goes, 'I can't stand this stupid school', and there's a photo of her doing something stupid, something really stupid at the toilets in the school. Somehow the teacher – we found out later on that the teacher was actually stalking, not stalking but monitoring Facebook. That's how they saw it and she was like, 'How did you find this photo?' and the Principal, 'Oh some student showed it to us,' when really they were the ones that were monitoring her Facebook. She got suspended for three days for that.

In this example, sexting becomes a justification for teachers to monitor students' use of social media. Even if sexting behaviour is not revealed, other forms of inappropriate behaviour can be identified through this increased monitoring.

Soft surveillance

Past indiscretions – sexual or otherwise – are beginning to follow young people into their later teens. There is evidence that in the US, colleges and universities use social networking websites as part of their evaluation of applications (Anderson, 2009). Similarly, a 2014 survey on a US job website found that 51 per cent of employers had not hired a candidate due to content, including provocative or inappropriate photos, that they had found on social media websites (CareerBuilder, 2014). This exchange indicates the ways in which future employers are beginning to use Facebook and other social media to make moral and risk judgements about the appropriateness of future employees:

Male 1: One of my best mates back at home, he had his first job interview after he graduated uni, and at the job interview, they brought him in and said like, 'Sign into your Facebook and Twitter accounts right now or you can leave'. My friend is lovely, he's a really smart, mature kid, that's fine. But a lot of people wouldn't be ready for that and see that, and like it was a bit ethical thing, is that right, that they can come into that – in much of a private sense. They've been doing news things back home that more and more employers are trying to do it.

Male 2: But I think they don't perceive it as a private sense, because it is public anyway.

Female 5: But also it's like if you're ashamed to let them see that, you must be hiding something. It's like can we trust you or are you trying to hide. …

Another noted that on joining the army, his social media accounts were subject to investigation and forced amendment, as expressed below:

Male 3: Yeah, I'm in the Army Reserve, I just got in. In my job application, it took me 18 months to get in but it didn't say anything about Facebook – but the day I got enlisted, I had to sign a declaration, swear allegiance and it said do you have Facebook, do you have this, do you have that and I ticked all the boxes. 'Cause they actually check you up even though your account is private, the government gets in and some people have been requested to take stuff down. But I have to now complete a security clearance pack for the Australian vetting agency and they also want to know all these details. So it can be a barrier to your employment, yeah. Especially if you want to become in the military, policeman or in the secret service, like ASIO.[5]

One respondent, who had worked for a company surveilling social media sites for prospective employers, offered insights into the ways in which technology is being used to influence decisions about individuals' futures based on their past activities.

Female 6: I used to be an Internet researcher, and my job was pretty much to find people's information on Facebook and send it to other people … it was a legitimate job … It was kind of like – I don't like to say it out loud, but you know those funny apps where you send …

Female 7: OMG, I was going to bring this up, you send out a message and you say someone's name?

Female 6: Yeah, find out information about blah, blah, blah.

Female 8: I've always wondered if you people existed.

Female 6: And then within three minutes, you'd get a reply back. So, you message this number, ask someone's name and within a few minutes, they write back and say so and so lives at, these guy friends ... people think it's amazing, they think it's some sort of tracking machine or something. It's actually not, it's heaps of Internet researchers researching people on Facebook, and all their Facebook friends.

Female 8: But how do they get into accounts that are blocked?

Female 6: We have like this separate Facebook account, it's like – we've got like 10,000 friends, so we've got connections to everyone, I don't know how that happens, but they just gave me that account, so pretty much you get access to everyone's information.

Resisting surveillance

Respondents also noted the range of strategies young people take to avoid surveillance or oversight of their online activities:

Male 3: I do know a lot of people that are using false names that are recognisable as being their names, but they're un-Google-able. So, if you say Ben Pikelet whoever, you go okay, I know who that is.

Female 9: I think with our age group too everything is so accessible, what is one click away you can find out anything you want. You can find out if they're single, you can find out what school they go to.

Clearly, respondents were aware of the potential repercussions of sexualised or 'inappropriate' behaviour being detected on social and other new technological media. The use of bogus accounts and false names offers at least the promise that their behaviour might be difficult to detect. However, the Internet lacks walls:

> The inherent replicability of bits and the power of search make most walls temporary at best. This is why most participants in networked publics live by 'security through obscurity' where they assume that as long as no one cares about them, no one will come knocking. While this works for most, this puts all oppressed and controlled populations (including teenagers) at risk because it just takes one motivated explorer to track down even the most obscure networked public presence. (boyd, 2007: 3–4).

Conclusion

The problematisation of childhood sexuality has a long history. This history is replete with both continuities and discontinuities as certain sexualised practices by young people are problematised, while others become normalised. As discussed, masturbation is a good example of a practice once maligned, but now generally seen as a natural part of childhood development. On the other hand, sexting has produced an enormous amount of discourse about the risks and dangers of the practice to young people.

These perceived risks and dangers have meant that there has been little drive to remove sexting from child abuse and child pornography legislation. However, as we have demonstrated elsewhere (Crofts *et al.*, 2015), research with young people indicated that their sexting is rarely motivated by maliciousness or the desire to exploit another young person, which would be reasons for criminalising it as child abuse or pornography. Nonetheless, the policy and legal frameworks for sexting have legitimated a range of hard and soft surveillance strategies aimed at detecting sexting by young people. These range from the monitoring of students' social media by schools to the checking of social media histories by prospective employers. However, young people are also demonstrating creative ways of resisting such surveillance. A popular strategy is to set up social media accounts under false names and identification.

Punitive approaches to young people who engage in sexting are not likely to have the desired effects of containing young people's exploration with sexual expression and identity. Instead of increasing the surveillance and regulation of young people, a much more productive approach might be to develop an appropriate education strategy around the practice to develop a set of 'sexual ethics' for young people who engage in consensual sexting (Carmody, 2014). This may discourage the riskiest behaviours of young people who sext, while acknowledging the reality that this practice, and the displays of childhood sexuality that accompany it, are here to stay – at least until the next leap forward in technology.

Notes

1 The age of a child for pornography offences is 18 years under the laws of the Commonwealth, Australian Capital Territory, Northern Territory, Tasmania and Victoria, while the age of consent in these jurisdictions is 16 years, aside from Tasmania where it is 17 years. In New South Wales, Queensland and Western Australia, the age for child pornography offences is the same as the age of consent, i.e. 16 years; in South Australia, both are 17 years.
2 From the available evidence, it appears that police use discretion to divert young people from formal proceedings unless there are aggravating factors, such as coercion, the involvement of adults or the commission of other offences.
3 Technical and Further Education.
4 Additional methodological details can be found in the study of Crofts *et al.* (2015).
5 Australian Security Intelligence Organization.

References

Anderson, L. (2009) 'To friend or not to friend? College admissions in the age of Facebook', *USA Today*. Available online at http://usatoday30.usatoday.com/news/education/2009-09-16-facebook-admissions_N.htm (accessed 12.12.2014).

Attorney-General's Department (2009) *Proposed reforms to commonwealth child sex-related offences*. Criminal Justice Division, Australian Government.

Beck, U. (1992) *Risk society: towards a new modernity*. London: Sage.

boyd, d. (2007) 'Social network sites: public, private, or what?', *Knowledge Tree*, 13, May. Available online at www.danah.org/papers/KnowledgeTree.pdf (accessed 12.12.2014).

CareerBuilder (2014) 'Number of employers passing on applicants due to social media posts continues to rise, according to new CareerBuilder survey'. Available online at www.careerbuilder.com/share/aboutus/pressreleasesdetail.aspx?sd=6%2F26%2F2014&id=pr829&ed=12%2F31%2F2014 (accessed 12.12.14).

Carmody, M. (2014) 'Sex and ethics'. Available online at www.sexandethics.net/ (accessed 12.12.2014).

Corby, E. K., M. Campbell, B. Spears, P. Slee, D. Butler and S. Kift (2015) 'Students' perceptions of their own victimization: a youth voice perspective', *Journal of School Violence*, 18: 1–21.

Crofts, T. and M. Lee (2013) '"Sexting", children and child pornography', *Sydney Law Review*, 35: 85–106.

Crofts, T., M. Lee, A. McGovern and S. Milivojevic (2015) *Sexting and young people*. Basingstoke, UK: Palgrave Macmillan.

Egan, D. and G. Hawkes (2008) 'Imperiled and perilous: exploring the history of childhood sexuality', *Journal of Historical Sociology*, 21(4): 355–67.

Explanatory Memorandum to the Crimes Legislation Amendment (Sexual Offences against Children) Bill 2010 (Cth), viewed 12 December 2014. Available online at www.austlii.edu.au/au/legis/cth/bill_em/claoacb2010554/memo_1. html (accessed 06.01.2016).

Faulkner, J. (2011) *The importance of being innocent: why we worry about children*. Melbourne: Cambridge University Press.

Fishman, S. (1982) 'The history of childhood sexuality', *Journal of Contemporary History*, 17: 269–83.

Foucault, M. (1990) *The history of sexuality*. Houndmills, UK: Penguin.

Grabosky P. (2007) *Electronic crime (Geis Master Series in Criminology)*. New Jersey: Prentice-Hall.

Jackson, S. (1982) *Childhood and sexuality*. Oxford: Basil Blackwell.

Jewkes, Y. (2011) *Media and crime*, 2nd ed. London: Sage.

Joint Select Committee on Cyber-Safety (2011) 'High-wire act: cyber-safety and the young', Commonwealth of Australia, viewed 12 December 2014. Available online at www.aph.gov.au/parliamentary_business/committees/house_of_representatives_committees?url=jscc/report.htm (accessed 06.01.2016).

Keeley, M., I. Katz, S. Bates and M. Wong (2014) 'Research on youth exposure to, and management of, cyberbullying incidents in Australia: synthesis report', Social Policy Research Centre, University of New South Wales.

Kellogg, J. H. (1877) *Plain facts about sexual life*. Michigan: Office of the Health Reformer.

Kimpel, A. F. (2010) 'Using laws designed to protect as a weapon: prosecuting minors under child pornography laws', *New York University Review of Law and Social Change*, 34: 299–338.

Law Reform Committee of Victoria (2013) *Report of the law reform committee for the inquiry into sexting*, Parliamentary Paper No. 230, Session 2010–13. Available online at www.parliament.vic.gov.au/images/stories/committees/lawrefrom/isexting/LRC_Sexting_Final_Report.pdf (accessed 12.12.2014).

Lee, M., T. Crofts, M. Salter, S. Milivojevic and A. McGovern (2013) '"Let's get sexting": risk, power, sex and criminalisation in the moral domain', *International Journal for Crime, Justice and Social Democracy*, 2(1): 35–49.

Lee, M. and T. Crofts (2015) 'Gender, pressure, coercion and pleasure: untangling motivations for sexting between young people', *The British Journal of Criminology*, 55(3): 454–73.

Livingstone, S. and P. K. Smith (2014) 'Annual research review: harms experienced by child users of online and mobile technologies: the nature, prevalence and management of sexual and aggressive risks in the digital age', *Journal of Child Psychology and Psychiatry*, 55(6): 635–54.

Marx, G. (2006) 'Soft surveillance: the growth of mandatory volunteerism in collecting personal information — "Hey buddy can you spare a DNA?"', in T. Monahan (ed.), *Surveillance and security: technological politics and power in everyday life*. Cullompton, UK: Willan.

O'Connor, B. (2010) *Commonwealth, parliamentary debates*, House of Representatives, 2051, 9 Mar.

Renold, E. and J. Ringrose (2011) 'Schizoid subjectivities? Re-theorising teen-girls' sexual cultures in an era of "sexualisation"', *Journal of Sociology*, 47(4): 389–409.

Ringrose, J., L. Harvey, R. Gill and S. Livingstone (2013) 'Teen girls, sexual double standards and "sexting": gendered value in digital image exchange', *Feminist Theory*, 14(3): 305–23.

Rosenberg, E. (2011) 'In Weiner's wake: a brief history of the word "sexting", *The Wire*. Available online at www.thewire.com/national/2011/06/brief-history-sexting/38668/ (accessed 12.12.2014).

Simpkins, L. (2010) *Commonwealth, parliamentary debates*, House of Representatives, 2046, 9 Mar.

Taylor, M., G. Holland and E. Quayle (2001) 'Typology of paedophile picture collections', *Police Journal*, 74(2): 97–107.

7 Media discourses of girls at risk and domestication of mobile phone surveillance

Jacqueline Ryan Vickery

> A middle-aged man is sitting in a monochromatic living room staring at a teenage boy seated across from him on a couch. He says, 'So, you're in my daughter's five,[1] huh?' The teenage boy responds, 'Yes, sir' and the camera backs up to reveal the boy's clearly nervous stance. The father leans forward, picks up his daughter's mobile phone laying on the coffee table. 'I'm in there too', he says, gesturing to the phone. He flips open the phone, shows it to the boy and says, 'My picture's right next to yours. It's almost like I'm watching you … *all the time*.' The boy laughs nervously as the father continues to hold his gaze while holding the phone. The camera pans back and forth to highlight the father's intimidation and the boy's visible discomfort. The teenage daughter then enters the room, approaches her father and asks, 'Is that my phone?' The father says 'Yes' and hands his daughter her phone as both he and the boy stand up. The daughter asks her date if he is ready to go, to which he eagerly replies, 'Yes!' The girl hugs her father and says, 'Bye daddy, I love you.' While she is hugging her father, we see him give an intimidating glare to her date. The boy exits with trepidation as he follows the girl out the door. The father tells them to 'Have a good night' while raising his eyebrows with an 'I'll be watching you' look directed toward the teen boy. (T-mobile Creepy Dad, 2007)

On the surface, this 2007 T-mobile commercial may be read as an example of a father monitoring his daughter's boyfriend. However, it is through the daughter's phone – which he readily accesses and views in the absence of his daughter – that he has constant and immediate access to her. The implication is that the daughter's perceived sexual innocence is at risk and her date represents a threat. The surveillance implied by her father reinforces the daughter's lack of sexual agency. This opening example serves as an à propos introduction to the overarching theme of this chapter: the increasing commodification and domestication of surveillance.

This chapter examines the media discourses surrounding mobile phone technology in the United States and how they serve to normalise surveillance in domestic spaces. The chapter has five parts. I provide a brief overview of risk as related to mobile phones, then briefly discuss the methodology of my research. My findings are presented in two parts: a discursive analysis of the ways media and mobile technology industries commodify and marketise the domestication of surveillance; and a qualitative analysis of how teen girls and their parents use mobile technology to enact or resist familial surveillance. Finally, I consider the ethics of mobile-phone-enabled surveillance of young people's lived experiences.

Risk, safety and telephony

Recent decades have seen an increase in the use of technology as a tool for parents to monitor their children's movements and behaviours within and beyond the home (Shade, 2011). This is what I refer to as the domestication of surveillance: that is, surveillance that originates in the home as a way for adults (namely, parents) to monitor adolescents. Increasingly, mobile devices enable parents to monitor not only their children's movements and whereabouts but also their social lives – with whom they are interacting, when, where and how. Because many parents are fearful of their children's social interactions via the mobile phone (Shade, 2011), it is productive to contextualise mobile surveillance within the context of risk and media panics. Doing so allows for an examination of the ways in which technology – and the mobile phone specifically – is simultaneously and paradoxically constructed as both risk and security, especially for girls.

Throughout the twentieth and twenty-first centuries, we have experienced an increased focus on the safety and well-being of young people, accompanied by increased anxiety and fear (Kelly, 2000; Stearns, 2003). While such a focus has its benefits (increased safety), it also gives rise to media panics about the risks young people inevitably encounter. Sociologist Ulrich Beck (1992: 21) defines risk as 'a systematic way of dealing with hazards and insecurities induced and introduced by modernization itself'. He continues, 'in the risk society the unknown and unintended consequences come to be a dominant force in history and society. They can be changed, magnified, dramatized or minimized within knowledge, and to that extent they are particularly open to social definition and construction' (Beck, 1992: 22–3). In other words, the ability for a society to identify, intensify and individualise risk may make us safer, but it also increases our anxiety and fear.

Media scholar Alice Marwick (2008) argues that modernity has given rise to moral panics over the well-being of adolescents; however, rather than address the far too prevalent realities of child poverty or neglect and abuse in the home, media panic discourses fuel concern about the risk of 'others'. This typically falls into the category of 'stranger danger', in which parents are disproportionately cautioned to protect their children from hypothetical unknown threats outside the home (predators, paedophiles, and so on). Additionally, as I have argued elsewhere (Vickery, forthcoming), media increasingly fuel concerns about peers as a threat to adolescents' well-being. Within news and popular media, mobile and social media are constructed as a dangerous space for young people, not only because of predators but also because of potential bullying and harassment from peers, referred to as 'peer fear' (Vickery, forthcoming). In the most extreme circumstances, suicides have been attributed to online bullying (Hinduja and

Patchin, 2010), which become part of the broader media panic that positions mobile and social media as dangerous, and also urges parents to monitor and surveil their children's mobile media practices (Prevent Cyberbullying, n.d.).

Moral panics are part of a historical trend in which new technologies lead to fear and anxiety (Marvin, 1998; Springhall, 1998; Thiel-Stern, 2014). Like its predecessor, the landline, the mobile phone has become a lightning rod for anxiety and panic. In the 1950s, when the landline telephone was a new domestic technology, parents were concerned that boys would have unrestricted access to their daughters in the privacy of their homes; and later even in the intimate space of the bedroom (Kearney, 2005). Additionally, there were concerns about strangers being able to invade the private space of the home and about interracial socialisation among peers (Kearney, 2005; Marvin, 1998). The mobile phone has been likewise constructed as an instrument of risk and harm because it renders young people accessible to others, even within the supposedly safe confines of the home. This has led to increased anxiety about young people accessing inappropriate content, such as porn, and concerns that they will be victims of inappropriate and harmful behaviours perpetrated by predators, bullies, peers and paedophiles (Herring, 2008; Shade, 2011; Vickery, forthcoming). As with the 1950s panics about protecting girls' sexual innocence, mobile phones are today sources of anxiety around female sexuality, particularly in regard to sexting (see Chapter 6).

These concerns work alongside the continual construction of youth, and more specifically girls, as at risk in order to provide justification for policies of surveillance, control, protection and monitoring. Kelly (2000: 470) writes, 'powerful narratives of risk, fear, and uncertainty structure a variety of emergent processes and practices aimed at regulating the behaviors and dispositions of populations of young people'. Moreover, because young people are uniquely dependent upon various institutional structures, their behaviours are often observed, regulated and scrutinised (Kelly, 2000). However, outside of formal institutional settings, Shade (2011: 261) argues that the 'protected child' has become an 'intrinsic facet of millennium parenting in North America', leading to increased domestication of surveillance as well. Because cell phones transgress public boundaries (by extending the private reach of the household beyond a physical presence and constraint), they provide increased opportunities for surveillance of young bodies outside the home (Horst, 2010).

Alongside discourses of the mobile phone as risk and threat, we also see it marketed and constructed as a technology of safety and security. In fact, in 2010, 94 per cent of US parents cited 'safety' as a reason to purchase a phone for their children; this was particularly true for mothers and girls (Lenhart *et al.*, 2010). In modern society, characterised by busy schedules and long commutes whereby the family unit is frequently separated across geography and time, the mobile phone offers parents and children a sense of security (Horst, 2010; Livingstone, 2009). The potential for constant and persistent communication produces what Turkle (2008) refers to as a 'tethered child', offering both parent and child a sense of security.

Yet, rather than functioning as merely a tool for communication, the mobile phone has also been marketed as a technology of surveillance (Richtel, 2006; Shade, 2011). The extension of the mobile phone from a tool for constant familial contact to a technology of surveillance repositions it within risk society and media panic discourses. Marketing the mobile phone as a technology of domestic surveillance reifies the panic of stranger danger and peer fear by amplifying the potential threats within a risk society.

Methodology

The two-part methodology and analysis adopted allows for an examination of both market expectations and family experiences related to the surveillance of teen girls via mobile media.

The next section of this chapter expands earlier research that examines how the four largest US mobile service providers market and normalise surveillance via their television commercials and services (Vickery, 2014).[2] The sample includes 42 US cell phone commercials from the period 2005–14; they were accessed via the mobile service providers' websites, YouTube and my personal recordings directly from television. Because the focus of this chapter is on young people and the domestication of surveillance, the sample only includes commercials that represent parents, children and families. In other words, commercials portraying professionals or non-parent adults are excluded from analysis. While the collection may not include every commercial from this time period, I am confident it encompasses a wide and representative sample. Drawing from feminist media studies, alongside discourse analysis, I consider the ways in which the commercials market and domesticate surveillance via mobile phones.

The following section shifts focus from representation of surveillance to an analysis of families' attitudes to surveillance via mobile media. The analysis focuses on three teenage girls – Gabriela, Selena and Jada – who participated as part of a larger ethnographic project.[3] I have chosen to focus on these three girls and their families because their experiences and perceptions reveal a diversity of perspectives of mobile surveillance. This research is qualitative and the case studies are not intended to be representative; rather, their stories highlight how access to technology, parent-child relationships and living situations mediate attitudes to and experiences with mobile media surveillance in the home.

The commodification and domestication of surveillance via the mobile phone

Although a common household technology in most US homes,[4] the mobile phone remains in a transitionary state of flux – the social norms, values, and adaptations of its everyday use are still evolving (Silverstone and Haddon, 1996). Media scholars refer to this as a period of 'interpretive flexibility' to describe the ways technology is incorporated into every day life through negotiations, contestations of meaning, localised social practices, and technological developments (Pinch and Bijker, 1984). Because youth and adults often have different constructions of technology and develop different communicative practices, it is important to consider how technology and social practices are adapted and developed within family units alongside the political economy of the consumer electronic industry.

Technology industries can play an integral role in shaping social norms and expectations, particularly in the early history of a technology's development, dissemination, adoption and domestication (Silverstone and Haddon, 1996). As an industry, mobile phone service providers have a significant economic and commercial stake in shaping discourse around young people and mobile devices. Examining mobile service providers accordingly affords a productive entry point for analysing the construction of mobile phones and girls' practices within a broader context of the domestication of surveillance.

Normative discourses of father-daughter surveillance

One way that mobile phone industries contribute to expectations of surveillance is via frequent visual representations of the domestication of surveillance in their television and online commercials. Within the commercials, the phone is frequently constructed and represented as a way to monitor girls' sociality within and outside the home. The example at the beginning of this chapter illustrates how mobile phone service providers frequently portray parents enacting some level of surveillance of their daughters via a mobile phone. A similar example of a father implicitly monitoring his daughter's sociality and sexuality is a 2008 T-mobile commercial called 'Derek with a Mustang':

> A white dad enters the home and says, 'Check it out gang, just got that new T-mobile family plan, now we can talk to our friends and family all we want.' His wife turns around and replies, 'Like Vivian' and his son (approximately 13-years-old) walks in the room and says, 'And Skinny Pete'. After another exchange, his teenage daughter walks up to her father and says, 'And I can call Derek?' She looks up at her father for confirmation, to which he responds, 'Derek with a moustache and Mustang Derek?'[5] The girl fiddles with her hands, smiles in a dreamy way while rocking back and forth on her feet, 'Yea'. Dad responds anxiously and abruptly with a nervous laugh, 'Yea, it's weird [looks at paper in his hand], there's a "no Dereks with moustaches clause" [points at paper]'. His daughter stands on her toes to try to read the brochure, but the dad moves it away. Dad continues, 'It's in the fine print'. [dad shakes his head, pretending to be sympathetic to his daughter, even though he's the one enacting the rule that she cannot add Derek to the plan]. 'What a drag, dude.'

Although intended to be humorous, the commercial also highlights the father's attempt at monitoring whom his teenage daughter can contact. By not allowing his daughter to add Derek to the phone plan, he essentially limits her ability to talk with him, which serves as a form of control and surveillance of her social and sexual life. In this way, surveillance is also gendered. Although the son suggested adding a male friend, arguably the commercial would not have worked had the dad attempted to prevent his son from adding a girl. In fact, in an AT&T commercial, we actually see a dad praising and encouraging his teenage son to add girls to the family plan (AT&T Sibling Rivalry, 2008). In this way, surveillance of girls' sociality is made possible via the phone plan, but is also explicitly framed as a way to monitor female sexuality, thus situating the commercials within a historical discourse in which female sexuality is portrayed as at risk via telephony (Kearney, 2005). Boys' sexuality, on the other hand, is not constructed as risky in the same way; hence, the father's implied justification for monitoring and surveilling whom his daughter can frequently contact via her phone.

Marketing surveillance services

Normative discourses of girls at risk

In addition to representing familial surveillance via mobile phone service provider commercials, surveillance is also normalised and commodified through actual surveillance service plans offered by the mobile phone service providers. These services are typically marketed to parents as a way to protect their children (Shade, 2007; Vickery, 2014). All four major US phone providers offer additional service options that allow phones – and, therefore, their users – to be tracked via GPS monitoring. Once the service is purchased and set up, anyone with access can log in and find out where the phone is currently located in real time and with accurate locational precision. Depending on the service, parents can even set up a feature that will automatically text them when their children arrive home. Additionally, on some plans, parents can set up 'safe zones'. If a child leaves a 'safe zone', parents will automatically receive a text alerting them of their child's whereabouts outside of the designated areas.

Unsurprisingly, these services are marketed to mothers as a way to protect their children, but more specifically, their daughters. In the opening scene of Sprint's promotional commercial for their family surveillance service, John Walsh, the host of *America's Most Wanted*, explains, 'It is a huge component of reality safety to know where your child is [at all times]'. In the next scene, a mother explains that her daughter forgot to text her after school. Rather than just calling or texting her, she enabled the family locator to find out exactly where her daughter was. Although she was safely at a friend's home, the mother explains how this feature gave her peace of mind (Sprint Family Locator, 2009).

The promo, thus, incongruously juxtaposes the threat of child predators alongside a girl who was 'missing' but completely safe. It exacerbates fears (and, thus, contributes to media panics), while also normalising and domesticating surveillance practices, particularly for girls, who are constructed as more vulnerable and in need of constant protection (that is, surveillance). All of the promotional videos on the service providers' websites specifically address and/or represent mothers as the ones charged with responsibility for managing the safety of their children. With one exception (AT&T Family Map, 2009), which includes a son and daughter, all the videos represent daughters as children in need of monitoring:

> In a Verizon commercial we see a mum and her teenage daughter at the mall together. The daughter walks away from her mum and heads down the escalator; she looks back over her shoulder to give mum a reassuring smile. Mum cranes her neck to watch her daughter get off the escalator as a picture of a US map appears above the daughter's head. We then see the mother check her phone; a layout of the mall is on the screen with a red arrow pinpointing her daughter's precise location in the mall. The daughter (still with an image of a map above her head) excitedly runs up to two other teen girls who exclaim, 'Hey, are you ready?' The three girls walk off together, the daughter turns around and waves and smiles one last time at her mum who is watching from the second-floor railing of the mall. Her mum smiles back at her and finally walks away. (Verizon Mall Moment, 2010)

Through T-mobile's Family Where (2012) app, mum can monitor her daughter and know if she leaves the mall (the presumption is that leaving the mall would put her daughter in danger). The commercial relies on a normative assumption that an unsupervised girl is inherently at risk in public. Rather than just having peace of mind that the daughter can call her if she gets into trouble (if a stranger abducts her?), the mother is able to actively watch her movements. The service highlights a broader societal context in which youth are the rationale for increased surveillance in society; in other words, the surveillance apps are justified because of the presumed vulnerability of adolescents. Surveillance is presented as an acceptable, normative, and even expected aspect for girls in public away from direct parental supervision.

As with the previous examples, this particular commercial would not be read in the same way were it a teenage boy being actively and knowingly surveilled by his mother. Because boys have historically been granted greater autonomy and are expected to occupy public spaces (Thiel-Stern, 2014), it would seem incongruous to have a mother surveilling her teenage son's movements throughout the mall; he is not presumed to be at risk in the same way girls are. The commercial subtly invokes fears about the girl's sexual innocence and vulnerability in distinctly gendered ways that would not work with a depiction of a teenage son. In other words, it plays off the accepted fears and normative constructions of girls (and their sexuality) as vulnerable and at greater risk in public spaces.

Surveillance as convenience

In addition to keeping daughters safe, the services are marketed as family management tools: that is, as a way to keep up with the family's hectic schedules.

As the voiceover in a Verizon commercial explains, 'Being a mom can feel like a balancing act' (Verizon Family Locator, 2012). Rather than merely calling or texting the family to coordinate plans, mothers can manage the household 'without interrupting their kids' by simply monitoring their locations (AT&T Family Locator, 2013):

> Sprint's promotional video introduces us to Emily, a busy teenager. Emily is portrayed as a cartoon character (racially ambiguous, but with fair skin), playing a musical instrument, going to soccer practice and karate lessons (markedly middle-class activities for this 'busy teen'). This is depicted by moving Emily across a 3-D map of her town. The voiceover tells us, 'The only person in Emily's family who's busier than she is is her mom.' Emily's mother, Sarah, appears on the screen holding both hands to her head looking frantic with 'question mark bubbles' popping out all around her. The voiceover tells us, 'Sarah needed an assistant, so she got Sprint Family Locator'. We then see Sarah at work on a computer and on her cell phone, checking to see exactly where Emily is (represented by a dot on a map). We also learn that 'Sarah gets a text letting her know that Emily got home on time or not'. On screen, we see Emily entering the front door, with a clock displaying 3:00 in full focus. The video ends by telling viewers, 'Never wonder where your kids are' and to sign up for a free trial of Sprint Family Locator. Throughout the entire promo, we see Emily smiling and happy; the implication is that her mother is able to monitor her without being intrusive. Sarah is also smiling, reassured by the ability to surveil Emily's movements and location in real time. (Sprint Family Locator, 2012)

The feature is promoted as a simple solution to a perceived problem for busy middle-class families. The implication is that mothers need to and are expected to know precisely where their children are – especially daughters – at all times. Again, as with similar surveillance commercials, rather than 'interrupting' children by calling or texting to ensure they make it home safely, parents can unobtrusively surveil their children's precise locations at any time. Thus, rather than overtly enacting fears around strangers, the domestication of surveillance is presented as a normal – and necessary – part of any busy family dynamic. A discourse of convenience and family management serves to sublimate the typical surveillance discourse of fear and risk. Instead of highlighting the risk-based justification of surveillance, the commercial further promotes, normalises and commodifies[6] the domestication of surveillance via a rhetoric of convenience.

In sum, many of the commercials rely on discourses of risk and safety to deny young girls agency over their social and sexual lives and, thus, promote the domestication of mobile surveillance. The commercial at the beginning of this chapter implies that the father does not trust his daughter to exercise sensible decisions regarding her own sexual agency. His ability to 'always watch' is a threat and is intended to keep her in line with her father's sexual rules and expectations. Similarly, in the commercial with 'Derek', the father also implies he does not trust Derek or, rather, his daughter's social interactions with Derek. Therefore, he enacts surveillance of her social and sexual life by denying her unlimited access to him. The commercials that more overtly portray surveillance – such as the mall commercial and the family locator commercials – invoke a discourse of risk by indicating mothers can only trust that their daughters are safe because of mobile surveillance. All these examples represent daughters as lacking agency; they cannot be trusted to make safe decisions. The message is that mobile phones – as a tool of safety – should be trusted instead. However, my interviews with teen girls and their parents in the next section reveal that their discourses of trust are from a people-first perspective – 'I trust my daughter'– not from a technology-first understanding of trust (evidenced by an absence of 'I trust technology' statements).

Familial perspectives of mobile media surveillance

As demonstrated, mobile phone service provider commercials represent the domestication of surveillance as a normative, necessary and natural aspect of family life. However, how do teen girls and their parents actually negotiate the surveillance potential afforded by mobile phones? Given the extent to which safety and surveillance discourses are typically gendered as female (Shade, 2007; Thiel-Stern, 2014; Vickery, 2014), this section highlights the experiences and perceptions of three families in central Texas. The three families include: Gabriela, a 16-year-old working-class Mexican-American and her father who earns a living installing windows; Selena, a 17-year-old low-income Latina and her unemployed single mother; and Jada, a lower-middle-class black 16-year-old and her mother who works at a hospital.

The three girls have different living situations, varied access to mobile technology and dissimilar relationships with their parent(s) – three factors that mediate the negotiation and domestication of surveillance. None of the families in this study used (nor could afford) family-monitoring apps, such as the ones offered by mobile phone service providers. It should also be noted that none of these families look like those portrayed in the mobile service commercials, who are all visibly middle class and white. For the families in this study, the mobile phone provided a way for parents to stay in contact with their daughters and gave parents access to their daughters' social media profiles and text conversations. The girls' families had different expectations of privacy and surveillance; and the interviews reveal the extent to which expectations of constant surveillance are privileged expectations that are not typically available to working-class families. Furthermore, unlike in the commercials, the girls exercise agency in negotiating expectations of surveillance and privacy.

Gabriela and her father: negotiating compliance and resistance

Gabriela lived in a three-bedroom suburban home with her little sister and her divorced, yet co-habiting, parents; she and her sister shared the master bedroom and her parents each occupied separate bedrooms. Gabriela's parents emigrated from Mexico to the USA before she was born. Her parents worked in service and labour jobs; they have done well for themselves and had middle-class aspirations for their daughters. Gabriela owned her own phone, which both of her parents paid for, and her own laptop, which was a gift from an uncle.

Although Gabriela described her relationship with her father as open and trusting, she also expected that he would monitor her social life via mobile and social media. In fact, her father actually teased her about having a password on her phone – something Gabriela did to prevent her friends from looking through her phone at school. However, at home, she disabled it, because her father interpreted her use of a password to mean that she was hiding something from him. Her willingness to take the password off – and, thus, grant her father unrestricted access to her phone – demonstrated her own expectation of and compliance with the fact that her father would monitor her social life via her mobile phone. She further acknowledged that her parents probably looked at her call log when they paid her mobile phone bill.

Gabriela expected that her father surveilled her interactions via her phone, as this was considered an acceptable and normalised practice of surveillance within the home. In an interview, her father confirmed that he occasionally looked through his daughter's phone when she left it sitting around the house and frequently asked her about her communications. His primary motivation was to make sure she was 'not getting into trouble with her friends'. In particular, he worried she would hang out with the 'wrong kind of Mexicans, the ones who go to parties, do drugs, and get in trouble'. Gabriela occasionally expressed frustration that her father did not trust her discretion when it came to friendships and her social life outside of the home.

Although Gabriela was, on the one hand, compliant with her father's expectations of surveillance, she also exercised agency via other aspects of her social life. One strategy for negotiating and resisting her father's access to her social life was by setting up private social media accounts that he did not know how to access. She and her boyfriend used a shared Tumblr account to secretly communicate with one another throughout the day. This afforded Gabriela more privacy – and, thus, relieved her from the consequences of surveillance – because she was not connected to her parents or extended family on Tumblr. And she did not anticipate that her dad would ever access or read her Tumblr if he looked through her phone; unlike Facebook, it was an app with which he was unfamiliar. In this way, Gabriela both conformed to and resisted familial surveillance in the home. She complied with her father's expectations by removing the password from her phone and knowingly granted him access, but she also agentively negotiated private modes of communication that afforded socialisation outside of familial surveillance. Unlike the depictions in the television commercials, Gabriela resisted monitoring and negotiated privacy even within a familial context of mobile surveillance.

Selena and her mother: class expectations of privacy

Selena shared a small two-bedroom apartment with her single and unemployed mother, a younger half-sister, an older brother, his girlfriend and their two young children. Needless to say, the home was constantly crowded and there were few expectations of spatial privacy. Selena's mobile phone access was precarious; her father occasionally helped pay the bill, but otherwise Selena tried to earn money doing odd jobs in the neighbourhood. Her pay-as-you-go mobile phone plan was frequently disconnected when she ran out of money to purchase more minutes and data. The family did not have Internet at home, so most of the time Selena depended on the school's Wi-Fi or friends' houses to access the Internet and mobile media. Unlike Gabriela, who presumed her dad would occasionally access her phone, Selena and her mother had a not-so-subtle agreement that they would not invade each other's mobile and social media privacy. In fact, it was Selena's mother who actually unfriended her daughter on Facebook because she did not want to see what her daughter was doing; likewise, she did not want Selena to see what she was doing online. As her mother explained to me:

> I'm trying to give them [my children] their space, but there's things they'll post that I don't agree on. I don't want to see it. I don't want to – there's certain pictures I might not want to see … They're kids and they tend to talk different than some of us adults and they put out things, whether it's cussing – a cuss word every other word – I don't want to see it. I don't want to associate with that.

In a household with limited access to mobile devices and low expectations of in-home privacy and personal space, the idea of familial surveillance shifts. Rather than mobile media providing a means through which mothers can keep tabs on their daughters, mobile phones become a space for both mother and daughter to exercise agency and privacy over at least some aspects of their social and domestic lives.

When Selena was out with friends, her mother would try to reach her via her mobile phone; however, Selena would deliberately turn it off (or claim to have run out of minutes on her pre-paid plan). Instead, she used a Wi-Fi-enabled iPod Touch as a way to communicate and text her friends, but not her mother. In other words, she was able to maintain contact with her peers, but she intentionally and deliberately made herself unavailable to her mother when she was not at home. Her mother was aware of this, to a certain extent; if she really needed to reach Selena, she called one of Selena's friends' phones or her friends' parents' phones:

> If I don't hear from her of course I'm going to worry. When her friends don't answer I'm like, 'Okay. Something's going on.' It could be bad or innocent – that's when I start calling parents but I try to stay away from having to do that because I don't want to be nagging. I try to give her her space.

For financial reasons – as well as Selena's deliberate strategies – her mother was required to rely on more traditional means of communication, rather than overt surveillance, as a way to check on her daughter. Calling her friends and her friends' parents was a way to monitor her daughter (what the commercials portray as 'invasive' and 'interruptive' means of communication), but in a way that is significantly different form other modes of constant surveillance.

Thus, in many ways, Selena's precarious and limited access to mobile media alleviated her burden of surveillance because her mother was unable – financially or technologically – to constantly surveil neither her daughter's movements outside the home nor her social interactions within the home. Selena and her mother's perspectives problematise the normative value of surveillance – not all parents expect or want to monitor their children in the way mobile phone industries suggest they should. The expectation and justification for constant surveillance are a class-based norm that not all families can afford nor desire. Surveillance services, which cost even more money in addition to phone plans – are a solution and tool available to only some families. Selena's home life reveals how the normalisation of mobile surveillance is an inherently privileged class expectation (for more information about how expectations of surveillance are class-based and gendered, see Franks, 2015). Unlike the middle-class mother-daughter representations within the mobile phone commercials, both Selena and her mother actively negotiate expectations of surveillance and enact strategies for mutual privacy.

Jada and her mother: trust and dialogue

Jada lived in a small three-bedroom home with her unmarried parents and a little brother and sister. The family shared a computer in the kitchen, but Jada had her own Wi-Fi-connected tablet. Her parents paid for her mobile phone and expected her to maintain communication with them: 'If they text and I can't answer, I have to respond. I let them know I'll call later.' Jada explained her parents could be strict compared to some of her friends, but she desired to please them, and was quick to add, 'It's ok though, they just worry about me.' For the most part, Jada had an open and trusting relationship with her parents. She was a good student and stayed perpetually busy with a part-time job, drill team and several other school activities. When I asked her about privacy at home, she explained that her parents trusted her and she did not think that they would ever monitor what she was doing.

Her mother reinforced an attitude of open dialogue and trust, but also explained that she could, would and, on occasion, had monitored her children via the computer and their mobile phones. After explaining that she insisted her children add her as a friend on her Facebook so she could monitor their behaviour, she continued:

> As for privacy in this house, they don't have a privacy. I need to know everything that goes on. If you're online and texting and you go out this door and I don't know where you are, I can always go back and see what you're doing. It's good to see what your child was doing. The last thing they were doing when they walked out the door. A lot of parents are like, 'My child was on the Internet before they walked out the door and I've never seen them again.' You can always check the history of computers.

When I asked Jada's mother the motivation for checking her children's phone records, Internet history and messages, she explained one of her biggest concerns was the negative effects of peer pressure. 'I think a lot of kids do that [pressure each other] because they want to fit in and don't want to be teased. It's very hard to be yourself. I think that's the number one thing because you hear about a lot of kids committing suicide and bullying.' Jada's mother explicitly referenced concerns about the potential dangers of her daughter's socialisation, concerns that are also invoked via mobile service commercials and media panics. However, she also continued to explain that the best form of intervention was open communication with her daughter. Although she admitted to surveilling her interactions, search history and phone logs on occasion, she also made it clear that she wanted to be in dialogue with her daughter about potential risks and harms. Jada echoed this in a separate interview, in which she said she felt she could and did talk to her parents about most things.

Jada's mother's perspectives are similar to the ways mobile media commercials construct mobile devices as a tool for both safety and risk. While she worried that mobile and social media could be a threat to Jada's safety and well-being, she also utilised the phone as a form of safety via monitoring and surveillance. Her perspectives, expectations and practices most closely reflected the rhetoric utilised by the media and mobile service providers: She monitored her daughter's mobile phone as a way to subtly enact a level of control over her daughter's socialisation. Additionally, Jada was the least resistant when it came to mobile surveillance; she was not overly concerned about her mother watching her or accessing her phone. Unlike Gabriela, she did not seek covert ways to digitally communicate with friends outside the purview of her parents. In part, this could possibly be explained by the fact that Jada was afforded a multitude of opportunities to socialise with her friends outside of the home and via her involvement in many after-school activities. However, it is also possible that her mom's surveillance of her mobile phone use discouraged Jada from socialising via social media as much as she might otherwise have done.

Conclusion: ethical considerations

What these three families reveal is the extent to which discourses of surveillance are often class-based and also how actual lived experiences are more complicated than media discourses typically portray. Gabriela's father reflects some of the ways surveillance has become an expected and normative aspect of contemporary parenting; however, Gabriela's privacy strategies reveal the way she negotiates and exercises agency even within a framework of familial surveillance. Selena's position highlights the extent to which reduced access to technology, combined with already compromised privacy within the home, actually leads to both mother and daughter resisting increased surveillance via mobile and social media. Their story further illustrates the ways in which discourses of risk and surveillance are continually shaped by class-based and privileged perspectives and expectations. Additionally, within the mediated discourses of risk, girls are frequently represented as lacking agency. However, the girls in the study demonstrate agentive strategies for resisting parental surveillance via their mobile devices.

Further, what is also strikingly absent from media discourses of surveillance, but significantly present in all three families in this chapter, is the discourse of trust. All three girls – Gabriela, Selena and Jada – frequently brought up the topic of trust when discussing privacy and surveillance within the home and beyond. Although their home lives and family rules differed, they all expressed a belief that their parents trusted them to make good decisions, to assess risk, to ask for help if they needed it, and to follow family expectations of acceptable behaviour. Likewise, their parents all invoked a discourse of trust as well. Although their expectations varied, they all trusted that their daughters were mostly making good decisions when it came to using mobile and social media. Likewise, they trusted that their daughters knew how to assess risk and to stay safe both within and outside of the home. Trust – as well as a respect for girls' agency and discretion – play important roles in shaping the ethics of the domestication of surveillance. However, by continually depicting teen girls as vulnerable and at risk (Shade, 2011), media discourses often presume that safety trumps teens' expectations of privacy.

Considering the mediated representations of girls, alongside girls' actual expectations and practices, is a productive space to ask: Who benefits from mediated representations of girls at risk and the domestication of surveillance? Is it problematic that the mobile service industry simultaneously contributes to discursive constructions of risk, yet financially benefits from surveillance services? As others have also reasoned (Shade, 2011), it can be argued that the industry is exploiting parental fears and capitalising on constructions of girls at risk. It is difficult to separate the domestication of surveillance from the market that is promoting and profiting from discourses of risk – discourses that engender fear and construct technology as the 'natural' and 'affordable' solution.

The normative aspects of familial surveillance work alongside stranger danger and peer fear rhetoric in a way that allows the mobile phone industry to capitalise on parental fears (by invoking an assumption that 'good parents' must surveil their daughters in the name of safety). Yet, they ignore girls' agency, as well as alternative mechanisms of safety – such as education and empowering girls to assess risk, make safe decisions and be secure outside of a framework of surveillance. As girls' studies scholar Leslie Shade writes (2011: 270), 'My [research] reinforces how media and public discourse still, with a few rare exceptions, constructs young women as susceptible to cyber-bullying, online sexual predation and therefore in need of technological solutions to assuage their parents' fears surrounding their mobility'.

Young people are afforded few spaces in which to question the normative value of surveillance at all levels – from home, to school, to corporate and governmental tracking; yet, surveillance increasingly plays an accepted and expected role in their lives. More so, what the commercials and the families highlight is the extent to which youth – specifically girls – is presented as justification for increased surveillance within and beyond the home. Parents and adolescents alike need to question discourses that position girls as inherently vulnerable and at risk, as well as messages that present mobile surveillance as the only and best solution to perceived threats. We should rather acknowledge girls' agency and enable them to safely navigate their social and sexual lives outside of a framework of surveillance.

Notes

1 Fave Five is a T-mobile feature that allows users to make unlimited calls to their favourite five contacts.

2 AT&T/Cingular (AT&T acquired Cingular in 2007), T-mobile, Verizon and Sprint (Lawson, 2013).

3 This chapter draws from data collected as part of the MacArthur Foundation's Digital Edge research project (S. Craig Watkins, PI). The ethnographic study included 18 ethnically diverse high school students, at least one of their parents or guardians and select teachers and administrators at a low-income high school in central Texas. The multi-method study included focus groups, participant observations in an after-school digital media club and one-on-one interviews with participants on a weekly basis over the course of the 2011–12 academic year. At the mid-point of the study, interviews were conducted at home with one of the girls' parents. All of the interviews were audio-recorded on mini-digital recorders and then transcribed and uploaded to a cloud-based qualitative software program for coding and analysis. For more information about the method and the larger project, see Vickery, 2012.

4 As of 2014, 90 per cent of US adults owned a mobile phone and 64 per cent owned a smartphone (Pew Research Center, 2014). As of 2013, 78 per cent of US teens owned a mobile phone and nearly 50 per cent owned a smartphone (Madden *et al.*, 2013).

5 A US sports car, the Ford Mustang.

6 In 2015, the services cost $5–$15 a month, depending on the service provider and the exact features of the plan.

References

AT&T Family Locator (2013) Video. Available online at www.youtube.com/watch?v=Aecbl8NBsmA (accessed 20.11.2015).

AT&T Family Map (2009) Video. Available online at www.youtube.com/watch?v=g2qv_6pVE7E (accessed 18.11.2015).

AT&T Sibling Rivalry (2008) video. Available online at www.youtube.com/watch?v=mmIj7_0-1kg (accessed 13.05.2013).

Beck, U. (1992) *Risk society: towards a new modernity*. Thousand Oaks, CA: Sage Publications Ltd.

Franks, M. A. (2015) 'The democratization of surveillance', paper presented at Privacy Law Scholars Conference, Berkeley, CA, 4–6 June.

Herring, S. C. (2008) 'Questioning the generational divide: technological exoticism and adult constructions of online youth identity', in D. Buckingham (ed.), *Youth, identity, and digital media*. Cambridge, MA: MIT Press.

Hinduja, S. and J. W. Patchin (2010) 'Cyberbullying and suicide', Cyberbullying Research Center. Available online at http://cyberbullying.org/cyberbullying_and_suicide_research_fact_sheet.pdf (accessed 21.11.2015).

Horst, H.A. (2010) 'Families', in M. Ito, S. Baumer, M. Bittanti, d. boyd and R. Cody *et al.* (eds.), *Hanging out, messing around, and geeking out: kids living and learning with new media*. Cambridge, MA: MIT Press.

Kearney, M. C. (2005) 'Birds on the wire: troping teenage girlhood through telephony in mid-twentieth-century U.S. media culture', *Cultural Studies*, 19(5): 568–601.

Kelly, P. (2000) 'The dangerousness of youth-at-risk: the possibilities of surveillance and intervention in uncertain times', *Journal of Adolescence*, 23: 463–76.

Lawson, S. (2013) 'Is AT&T, Sprint, or Verizon the largest U.S. mobile phone carrier? It may not matter', *Tech Hive*. Available online at www.techhive.com/article/2044580/is-atandt-sprint-or-verizon-the-largest-u-s-mobile-phone-carrier-it-may-not-matter.html (accessed 20.05.2013).

Lenhart, A., R. Ling, S. Campbell and K. Purcell (2010) 'Teens and mobile media', Washington, DC: Pew Research Center. Available online at www.pewinternet.org/2010/04/20/teens-and-mobile-phones/ (accessed 18.11.2015).

Livingstone, S. (2009) *Children and the Internet*. Malden, MA: Policy Press.

Madden, M., A. Lenhart, M. Duggan, S. Cortesi and U. Gasser (2013) 'Teens and technology report', Washington, DC: Pew Research Center. Available online at www.pewinternet.org/files/old-media/Files/Reports/2013/PIP_TeensandTechnology2013.pdf (accessed 18.11.2015).

Marvin, C. (1998) *When old technologies were new*. Oxford: Oxford University Press.

Marwick, A. E. (2008) 'To catch a predator? The MySpace moral panic', *First Monday*, 13(6). Available online at http://firstmonday.org/htbin/cgiwrap/bin/ojs/index.php/fm/article/view/2152/1966 (accessed 20.05.2013).

Pew Research Center (2014) 'Mobile technology fact sheet'. Available online at www.pewinternet.org/fact-sheets/mobile-technology-fact-sheet/ (accessed 20.11.2015).

Pinch, T. J. and W. E. Bijker (1984) 'The social construction of facts and artefacts: or how the sociology of science and the sociology of technology might benefit each other', *Social Studies of Science*, 14(3): 399–441.

Prevent Cyberbullying (n.d.) Washington, DC: US Department of Health and Human Services. Available online at www.stopbullying.gov/cyberbullying/prevention/#Be Aware of What Your Kids are Doing Online (accessed 20.11.2015).

Richtel, M. (2006) 'Selling surveillance to anxious parents', *New York Times*, 3 May. Available online at www.nytimes.com/2006/05/03/technology/techspecial3/03locate.html?pagewanted=all (accessed 03.02.2010).

Shade, L. R. (2007) 'Feminizing the mobile: gender scripting of mobiles in North America', *Continuum*, 21(2): 179–89.

Shade, L. R. (2011) 'Surveilling the girl via the third and networked screen', in M. C. Kearney (ed.), *Mediated girlhoods: new explorations of girls' media culture*. New York: Peter Lang.

Silverstone, R. and L. Haddon (1996) 'Design and the domestication of ICTs: technical change and everyday life', in R. Silverstone and R. Mansell (eds.), *Communication by design: the politics of information and communication technologies*. Oxford: Oxford University Press.

Springhall, J. (1998) *Youth, popular culture, and moral panics: penny gaffs to gangsta rap, 1830–1996*. London: Macmillan Press Ltd.

Sprint Family Locator (2009) Video. Available online at www.youtube.com/watch?v=3ZDguyCnUuk (accessed 20.05.2013).

Sprint Family Locator (2012) Video. Available online at www.youtube.com/watch?v=7Yx87oN-_-s (accessed 17.11.2015).

Stearns, P. N. (2003) *Anxious parents: a history of modern childrearing in America*. New York: NYU Presse.

T-mobile Creepy Dad (2007) Video. Available online at www.youtube.com/watch?v=1ltYQlFuzrg (accessed 18.11.2015).

T-mobile Derek with Mustang (2008) Video. Available online at www.youtube.com/watch?v=muRMsfrbc10 (accessed 18.11.2015).

T-mobile Family Where (2012) Video. Available online at www.youtube.com/watch?v=7R9nPHJisH8 (accessed 18.11.2015).

Thiel-Stern, S. (2014) *From dance halls to Facebook: teen girls, mass media, and moral panic in the United States, 1905–2010*. Amherst, MA: University of Massachusetts Press.

Turkle, S. (2008) 'Always-on/always-on-you: the tethered self', in J. E. Katz (ed.), *Handbook of mobile communication studies*. Cambridge, MA: MIT Press.

Verizon Family Locator (2012) Video. Available online at www.youtube.com/watch?v=Zsx9zBwToSA (accessed 20.05.2013).

Verizon Mall Moment (2010) Video. Available online at www.youtube.com/watch?v=YPJbcd9AmJA (accessed 20.05.2013).

Vickery, J. R. (2012). Worth the risk: the role of regulations and norms in shaping teens' digital media practices. PhD dissertation. University of Texas at Austin. Available online: https://repositories.lib.utexas.edu/bitstream/handle/2152/ETD-UT-2012-08-6246/VICKERY-DISSERTATION.pdf?sequence=1.

Vickery, J. R. (2014) 'Talk whenever, wherever: how the U.S. mobile phone industry commodifies talk, genders youth mobile practices, and domesticates surveillance', *Journal of Children and Media*, 9(2): 387–403.

Vickery, J. R. (forthcoming) *Digital expectations: a generation at risk and why we're worrying about the wrong things*. Cambridge, MA: MIT Press.

8 'Where are you, who are you with, what are you doing?'

Children's strategies of negotiation and resistance to parental monitoring and surveillance via mobile phones

Carol Barron

Introduction

The monitoring of children via technological devices has become a characteristic of modern childhood (Qvortrup, 1993; Rasmussen, 2004; Rooney, 2010); yet, the effects are largely unknown. This chapter is concerned with mobile phones as the fastest-spreading technology in human history (Silva, 2012) and the ways in which parents have appropriated the devices to monitor their children in time and space. It contributes to an emerging body of knowledge on this topic from an anthropological perspective. Findings are drawn from a year-long ethnographic study of children in middle childhood (8–12 years), examining their play, play spaces and independent mobility. There are myriad ways in which mobile phones can and are utilised by parents to surveil their children (see also Chapters 6, 7 and 9 in this collection). This chapter focuses on how texting and phone calls are used to monitor children in real time. Analysis reveals that mobile phones have a significant impact on children's mobility, at times enabling and other times severely restricting movement. The chapter starts by synthesising the existing literature about the use of mobile phones as a form of surveillance in childhood, followed by an explanation of the fieldwork sites and methodology, before detailing the different ways that children negotiate and resist surveillance via mobile phone technologies to maintain and enhance their independent mobility.

Surveillance, childhood and mobile phones

The International Telecommunications Union (2014) claims that mobile cellular subscriptions were expected to reach almost 7 billion globally by the end of 2014. Mobile phones have, therefore, rapidly become a fundamental artefact of everyday life (Strandell, 2014), and this is true for children as well as adults (Fyhri *et al.*, 2011). Moreover, non-ownership of mobile phones may lead to social exclusion for children (Leung and Wei, 1999). We also know that children are using mobile phones at increasingly younger ages (Goggin, 2006). Steeves (2014) illustrates this rise in mobile phone ownership among Canadian children over the last decade; in 2005, only 6 per cent of children aged 9–10 years surveyed owned mobile phones; by 2013, this figure had quadrupled to 24 per cent for the same age group.

It is unsurprising then that the mobile phone and various software applications are becoming one of the most common mechanisms for parents to monitor and surveil their children. Green (2002) informs us that mobile phones have brought surveillance, traditionally associated only with the state and corporate bodies, into the realm of the individual's personal relationships, including between the parent and child. It is argued that this development is normalising the societal perception that all children should be accessible and accountable to others at any time and in any given place.

Surveillance has differing facets. It is no longer just about discipline and control, but also used or perceived as a form of child 'care' (Rasmussen, 2004; Rooney, 2010). Parents are encouraged to invest in surveillance technologies to keep children 'safe' and be a 'good parent' (Marx and Steeves, 2010). Parental concerns about 'stranger danger', traffic congestion and difficulties with the built environment (Valentine and McKendrick, 1997) may restrict children's lives and experiences through decreased independent mobility (Valentine, 2004) and increase their dependence on adults (Christensen and Romero Mikkelsen, 2008). Monitoring and surveillance by mobile phones has the potential to add to these restrictions and further increase children's dependence on adults, while simultaneously having the potential to enhance children's independent mobility.

Rooney (2010) argues that child surveillance technologies are promoted as enabling a risk-free environment, with 'risk reduction' or indeed 'risk avoidance' as the key attainable goal. The 'risk-reduction' rhetoric underpinning much of the monitoring and surveillance of children using mobile phones is a reflection of the 'risk adverse' society in which many of us live. Yet, as Giddens (1991: 124) argues, it is not that societies are more dangerous now than in previous times, but rather that 'thinking in terms of risk and risk assessment is a more or less ever-present exercise', which companies promoting surveilling apps make good use of in their marketing strategies. This is not without important implications for childhood. Livingstone (2002) suggests that children need opportunities to interact with the world without being monitored to assist in the development of personal autonomy and independence. A degree of 'risk engagement' is an important component of how children learn, and children have a greater ability to manage risks than adults perceive (Christensen and Romero Mikkelsen, 2008). It is clear, however, that parental surveillance using mobile phones is expanding and that this can take on a variety of forms, while the full consequences are yet to be understood.

Ling (2007: 60) suggests that teenagers often view the mobile phone as 'a reluctantly accepted umbilical cord to their parents', albeit a very elastic cord, which enables contact between the teenager and his/her parents, acknowledging the tension that this may create between them. Fotel and Thomsen's (2004) work on the surveillance of children's mobility in Denmark reports that parents keep track of their children's geographical location by having the child call during the day, whereas Williams and Williams (2005) inform us that teenagers and parents in England use the mobile phone to negotiate spatial boundaries.

Similarly, Ito, Okabe and Matsuda (2005) have reported how mobile phones have become a key part of social and personal lives in Japan.

Porter et al. (2012) conducted a large-scale study of children and young people's phone usage in sub-Saharan Africa (Ghana, Malawi and South Africa) and reported the monitoring and surveillance of children by their parents via mobile phones. In their study, surveillance took two forms: first, parents would call their children to identify their physical whereabouts and, while a minority of children viewed this practice as acceptable, for most it was a source of potential tension between the teenager and their parents. Second, parents checked their child's call and text history, as well as their contact list. This monitoring was done overtly and covertly by parents and elicited negative responses from the children. The dominant form of resistance to parental monitoring was to delete their text history: as one child stated, 'I usually delete all my texts when returning the phone [to mother] because I feel it is an invasion of privacy' (rural Malawi, 15-year-old girl). None of the parents reported using any additional tracking methods or software with the mobile phone – the monitoring was conducted solely through calls, texts and examination of the call and text history on the phone. In contrast, Ribak (2009) in her study in Israel reports that teenagers did not filter or reject parental calls, even though some found the practice frustrating. This is not reflected in other research findings. Ribak proposes it may be a combination of cultural differences and the significant presence of Israeli parents in their children's lives.

From the existing research, it would appear that the surveilling and monitoring of children and young people via the mobile phone are increasingly a global phenomenon. The majority of research examined has been conducted with young people, teenagers and parents; as yet, the views and experiences of children in middle childhood (8–12 years) are largely unknown. This chapter aims to add to the small body of research addressing the surveillance of children using mobile phones in this age group, and their strategies of negotiation and resistance.

Fieldwork setting

The findings reported here are part of a larger study on children's play spaces and mobility utilising an ethnographic approach. The fieldwork took place in Ireland. From November to the end of February, it gets dark between 4 and 4:30 pm. Both the climate (high rainfall) and the dark evenings have an effect on children's independent mobility and, therefore, their parents' monitoring of them in time and space. Rathvarna (the pseudonym for the urban setting in which the fieldwork took place) is situated in Kildare, which borders the capital, Dublin, and has a population of 19,537 (Central Statistics Office, 2012). Most families living in Rathvarna were not born there but migrated to the area for purposes of work, study and/or because of the lower cost of accommodation (Waddington, 2000). Hence, very few of its inhabitants (adults or children) have any extended family within the town, similar to many 'commuter belt' settings throughout Ireland and elsewhere.

The built environment is a mix of the old and new. Old narrow side streets, with (and without) narrow pavements lie in close proximity to insulated housing estates.

Methodology

As ethnography attempts to place the participants' own perspectives centrally (Hammersley and Atkinson, 2007), it is eminently suited to examine the lived experiences of children in relation to their play spaces and mobility and the surveillance and monitoring of their daily lives. In addition, a child-centred anthropology views children as the best informants of their own lives and worlds (Montgomery, 2005). Children are competent social actors and, therefore, need to be involved in the construction of new understandings about their worlds. To this end, participatory data-collection techniques, such as visual ethnography and draw and write techniques, were employed to generate children's own data *on* and *about* their play spaces and mobility. These were used alongside the more traditional methods of participant observation in two single-sex school settings and the housing estates in which the students lived over a school year. Participant observation took place in 4th, 5th and 6th classes (aged 8/9–12 years) in both schools. Ethical approval for the research was sought and received prior to the commencement of the study. Written informed consent was received from the parents and written informed assent from the children. The findings reported in this chapter focus on the analysis of the year-long field notes in both schools, as well as 11 photo-elicitation interviews with 60 children (32 girls, 28 boys) whose pseudonyms were selected by the children.

Findings and discussion

The following section of this chapter focuses on the research findings related to the children's understanding of mobile phones for 'emergency' use, who actually owns the mobile phone, and examines children's negotiation and resistance to monitoring and surveillance of their person in time and space.

'For emergencies'

All of the children in the 5th and 6th classes (10–12 years) had mobile phones and approximately 25 per cent of the 8- and 9-year olds in 4th class, which is a year younger for phone ownership than reported by Steeves (2014). School is a very important space and place for children in middle childhood (Bond, 2013; Taylor, 2013) and, like public spaces, it imposes its own set of rules, regulations and restrictions on children in relation to mobile phones. In both schools, the rules specified that the children had to keep their mobile phones switched off and in their school bags during the school day. In both schools, a practice of confiscation was used for transgressions of the rules in relation to mobile phones. As Aisling (12) explains, 'Like if your phone is in your pocket, even if it's off and the teacher sees it, she takes it off you.' Children did subvert the rules and mobile phones were in blouse, trouser and coat pockets at break times; however, this also occurred accidentally where children just 'forgot' to place the phone in their school bag. Outside of the school day, they kept their mobile phones on their person.

When the children were asked why they brought their phones to school when they could not use them, the consistent and repeated answer from boys and girls between 8 and 12 years was 'for emergencies', 'my mum makes me bring it for emergencies', 'emergency use only'. The exact interpretation of what constitutes an 'emergency' remained unclear to the children throughout the study; however, they recounted stories of their parents calling them to make sure they had arrived home after school, arrived at organised after-school activity, to check who they were with, and so forth. 'Emergencies', in this context, stem from the parental desire to monitor and surveil who their children are with and where their children are geographically, at certain times during the day, specifically after school finished. This focus on after-school surveillance may be because many of the children were driven to school in the mornings, as well as the parents' work patterns. This monitoring of children in time and space via text and phone appears to provide parents with the feeling of control and, thus, minimise their risk perception. The children, however, were very clear that they view the mobile phone as a form of communication, specifically textual as opposed to oral – 'mobile phones are for texting my mates' (Tony, 10 years).

Who owns the mobile phone?

Initially in Ireland, empirical evidence suggests that children started receiving mobile phones from parents as 'gifts' as part of a 'rite of passage': for example, transition from primary to secondary school; on their confirmation into the Catholic church at 11 or 12 years, in their final year of primary school; as well as the traditional birthday or Christmas present. However, the 'gifting' of mobile phones to children from parents rapidly started to occur at younger and younger ages and can no longer claim to be associated with particular rites of passage. Consistent with findings from other studies (see Ribak, 2009, for example), all the mobile phones owned by the children in this study were purchased by their parents, who also pay the bills, predominantly employing the 'top up' or 'pay as you go' system of credit. While one could argue, therefore, that the children did not in fact 'own' the mobile phone, in reality, the children felt total ownership over the phone and saw no paradox in parents paying the bills.

Like teenagers internationally (Ribak, 2009), the younger children 'objectified' (Silverstone *et al.*, 1992) their mobile phones in specific ways – they displayed individualised images as their background, added stickers as adornments on the phone and personalised the ring tone. The last was perceived as 'fun' – 'It's fun, putting the ring tones on, it is fun' (Sean, 10) – as they could be 'cool ring tones' (Saoirshe, 9). This personalisation of the mobile phone serves to visually display 'ownership' of the object. As Owen (9) succinctly portrayed the children's view of their mobile phones, 'you need it'. The children in this study view the mobile phone as a necessity, or as indispensable to their daily lives as watches were a century ago (Strandell, 2014). However, parents were also invested financially and psychologically with the same phone. They also 'needed it' to enable them to reduce their anxieties about where their children are, what they are doing and who they are with. Thus, they purchase the phone with an unconscious perception of duality of ownership or partial ownership that remained unarticulated by either parent or child.

Strategies of negotiation

While parents – predominantly mothers – use the mobile phone, in part, as a method of monitoring at a distance, children employ strategies of negotiation. The monitoring of children's mobility unfolds in an ongoing dialogue between parents and children, as the extract below demonstrates:

> Gus (10): I tell my ma to text me, not ring me, when I'm with me friends.
> Carol: Why text only?
> Gus: Because it's embarrassing you know, it's embarrassing if your mother checks up on you, if she texts then they don't know it was her [who texted] that's OK.
> Carol: So if you're with your friends does your mum ring or text you?
> Gus: She texts me.

Children actively engage in planning their own movement and are not merely objects of their parents' remote control. Many of the children throughout the year's fieldwork recounted getting their parents to text them rather than call. Moreover, the children encultured the parents into their preferred form of communication by ignoring calls yet responding quickly to text messages, as Ailbhe (11) explains: 'I keep my phone on "silent" so when my mam rings I miss the call, but then she will text me and I will text her back'.

Discussions of the power relationships between children and parents frequently portray the child as powerless or less powerful (Christensen, 2004; Lynch and Lodge, 2002). However, family power relationships are not static, and children clearly demonstrate the ability to negotiate with their parents over the monitoring of their everyday lives. Texting is a modern-day example of a negotiated compromise between parent and child. Williams and Williams (2005) examined child/parent negotiation with young people (15- and 16-year-olds) and found that young people see themselves gaining a degree of empowerment from the mobile phone, which in fact has become a significant facilitator of negotiations between parents and young people. Children become increasingly skilful negotiators by ongoing renegotiation in their relations with their parents. At the same time, parents are using the mobile phone to enter into their children's time and space as an 'absent other', and see this as a means of extending parental authority and control (Williams and Williams, 2005).

Strategies of resistance

Both boys and girls recounted how they resisted the restrictions on their mobility using avoidance strategies, as with Sorcha and Sean in the extracts below:

> If my mum rings me and I am up at Lauren's [where she is not allowed to go on her own], I don't answer it and then pretend that it was on silent like and I did not hear it. (Sorcha, 9)

> If I am in the shops [on the way home from school] with my mates and my mam rings, I won't answer cause I am not supposed to buy sweets after school. (Sean, 10)

Josh (11) recounts another frequent strategy of resistance used by the children: 'the battery was flat'. This strategy included both deliberate and accidental failure to recharge the mobile phone, as well as the falsification that the mobile was uncharged when that was not true. Teenagers also use these strategies (for example, see Devitt and Roker, 2009). Both boys and girls recounted stories of telling their mothers 'I forgot to turn it on after school', 'I had no credit to ring you back' or 'it was on silent and I did not notice'. The avoidance of parental monitoring with the strategy of 'I had no credit to ring you back' was very common in middle childhood, perhaps because they did frequently run out of credit and, thus, it was viewed as a very justifiable and believable excuse to employ in their avoidance of parental monitoring.

Some children deliberately gave false information about their physical location when parents texted to ask where they were:

> Paul (12): I text her back and say I am just outside on the green when really I am in Tom's house [in the next housing estate where he is not allowed without permission].
>
> Isabella (11): If I am in Áine's garden playing then I text her and say I am nearly home. [Áine's house is in a neighbouring housing estate and Isabella knows she needs her parents' permission to leave her housing estate.]

Williams and Williams (2005) point out that parental 'authority-at-a-distance' is in some sense illusionary, since parents have little way of ascertaining the exact location of their children, especially when monitoring using text or phone calls only. This may change if parents make more use of tracking systems built into their children's phones. While children deliberately thwart parents' attempts to monitor their mobility and are sometimes less than truthful about their whereabouts, none of the children in this study went any significant geographical distance from the home (less than 1.2 km); and this was predominantly to visit friends in neighbouring estates, go to a local space not 'allowed' by their parents or to go to sweet shops on the way home from school. Echoing the overall findings of Romero Mikkelsen and Christensen's (2009) examination of children's independent mobility, this study found that the mobility of both boys and girls in middle childhood is primarily social; that is, the children's mobility patterns focused on socialising with their peers, an unsurprising finding, bearing in mind the importance of the peer group to this age group. Children like to play close to their home in their own neighbourhood (Barron, 2013; Meire, 2007). Ireland has become an increasingly globalised society; yet, the importance of the local is still apparent.

Another common strategy of resistance employed by both boys and girls, especially the 11- and 12-year-olds, was to delete their text messages almost on a daily basis. Orla (12) clearly articulates her desire for personal privacy:

> Orla: I delete my text messages all the time.
> Carol: Why?
> Orla: 'Cause like, it's my business, like it's private and I don't want other people reading them.

This deletion of texts by children in middle childhood is not only to prevent parents monitoring their texts but also to prevent *anyone* (peer, parent or sibling) monitoring them. Porter *et al.* (2012) in their work in sub-Saharan Africa found the same strategy of resistance employed by older children. In a similar vein, Livingstone (2002) reports that children deleted their web-surfing histories. Under the United Nations Convention on the Rights of the Child (UNCRC, 1989), children have a right to privacy; yet, despite this international treaty, children's right to privacy has not been broadly debated, notwithstanding the current emphasis on privacy concerns regarding adults (Hanafin *et al.*, 2010). Nihlén Fahlquist (Chapter 9) argues that there is a strong case for children's right to privacy, albeit not necessarily as wide-ranging as the adult equivalent and that it is reasonable for children to have some private space. The children in this study articulated their desire for, and awareness of, strategies to achieve personal privacy when using their mobile phones from the surveillance of parents, peers and influential others.

A final strategy of resistance to be discussed here is the use of texting language itself. Particular aspects of mobile phone culture are strongly associated with young people (Goggin, 2006), especially text messaging (Harper *et al.*, 2005). The language of texting has developed out of the need to compress words sent by mobile phones due to limitations of space. Furthermore, conducting a conversation in real time also calls for speed in the writing of the message. The language used in messaging by the children is markedly informal and in some ways reminiscent, according to Albero-Andres (2004), of the language used in quickly scribbled notes that were passed from child to child in the classroom setting in previous generations.

While the study revealed a use of language in the children's mobile phone texts similar to that found by Albero-Andres (2004) – for example, 'eya wdc wyu2' (Heya, what the craic [a Gaelic term meaning fun and/or what's happening], what you up to?); 'cuL8er' (see you later); 'up2u' (up to you); 'were r u' (where are you?); 'tnkz' or 'tanks' (thanks); kwl (cool); clas (class, meaning brilliant, great) – the study also uncovered further compression of words into single letters, even when space is not the issue. This may be due to the speed of real time conversation coupled with the use of a textual language (Barron, 2014) virtually impenetrable to parents, such as 'k ttyl' (OK, talk to you later). This further compression of written language was used both on its own – for example, 'k' (OK) as a response to a text – and in combination with words that had already been compressed. See, for example, the exchange below between Hannah and Orlaigh (both 12):

> Orlaigh: heya hun wyu2 wdc plz wb im reli bored (heya, hun, what you up to? Please write back, I'm really bored).
>
> Hannah: nm jus on d laptop r u goin ta K8s party (nothing much, just on the laptop. Are you going to Kate's party?).
>
> Orlaigh: prob f im alowd u (probably, if I'm allowed. You?).
>
> Hannah: yeah cnt w8 hop il c ya dere (yeah, can't wait. Hope I'll see ya there).
>
> Orlaigh: same g2g having mi dinner tty wen im done … ly x x x x x (same, got to go, having my dinner, talk to ya when I'm done, love ya kiss, kiss kiss, kiss, kiss),
>
> Hannah: k ttyl (OK, talk to you later).

The compression of words enables children to communicate with each other in almost real time. Texts are composed, sent, a response developed and delivered in seconds. This dance of texting communication moves back and forwards between two players very rapidly. Note in the example given how children incorporate culturally specific terms into the text using a single letter of the alphabet, for example, c (craic) and wdc (what's the craic?). The use of a question mark is not used in the written text but it is implied. 'Ya' does mean 'you', but in Ireland it can also be pronounced as 'ya' – for example, 'ya doing anything this weekend?'. Children have learned to transform and adapt written and verbal language into a format that is comprehensible to them and enables them to conduct textual conversations with their peers in virtual real time. The medium of texting can, to some degree, resist parental monitoring by virtue of the fact that parents may find the language used in text messages difficult to decipher. This finding is consistent with boyd's (2012) work with teenagers: that children rely on 'encoded messages', which can minimise adult understanding of the information within text messages.

Conclusion

Irish children in middle childhood are part of what Malone (2007) refers to as 'Generation Z' – they are so-called 'digital natives' (Livingstone, 2002) who have always lived in a world with mobile phones, the Internet and social media sites. Technology provides parents with numerous opportunities to monitor children, the mobile phone being one of the most readily available. A substantial advantage of this technology is the potential for enhanced safety, security and easing parents' anxiety and fear. Moreover, the mobile phones can be used by parents to have a 'childcare' role, answering 'where are you, what are you doing, who are you with?' Alongside the evolution in communication technologies is the 'bubble-wrapping' (Cadzow, 2004) and over-protection of children against encounters with risk (Furedi, 2002), all of which has culminated in a dramatic increase in children's surveillance by parents and society more widely.

Nevertheless, children are not passive, powerless recipients of surveillance (MediaSmarts, 2012). Their resistance takes several differing forms. First, negotiation and ongoing discussion and renegotiation between the child and parent was a very common practice with most of the boys and girls who owned mobile phones. Second, children at times wanted to avoid parental mobile communications and employed predominantly the following strategies to achieve their goal: left the mobile phone on silent or switched off; let the battery run flat; no credit to ring back; and so forth. Third, children in middle childhood have a need for and value privacy; this is reflected in their resistance strategies of deleting text and call histories, although it should be noted that these practices were to maintain their privacy from all individuals and not just their parents. They also used textual language that had a duality of purpose: The compression of words and letters allowed for almost real-time communications whilst being almost indecipherable by their parents. Many of these strategies of resistance are also used by teenagers/young people, as discussed in the beginning of this chapter. The issue of parental and child trust in relation to child surveillance is evolving, and children in middle childhood clearly resented being monitored via the mobile phone by parents. As Rooney (2010) points out, the underlying problem is not the type of surveillance being used but rather that it is used at all.

Parents of children in middle childhood in this study did not use GPS tracking or dedicated software applications on their children's mobile phones; rather, the surveillance was primarily undertaken by text messages to the children, with some parents calling their children. The predominant reason for parental monitoring was a combination of 'child care' and 'good parenting'. Mothers wanted to know where their child was, who they were with and what they were doing. This surveillance occurred predominantly after school hours.

A final word of caution must be expressed: Mobile phone monitoring and surveillant technology have advanced faster than researchers can keep abreast with. Whilst there is a proliferation of products available to parents, the uptake of these products and the specific variables that influence the parental decisions nationally and internationally are still largely unknown. Until we can identify and address these issues, the full effects of monitoring and surveillance of children and childhood will continue to require further consideration.

References

Albero-Andres, M. (2004) 'The Internet and adolescents: the present and future', in J. H. Goldstein, D. Buckingham and G. Brougere (eds), *Toys, games, and media*. New Jersey: Lawrence Erlbaum Associates.

Barron, C. (2013) 'Physical activity play in local housing estates and child wellness in Ireland', *International Journal of Play*, 2(3): 220–36.

Barron, C. (2014) '"I had no credit to ring you back": children's strategies of negotiation and resistance to parental surveillance via mobile phones', *Surveillance and Society*, 12(3): 401–13.

Bond, E. (2013) 'Managing mobile relationships: children's perceptions of the impact of the mobile phone on relationships in their everyday lives', *Childhood*, 17(4): 514–59.

boyd, d. (2012) 'Networked privacy', *Surveillance and Society*, 10(3): 348–50.

Cadzow, J. (2004) 'The bubble-wrap generation', *Sydney Morning Herald*, 17 Jan.: 18–21.

Central Statistics Office (2012) *Census 2011, Volume 1:* Population Classified by Area. Dublin: Stationery Office.

Christensen, P. (2004) 'Children's participation in ethnographic research: issues of power and representation', *Children and Society*, 18(2): 165–76.

Christensen, P. and M. Romero Mikkelsen (2008) 'Jumping off and being careful: children's strategies of risk management in everyday life', *Sociology of Health and Illness*, 30(1): 112–30.

Devitt, K. and D. Roker (2009) 'The role of mobile phones in family communication', *Children and Society*, 23: 189–202.

Fotel, T. and T. Thomsen (2004) 'The surveillance of children's mobility', *Surveillance and Society*, 1(4): 535–54.

Furedi, F. (2002) *Culture of fear: risk-taking and the morality of low expectation*, 2nd ed. London: Continuum.

Fyhri, A., R. Hjorthol, R. MacKett, T. Nordgaard Fotel and M. Kytta (2011) 'Children's active travel and independent mobility in four countries: development, social contributing trends and measures', *Transport Policy*, 18: 703–10.

Giddens, A. (1991) *Modernity and self-identity self and society in the late modern age*. Cambridge: Polity Press.

Goggin, G. (2006) *Cell phone culture: mobile technology in everyday life*. New York: Routledge.

Green, N. (2002) 'Who's watching whom? Monitoring and accountability in mobile relations', in B. Brown, N. Green and R. Harper (eds), *Wireless world: social, cultural and interactional issues in mobile technologies*. London: Springer.

Hammersley, M. and P. Atkinson (2007) *Ethnography: principles in practice*, 3rd ed. London: Routledge.

Hanafin, J., T. Donoghue, M. Flynn and M. Shevlin (2010) 'The primary school's invasion of the privacy of the child: unmasking the potential of some current practices', *Educational Studies*, 36(2): 143–52

Harper, R., L. Palen and A. Taylor (2005) *The inside text: social, cultural and design perspectives on SMS*. Houten: Springer.

International Telecommunications Union (2014) 'Mobile-broadband penetration approaching 32 per cent. Three billion internet users by end of this year. Available online at www.itu.int/net/pressoffice/press_releases/2014/23.aspx (accessed 28.10.2015).

Ito, M., D. Okabe and M. Matsuda (eds) (2005) *Personal, portable, pedestrian*. London: MIT Press.

Leung, L. and R. Wei (1999) 'Who are the mobile phone have-nots?', *New Media and Society*, 1(2): 209–26.

Ling, R. (2007) 'Children, youth, and mobile communications', *Journal of Children and Media*, 1(1): 60–7.

Livingstone, S. M. (2002) *Young people and new media: childhood and the changing media environment*. London: Sage Publications.

Lynch, K. and A. Lodge (2002) *Equality and power in schools: redistribution, recognition and representation*. London: Routledge Falmer.

Malone, K. (2007) 'The bubble-wrap generation: children growing up in walled gardens', *Environmental Education Research*, 13(4): 513–27.

Marx, G. and V. Steeves (2010) 'From the beginning: children as subjects and agents of surveillance', *Surveillance and Society*, 7(3/4): 192–230.

MediaSmarts (2012) *Young Canadians in a wired world, phase iii: talking to youth and parents about life online*. Ottawa: MediaSmarts.

Meire, J. (2007) 'Qualitative research on children's play: a review of recent literature', in T. Jambor and J. V. Gils (eds), *Several perspectives on children's play*. Antwerp: Garant.

Montgomery, H. 2005. 'Gendered childhoods: a cross disciplinary overview', *Gender and Education*, 17(5): 471–82

Porter, G., K. Hampshire, A. Abane, A. Munthali, E. Robson, M. Mashiri and A. Tanle (2012) 'Youth, mobility and mobile phones in Africa: findings from a three-country study', *Information Technology for Development*, 18(2): 145–62.

Qvortrup, J. (1993) *Nine theses about childhood as a social phenomenon: an introduction to a series of national reports*. Vienna: European Centre for Social Welfare Policy and Research.

Rasmussen, K. (2004) 'Places for children — children's places', *Childhood*, 11(2): 155–73.

Ribak, R. (2009) 'Remote control, umbilical cord and beyond: the mobile phone as a transitional object', *British Journal of Developmental Psychology*, 27: 183–96.

Romero Mikkelsen, M. R. and P. Christensen (2009) 'Is children's independent mobility really independent? A study of children's mobility combining ethnography and GPS/ mobile phone technologies', *Mobilities*, 4(1): 37–58.

Rooney, T. (2010) 'Trusting children: how do surveillance technologies alter a child's experience of trust, risk and responsibility?', *Surveillance and Society*, 7(3/4): 344–55.

Silva, A.R. (2012) 'On emotion and memories: the consumption of mobile phones as "affective technology"', *International Review of Social Research*, 2(1): 157–72.

Silverstone, R., E. Hirsch and D. Morley (1992) 'Information and communication technologies and the moral economy of the household', in R. Silverstone and E. Hirsch (eds), *Consuming technologies: media and information in domestic spaces*. London: Routledge.

Steeves, V. (2014) *Young Canadians in a wired world, phase iii: life online. Talking to youth and parents about life on line*. Ottawa: MediaSmarts.

Strandell, H. (2014) 'Mobile phones in children's after-school centres: stretching of place and control', *Mobilities*, 9(2): 256–74.

Taylor, E. (2013) *Surveillance schools: security, discipline and control in contemporary education*. Basingstoke: Palgrave Macmillan.

Valentine, G. (2004) *Public space and the culture of childhood*. London: Ashgate.

Valentine, G. and J. McKendrick (1997) 'Children's outdoor play: exploring parental concerns about children's safety and the changing nature of childhood', *Geoforum*, 28(2): 219–35.

Waddington, S. (2000) 'Changing life in the towns of north Kildare', *Irish Geography*, 33(1): 74–89.

Williams, S. and L. Williams (2005) 'Space invaders: the negotiation of teenage boundaries through the mobile phone', *Sociological Review*, 53(2): 314–31.

9 Ethical concerns of using GPS to track children

Jessica Nihlén Fahlquist

Most people would probably agree that the most important task, as a parent, is to protect one's child. Whereas it used to be enough to keep an eye on the child and trust other adults to do the same, modern technology provides novel tools to perform this task to a previously unimaginable extent. Global positioning system (GPS) technology is such a tool. Its substantial advantage is, of course, associated with safety, security and easing parents' anxiety and fear. It is of particular interest, since it makes possible constant monitoring of children, 24 hours a day, throughout their childhood and teens.

However, using GPS to track children is ethically problematic. In this chapter, I first explore and discuss the concept of parental responsibility in the context of GPS and children. Second, against the background of psychological research, I argue that it is not conducive for children's sense of responsibility to be constantly monitored. Third, I discuss whether children have a right to privacy. I conclude that due to the considerable uncertainty concerning the effects of constant monitoring, as well as the ethical problems arising, we ought to adopt a cautious attitude to using GPS to track children.

GPS and children

'Don't you want to know where your [child] is? Keep track of your [children]' read a promotional campaign during the autumn of 2011 by Lociloci, in one of the biggest-circulation newspapers in Sweden, *Dagens Nyheter*. The company was eager to encourage parents to use GPS technology in mobile phones to track their children. Similarly, in 2009, the British company Lok8u launched the Num8 wristwatch with GPS tracking technology that allows parents to receive text messages with the child's location (Johnson, 2009; Lok8u, 2012). But it's not just parents who are seen as viable monitors of children; in Sweden, for example, a number of preschools have started to use GPS as a means to keep track of pupils (*Svenska Dagbladet*, 2011). One company, Momenta, provides 100–150 Swedish preschools with GPS tags for clothing (*Göteborgsposten*, 2011). Similarly, in the United States, some schools have introduced GPS tracking as a part of an anti-truancy programme (Cargile, 2012; Santa Cruz, 2011).

In addition to mobile phones and watches, there is now clothing, including jackets and shoes, equipped with GPS technology. One of the products on the market, the Loc8u's so-called 'nu.m8+' is securely fastened to a child's wrist and cannot be removed by the child. It stays locked until deactivated by a parent (Lok8u, 2012). Another product, called Amber Alert GPS V3, alerts the parent regularly, has an SOS button and a 'mom-friendly tracking portal', which allows parents to set zones – for example, school and home – and receive alerts when the child enters or exits those zones. Furthermore, the history can be checked in order to know where your child has been during the day or week (Amber Alert, 2012).

Different GPS tracking devices are targeted by companies like Garmin and Magellan across the spectrum of ages, from toddlers to teenagers. If, for example, you want to know where your teenager has been with the family car, or how fast they were travelling, this is possible using their technology. This type of monitoring is not limited to the purview of parents, and the potential for actuarialism has captured the imagination of insurance companies. For example, some US insurance companies have even expressed an intention of giving discounts to owners of cars equipped with GPS (Kidsgpsguide, 2012).

Many reasons have been put forth to encourage parents to utilise GPS to track their children, but most centre on safety, security and anxiety relief, exemplified by the slogan on a website marketing GPS tools used to track children: 'Create safety for you and your child' (Barngps, 2012).[1] The idea of creating safety for our children and putting ourselves at ease as parents is, of course, extremely alluring for risk-conscious parents. On websites marketing these products, protection against kidnappers and child molesters as well as the risk of getting lost in the woods are mentioned (Barngps, 2012). AmberAlert describes how camping trips sometimes turn into scary events that do not always end well – it can be so easy for a child of any age to wander off from camp and get lost in the woods, where finding them can be difficult (AmberAlert, 2010).

Conversely, rather than focusing on control, Lociloci states that GPS provides an opportunity to give children more freedom. Instead of forbidding one's 8-year-old daughter to go on a bike adventure, the parent will be able to let her go if she uses the tracking device, thereby allegedly increasing her freedom (Lociloci, 2012). The same argument is made by the British company Lok8u's Steve Salmon, who hopes that the Num8 wristwatch will be used as a way to give children more freedom, instead of promoting lazy parenting: 'Only 20 per cent of children are now allowed to go out and play. It's my profound hope that Num8 will help parents feel more comfortable about letting their children go out to play' (cited in Johnson, 2009).

Companies also appeal to feelings of anxiety and fear. This kind of marketing fits well into the contemporary obsession with risks and threats. Beck and Giddens famously argue that we live in a 'risk society' (Beck, 1992; Giddens, 1999). Similarly, it has been suggested that we live in a 'culture of fear' (Furedi, 2006). There has been a 'domestication' of children's lives, whereby they are removed from the streets, and an institutionalisation, whereby their activities are confined to separate settings and supervised by professionals (Prout, 2005; Zeiher, 2001).

Altheide (2009) describes contemporary discourse as characterised by fear and suggests that a 'key element in the contemporary discourse of fear is children'. Thus, the idea and practice of protecting children are highly prevalent in society. Surveillance of children and marketing of devices that parents and schools can use to monitor children fit into this discourse (Marx and Steeves, 2010). Parents' anxieties are appealed to:

1 Millions of parents all over the globe worry about their children. They want to keep them safe and secure and in a loving environment.
2 Imagine trying to find out where your son or daughter has wandered off to and then feeling that sinking feeling in your stomach when you cannot find them. Or perhaps your worst fears are realised and your child is a victim of a kidnapping. (Kidsgpsguide, 2012)

Although fear is effective in making us aware of risks to ourselves and our children, levels of fear are often disproportionate to the risk, which is often the case with crime (Millie and Herrington, 2005). Fear that children will be exposed to crime causes parents to prevent their children from playing outside and there is now a flourishing 'market in fear' (Furedi, 2006). Fear, in contemporary society, is 'free-floating' and what we fear can change from one day to the other. The free-floating dynamic, Furedi (2006: 6) argues, 'is promoted by a culture that communicates hesitancy and anxiety towards uncertainty and continually anticipates the worst possible outcome'. The culture of fear encourages society to approach every conceivable human experience as a risk to our safety that should be managed (Furedi, 2006).

In such a context, it is hardly surprising that the issue of protecting our children receives special attention. What used to be called play is symptomatically called 'unsupervised children's activity' and treated as a risk. Parental responsibility is equated with supervising one's children (Furedi, 2006). In sociological research and childhood studies, the increased tendency to regulate and attempt to control children's lives, possibly due to a perceived 'childhood in crisis', has been extensively discussed (James and James, 2001; Valentine, 1996; Wyness, 2000).

Parental responsibility

GPS is used to monitor children in order to protect them from others but also to protect them from themselves. The child is 'equally vulnerable and dangerous, both unable to care for himself and yet more skilled than the adults in his life', making protection and control the dual goal of monitoring children (Marx and Steeves, 2010: 217).

For parents who already do what they can to keep track of their children at all times, GPS will be an added tool aimed at managing parental anxiety. Once it has become a natural part of everyday life in a family or in a school, there is a potential element of peer pressure. The norms are changing and if a parent sees all the other parents tracking their children, she may feel obliged to also do so. In the context of genetic information, there is debate about 'the right not to know' one's genetic makeup in order to avoid serious psychological consequences (Andorno and Laurie, 2004). Similarly, it is imaginable that having constant access to information about one's child's whereabouts may cause psychological problems, such as increased, as opposed to decreased, anxiety.[2] Some parents may not want to have this information and the question is whether it will be possible to opt out if GPS becomes a standard tool for parents and teachers.

As I have suggested elsewhere, the core of parental responsibility can be understood as a virtue (Nihlén Fahlquist and van de Poel, 2012). As a virtue, parental responsibility could be said to consist of different obligations that should be met and a more long-term 'meta-virtue', described by Ruddick (1989) as attentive love. In addition to the meta-virtue of attentive love, Ruddick argues that there are three dimensions of such practice: preservation (preserving the child's life does not require love, just seeing vulnerability and responding to it); growth (such as fostering the child's emotional and intellectual development); and acceptability (making sure the child adjusts to societal norms).

Attentive love is the foundation of maternal (parental) work and it consists of a cognitive ability (attention) and a virtue (love) (Ruddick, 1989). As Nihlén Fahlquist and van de Poel (2010) argue, a fourth reasonable requirement of parental responsibility is to inspire the child to think independently and have a critical perspective on current norms and values. This could be seen as an additional feature or as part of the requirements associated with nurturance. Although difficult, this is important to help children become morally autonomous agents and perhaps also to develop a sense of self-worth (Nihlén Fahlquist and van de Poel, 2010). Arguably, this is also crucial for society at large, in order to facilitate moral progress. Democratic societies need critically reflecting citizens.

The ideals of protecting a child and promoting their independence can come into conflict with each other. Using technology to track children puts this potential conflict to the fore: How do we protect our children without impeding their growth as individuals? A distinction should be made between gut reactions and reflective moral emotions (Roeser, 2010). One such moral emotion could be the intuition that if a child is overprotected, he/she will not learn how to become a responsible human being who is able to take care of himself/herself and to manage risks and challenges. The prospect of using GPS to monitor children could be seen as surfacing a conflict between the gut feelings related to preservation – urging a parent to protect their child – and the more reflective moral emotions associated with nurturance – inspiring one's child to grow intellectually and emotionally. An important insight from the ethics of care is that care is a relation where one has to consider the effect on the recipient of care in order to determine if it is genuine care as opposed to merely a caring attitude (Noddings, 2002). Against this background, it is important to find out how children experience being tracked by GPS.

By placing children at daycare centres and schools, parents delegate parts of their responsibility. This includes both the aspect of keeping them safe and the idea that children should learn by mistakes and grow as independent human beings.

If safety were our only goal as parents, we should not allow children to climb trees, explore the woods, use scissors, and so on. In order to become independent grown-ups on the other side of the parenting process, children need to learn how to go about in the world. Furthermore, we should think critically about what we are communicating when making children carry a device equipped with an SOS button, which allows us to be alerted when they enter and exit zones and to know the exact history of a child's daily whereabouts. The message is, arguably, that the world is not a safe place and that the child is not trustworthy or responsible enough to manage in this dangerous world.

When daycare and school staff use GPS, the question may be even more difficult because of the potential double delegation: Parents delegate responsibility to staff, who possibly delegate responsibility to technology. Imagine that a child gets lost in the woods on a school excursion and the GPS technology was defective. The ethically crucial question is which actor is to be considered responsible for the child in such a situation.

Psychologists have studied the relationship between parental monitoring and children's adjustment and behaviour. The definition of 'parental monitoring' used in such studies is often vague, and there is little agreement on what is involved (Jensen Racz and McMahon, 2011). According to Jensen Racz and McMahon (2011), the term 'parental monitoring' is often conflated with 'parental knowledge'. Noticing the conceptual conflation, Kerr and Stattin (2000), in an extensively cited work, distinguish between three different sources of parental knowledge: child disclosure (children voluntarily tell their parents about their activities); parental solicitation (parents ask children and/or their friends for information); and parental control (parents use rules and restrictions to limit children's ability to participate in activities about which parents lack information) (see also Jensen Racz and McMahon, 2011).

Kerr and Stattin's (2000) findings indicate that spontaneous and voluntary child disclosure is the most important source of parental knowledge. They hypothesise that the extent to which parents have listened actively since the child was younger and how warm and accepting they are affect the extent to which an adolescent is willing to disclose information about his/her activities (Kerr and Stattin, 2000). Not only does voluntary disclosure appear to be the most effective way of achieving the parents' goal of gaining knowledge about their child's activities but also excessive parental solicitation and control may have negative effects on children's adjustment and behaviour, as well as on their well-being (Jensen Racz and McMahon, 2011; Kerr and Stattin, 2000). This is confirmed in a Japanese study investigating the increased use of information and communication technology (ICT) to monitor children (Nakayama, 2011).

During the last decades, crime has been reduced worldwide, yet levels of fear are higher than ever. This has been called the 'reassurance gap': high levels of fear of crime and low levels of trust in policing (Millie and Herrington, 2005). For example, although reported crime in Japan has decreased by 40 per cent from 2002 to 2010, people perceive public safety as deteriorating. This, combined with the natural tendency of parents to worry about their children's safety, has led to an increased interest in using ICT to monitor children. The Japanese study investigated the correlation of parenting style – 'responsiveness' or 'control' – with the intention to use ICT to monitor their children. The result shows that where parents and children describe parenting style as high in control, the intention to use the technology is higher. However, children are more likely to accept being monitored if the parenting style is higher in responsiveness.

As Nakayama (2011) suggests, a child may be more willing to accept being monitored when the relationship between parent and child is affectionate because it is then seen purely as a security measure. If, on the other hand, the relationship is characterised by overprotection and a controlling parenting style, the monitoring may instead be seen as an expression of that relationship and a parental tool to exercise that control. Studies in attachment theory have indicated that children with responsive parents are more likely to contribute to parental monitoring (Kerns *et al.*, 2001). This could mean that a secure attachment leading to more disclosure would at least reduce the need to monitor children because of a perceived risk that they expose themselves and others to danger.

These findings illuminate an interesting link between preservation and nurturance. By focusing parental efforts on nurturance, the parent may simultaneously contribute to preservation. When focusing on encouraging one's child to become self-regulating and independent, intellectually and emotionally mature, the child is more likely to share information, thereby contributing to his/her own preservation.

Sociologists have noted increased societal and parental concern about risks to children and risks posed by children and the perceived need to control all aspects of their lives (for example, James and James, 2001; Prout, 2005; Scraton, 1997; Wyness, 2000; Zeiher, 2001). Against this background, James and Richards (1999) argue that children should be seen as social actors with rights. In addition to the psychological research supporting a receptive style of parenting, then, there are good reasons to argue that relationships between adults and children should be based on respect and trust as opposed to control and regulation.

Autonomy and responsibility

In addition to parental responsibility, GPS tracking raises the question of children's developing sense of responsibility. Nurturance, as presented above, aims to promote the growth of children. Children need to become autonomous individuals, able to take care of themselves and others. They need to develop a sense of responsibility and this requires practice. A study by Kakihara *et al.* (2010) found that youths with parents who had more rules decreased in norm-breaking but also in self-esteem. This study suggests that when parental control limits choice, this may compromise the psychological autonomy of youths. A loss in self-esteem and sense of autonomy are likely to be counter-productive to developing responsibility as a virtue.

Whereas the studies mentioned above tested parental control generally, GPS and similar technology may be seen in light of more general research concerning parental control and children's sense of autonomy and responsibility. If a child's parents use GPS and know all of his/her whereabouts, this sends the message that someone else is in control and presumably also takes responsibility. If young people experience parental control dually as care and a sign that the parents regard them as incompetent (Pomerantz and Eaton, 2000), this presumably does not merely counteract trust but also their developing sense of responsibility. Parental control needs to be adjusted gradually to fit the child's developmental abilities and progress towards self-sufficiency (Kakihara *et al.*, 2010). Children with parents who provide opportunities for self-regulation and participation in decision-making are more likely to develop self-worth and avoid depression (Smetana *et al.*, 2004).

Consequently, children need freedom for psychological reasons. From a normative perspective, this is also highly reasonable. Children have a strong interest in a certain amount of freedom to develop into autonomous and responsible individuals. Arguably, this interest should be the foundation of a right, with the corresponding duty of the adult world to make sure the right is respected.

Children and privacy

So far, we have discussed parental responsibility and children's sense of responsibility. GPS technology used to track children also illuminates the question of whether children have a right to privacy. Usually, the right to privacy is discussed in the context of the government tracking citizens. In this case, the context is somewhat different and involves several relationships: parent–child, teacher–child; parent–teacher/school; and parent–industry. One interesting aspect of children and privacy is that, on the one hand, children are often seen as belonging to the private sphere by their very nature as dependents of their parents and because they are not normally considered moral agents. On the other hand, when children play in public spaces, for example, in school playgrounds, they are located in the public sphere, which if they were adults would raise the issue of 'privacy in public' (Nissenbaum, 1998, 2004).

Legally, children have a right to privacy (UNCRC, 2012). Apart from the Convention on the Rights of the Child, children's right to privacy has not been widely discussed in spite of the current focus on adult privacy issues (Hanafin *et al.*, 2010). However, a discussion concerning children's right to privacy in the school context has recently been initiated. For example, it has been argued that if human beings have a right to privacy, then pupils who are children must also have this right (Davis, 2001).

There is a strong case for children's moral right to privacy, albeit not necessarily as extensive as the adult equivalent. There are two primary reasons for granting children a right to privacy. First, although there are differences, developmentally, psychologically and physiologically, between adults and children, they are not substantial but gradual differences. Children, like adults, have human rights and it is reasonable that children have some private space. We should care and empathise with children to the extent that we take into account how privacy intrusions are experienced by them, for example, how they feel about being constantly monitored. In a study of the use of CCTV cameras in British schools, pupils were asked how they experienced being monitored. Most felt that the cameras undermined privacy and represented a manifestation of mistrust (Taylor, 2010). Hence, not only do children dislike being monitored through technology but such surveillance also affects the trust and relationship between adults and children. The current increase in regulation and monitoring of children potentially infringes on children's right to privacy. The balance between protection and children's right to privacy should be discussed in society to prevent the norms from changing in unreasonable ways.

Sociologists and childhood scholars have argued that we should start seeing children not as subordinate, inferior and in need of control, restriction and protection but as 'competent social actors' (Prout, 2005; Wyness, 2000). As competent social actors, they, just like adults, should have a private sphere. A second reason is instrumental. From a psychological perspective, privacy is considered an important prerequisite for the development of a self and for regulating the boundaries between self and society (Parke and Sawin, 1979).

Conclusion

Most parents have moments when they wish they could keep better track of their children, and we can all imagine the horror of having a child abducted. Teachers, as professionals taking care of children, are likely to share this concern to some extent. However, the benefits of tracking technology should not distract us from seeing the bigger picture. While potentially protecting children and possibly making parents and teachers feel more secure (although it is questionable whether they actually do feel more secure), it also removes children's freedom and may damage their growth as independent, creative and responsible individuals. It truly should be negotiated between adults and children and the power inequality between adult and child should not be abused. Parent–child, and teacher–child relationships should be based on trust and a gradual transfer of responsibility, things that may be hampered by using monitoring technology without careful deliberation. There may be cases when GPS and other monitoring technology is a good supplement to achieve security and safety for our children, but we should always keep in mind the ethical questions that arise when we want to use them. We need to separate gut feelings associated with preservation from reflective moral emotions associated with nurturance and growth. There may be ways to benefit from the advantages of GPS while reducing the ethical problems: for example, limiting its use to toddlers, with rules to prevent misuse. A first step would be to discuss these issues with the industry and in society at large.

Notes

1 Author's translation from the Swedish 'Skapa trygghet för dig och ditt barn'.
2 I would like to thank Peter Kroes for making this point in a colloquium discussion.

References

Altheide, D. L. (2009) 'The Columbine shootings and the discourse of fear', *American Behavioral Scientist*, 52(10): 1354–70.

AmberAlert (2010) Julia Howard, Smart Family Blog: 'Using the amber alert child locator while on camping trips', 4 Mar. Available online at www.amberalertgps.com/using-the-amber-alert-child-locator-while-on-camping-trips (accessed 06.03.2015).

AmberAlert (2012) Website. Available online at www.ambertalertgps.com (accessed 29.09.2012).

Andorno, R. and G. Laurie (2004) 'Right not to know: an autonomy based approach', *Journal of Medical Ethic*, 30(5): 435–40.

Barngps (2012) Website. Available online at http://barngps.se/ (accessed 08.05.2012).

Beck, U. (1992) *Risk society: towards a new modernity*. London: Sage.

Cargile, E. (2012) 'AISD: GPS tracking to boost attendance', *Kxan.com*, 27 Aug. Available online at www.txwclp.org/2012/08/aisd-gps-tracking-to-boost-attendance/ (accessed 06.01.16)

Davis, A. (2001) 'Do children have privacy rights in the classroom?', *Studies in Philosophy and Education*, 20(3): 245–54.

Furedi, F. (2006) *The culture of fear revisited*. London: Continuum.

Giddens, A. (1999) 'Risk and responsibility', *Modern Law Review*, 62(1): 1–10.

Göteborgsposten (2011) 'Allt vanligare med gps på förskolan', 21 Sept.

Hanafin, J., T. Donoghue, M. Flynn and M. Shevlin (2010) 'The primary school's invasion of the privacy of the child: unmasking the potential of some current practices', *Educational Studies*, 36(2): 143–52.

James, A. L. and A. James (2001) 'Tightening the net: children, community and control', *British Journal of Sociology*, 52(2): 211–28.

James, A. L. and M. Richards (1999) 'Sociological perspectives, family policy, family law and children: adult thinking and sociological tinkering', *Journal of Social Welfare and Family Law*, 21(1): 23–39.

Jensen Racz, S. and R. J. McMahon (2011) 'The relationship between parental knowledge and monitoring and child and adolescent conduct problems: a 10-year update', *Clinical Child and Family Psychological Review*, 14: 377–98.

Johnson, B. (2009) 'GPS wristwatch helps parents track children', *Guardian*, 12 Jan.

Kakihara, F., L. Tilton-Weaver, M. Kerr and H. Stattin (2010) 'The relationship of parental control to youth adjustment: do youths' feelings about their parents play a role?', *Journal of Youth Adolescence*, 39: 1442–56.

Kerns, K. A., J. E. Aspelmeier, A. L. Gentzler and C. M. Grabill (2001) 'Parent-child attachment and monitoring in middle childhood', *Journal of Family Psychology*, 15(1): 69–81.

Kerr, M. and H. Stattin (2000) 'What parents know and how they know and several forms of adolescent adjustment: further support for a reinterpretation of monitoring', *Developmental Psychology*, 36(3): 366–80.

Kidsgpsguide (2012) Website. Available online at www.kidsgpsguide.com (accessed 08.05.2012).

Lociloci (2012) 'Lociloci — a family phone tracker — know where your loved ones are right now'. Available online at www.lociloci.com/en/ (accessed 06.01.2016)

Lok8u (2012) Website. Available online at www.lok8u.com/products.html (accessed 08.05.2012).

Marx, G. T. and V. Steeves (2010) 'From the beginning: children as subjects and agents of surveillance', *Surveillance and Society*, 7(3/4): 192–230.

Millie A. and V. Herrington (2005) 'Bridging the gap: understanding reassurance policing', *Howard Journal*, 44(1): 41–56.

Nakayama, M. (2011) 'Parenting style and parental monitoring with information communication technology: a study on Japanese junior high school students and their parents', *Computers in Human Behavior*, 27: 1800–5.

Nihlén Fahlquist, J. and I. van de Poel (2012) 'Technology and parental responsibility: the case of the V-chip', *Science and Engineering Ethics*, 18(2): 285–300.

Nissenbaum, H. (1998) 'Protecting privacy in an information age: the problem with privacy in public', *Law and Philosophy*, 17: 559–96.

Nissenbaum, H. (2004) 'Privacy as contextual integrity', *Washington Law Review*, 79(1): 119–57.

Noddings, N. (2002) *Starting at home: caring and social policy*. Berkeley: University of California Press.

Parke, R. D. and D. B. Sawin (1979) 'Children's privacy in the home: developmental, ecological, and child-rearing determinants', *Environment and Behavior*, 11(1): 87–104.

Pomerantz, E. M. and M. M. Eaton (2000) 'Developmental differences in children's conceptions of parental control: "they love me, but they make me feel incompetent"', *Merrill-Palmer Quarterly*, 46: 140–67.

Prout, A. (2005) *The future of childhood*. New York: Routledge.

Roeser, S. (2010) 'Emotional reflection about risk', in S. Roeser (ed.), *Emotions and risky technologies*, International Library of Ethics, Law and Technology, Vol. 5. Dordrecht: Springer.

Ruddick, S. (1989) *Maternal thinking*. Boston: Beacon Press.

Santa Cruz, N. (2011) 'For chronic truants, a GPS program can help them make the grade', *Los Angeles Times*, 25 Feb.

Scraton, P. (1997) *Childhood in 'crisis'*. London: UCL Press.

Smetana, J. G., N. Campione-Barr and C. Daddis (2004) 'Longitudinal development of family decision making: defining healthy behavioral autonomy for middle-class African-American adolescents', *Child Development*, 75: 1418–34.

Svenska Dagbladet (2011) 'Allt vanligare med GPS på förskolan', 21 Sept.

Taylor, E. (2010) 'I spy with my little eye: the use of CCTV in schools and the impact on privacy', *Sociological Review*, 58(3): 381–405.

UNCRC (2012) United Nations Convention on the Rights of the Child (CRC). Available online at www.unicef.org/crc/ (accessed 25.09.2012).

Valentine, G. (1996) 'Children should be seen and not heard? The role of children in public space', *Urban Geography*, 17(3): 205–20.

Wyness, M. (2000) *Contesting childhood*. London: Routledge.

Zeiher, H. (2001) 'Children's islands in space and time: the impact of spatial differentiation on children's ways of shaping social life', in M. du Bois-Reymond, H.-H. Krüger and H. Sänger (eds), *Childhood in Europe: approaches, trends, findings*. New York: Peter Lang.

10 Childhood, surveillance and mHealth technologies

Emma Rich

In recent years, the growth and development of 'mHealth' technologies within the health professions have driven significant transformations to healthcare systems and health practices. The World Health Organisation (WHO) describes mHealth as 'medical and public health practice supported by mobile devices, such as mobile phones, patient monitoring devices, personal digital assistants (PDAs), and other wireless devices' (WHO, 2011: 6). In policy terms, mHealth technologies are often framed as essential cost-effective 'solutions' to health care since they not only enable health professionals to predict, treat, monitor and regulate health but, increasingly, provide the means through which users can actively participate in their own health care. mHealth can, thus, act as a means through which 'preventative medicine may be realized through participatory health initiatives' (Swan, 2012).

Governments and health organisations are therefore investing in mHealth in order to deliver a more effective healthcare system (European Commission, 2014) and foster a 'digitally engaged patient' (Lupton, 2013). Digital health is a priority focus in a range of UK and European policies and consultations (European Commission, 2014), and the digital agenda is seen as a flagship initiative for public health as part of the Europe 2020 growth strategy. In the UK, the National Health Service (NHS) has launched the 'Health Apps Library' which includes an 'expanding set of NHS accredited health apps that patients will be able to use to organise and manage their own health and care' (NHS England, 2014: 32).

According to Fox and Duggan (2013), some 80 per cent of the population in Europe have carried out a health-related search on the Internet, while 52 per cent have done so through their smartphone, representing a turn towards mobile technologies to access health information. Digital technologies, such as mobile software applications (apps), provide relatively low-cost means through which individuals can track, quantify and monitor various aspects of their lifestyles and health behaviours. For example, diet and levels of physical activity can be tracked and users can potentially modify their behaviours in accordance with feedback on this data. As such, many of these apps have been integrated into people's everyday lives. Sources elsewhere indicate that currently, there are 97,000 mHealth apps available and the global market for the mHealth industry is predicted to reach $42.12 billion by 2020 (Grand View Research Inc, 2015). More recently, the parameters of these mHealth technologies look set to expand with the advent of Web 3.0 and the 'internet of things'. As Lupton describes it,

> An internet of things is now beginning to develop (also often referred to as 'Web 3.0') in which digitised everyday objects (or 'smart' things) are able to connect to the internet and with each other and exchange information without human intervention, allowing for joined-up networks across a wide range of objects, databases and digital platforms (2014: 9).

A growing range of wearable technologies are available to monitor health behaviour. Those with sensors, such as bands, patches and GPS technologies, enable users to record and log data on their bodies, such as body mass index, calories burnt, heart rate and physical activity patterns. Wristbands such as Fitbit, Nike+ Fuelband and Jawbone wristbands, fitted with motion sensors and algorithms can track everyday activities, for example, steps taken or sleep patterns.

Questions are beginning to emerge about how these technologies are being taken up by individual, organisations and institutions to monitor others. Young people, in particular, may be exposed to these technologies with the recent trend towards 'eHPE', where health and physical education (HPE) is becoming increasingly digitised and schools are using 'digital devices and software that allow students to collect, track, manipulate and share health-related data' (Gard, 2014: 838). These trends raise questions about how and what young people are learning about their own and others' bodies as good, healthy and active, in the pursuit of 'health' within these digital environments.

Despite the exponential market growth in these types of mHealth technologies, there is very little scrutiny of their role and, hence, a growing need to understand their potential impact, particularly in relation to young people. This chapter examines the ethical and moral implications the use of mHealth technologies might be doing to the subjectivities and bodies of young people through examining the increasing use of mobile health technologies as part of a broader health promotion strategy to tackle obesity.

Many of the mHealth apps available for monitoring weight and health are categorised as 'wellness and lifestyle' apps. Although mHealth technologies now represent a critical mass in the digital health landscape, they are not subject to the same forms of regulation (Powell *et al.*, 2014) as medical devices. I use the example of obesity to argue that a simple distinction between potentially harmful medical devices and more commercially oriented 'wellness' mHealth technologies might be misleading, particularly when considering the potentially harmful impact on young people's subjectivities and bodies. This, I argue, warrants the immediate focus of scholars and health practitioners in developing more critical frameworks of understanding mHealth use and experience that can inform broader debates about mHealth regulation.

In recent years, more critical approaches to the digitisation of health have begun to emerge (Gard, 2014; Lupton, 2014; Rich and Miah, 2014).[1] This chapter makes a case for building on this critical work, pointing towards a public pedagogy perspective of mHealth (Rich and Miah, 2014) and raising a number of questions from a more contextualised, socio-political perspective of mHealth. As such, the chapter examines the implications of mHealth in socio-cultural and political contexts where 'weight stigma' is pervasive and damaging (Bombak, 2014) and intimately connected to practices of surveillance.

mHealth, regulation and children

Whilst mHealth is being positioned as a core driver of future health care, there is a lack of research on the impact of these technologies on users' health practices and behaviours (Mager, 2012). The blurring of the distinction between the provision of health care and self-administration has prompted the medical community to consider the potential risks and harm that might be realised through mHealth. The classification of mobile health technologies and their potential risk brings these debates into complex terrain. Mobile health care is subject to the medical device regulation and regulatory frameworks that govern the design, development and use of these technologies. One of the key considerations with these frameworks is the 'intended use' or purpose of the product to determine, in part, whether or not it is considered to be a medical device. Under the European Directive 2007/47/EC (21 March 2010) amendment to the Directive 93/42/EEC, a medical device is:

> [A]ny instrument, apparatus, appliance, software, material or other article, whether used alone or in combination, including the software intended by its manufacturer to be used specifically for diagnostic and/or therapeutic purposes and necessary for its proper application, intended by the manufacturer to be used for human beings for the purpose of: diagnosis, prevention, monitoring, treatment or alleviation of disease, diagnosis, monitoring, treatment, alleviation of or compensation for an injury or handicap, investigation, replacement or modification of the anatomy or of a physiological process, control of conception, and which does not achieve its principal intended action in or on the human body by pharmacological, immunological or metabolic means, but which may be assisted by such means.

However, as mentioned above, a large proportion of the mHealth apps available, particularly those aimed at young people, would be categorised as 'wellness' or 'lifestyle' apps; yet, they perform various functions enabling users to track their exercise behaviour, body weight and food consumption. Indeed, Google announced 2014 as the year of health and fitness apps (Boxall, 2014), recording this as their fastest-growing app category. Yet, 'the bewildering diversity of apps available has made it difficult for clinicians and the public to discern which apps are the safest or most effective' (Powell *et al*., 2014). Given their capacity for surveillance, these are significant issues, particularly as commercial mobile apps and wearable devices are increasingly targeted at children. For example, in 2014, a fitness band designed for children aged as young as four was launched, promoted by its manufacturer as 'the only activity tracker just for kids that encourages active play and healthy habits with a customisable pet pal' (Leapfrog, 2014). The band includes a small screen with a virtual pet, which can be given snacks and rewards, as the child completes certain levels of physical activity.

This is one example of the digital platforms providing mechanisms of surveillance of young people's bodies. Through tracking, measuring and monitoring, our bodies, behaviours and health practices are often reduced to data, such as body mass index (BMI), caloric consumption or levels of physical activity. Users are encouraged to acquire information and data about their bodies using self-tracking processes (Ruckenstein, 2014) and subsequently undertake self-management of their health, bodies and lifestyle (Lupton, 2012; Mort *et al*., 2013). mHealth users can collect and log data on various aspects of lifestyle, such as exercise habits, diet and weight, with reward systems, motivational tools and links to upload and publicise results through social media platforms, such as Facebook or Twitter. This popular 'quantified self' (Smarr, 2012; Swan, 2012) trend involves 'the practice of gathering data about oneself on a regular basis and then recording and analyzing the data to produce statistics and other data (such as images) relating to one's bodily functions and everyday habits' (Lupton, 2013: 25). Users are, thus, taking a more active role in managing their lifestyles through data gathered via mHealth technologies.

Little is known about young people's experiences of these technologies, their actual impact on health practices, and the ethical risks or harms they present. We don't know, for example, whether children are taking a lead role in this or whether it is something adults are deciding to do as a way of surveilling children's bodies. The influence of mHealth practices for those interested in the surveillance of children's bodies is a pressing matter for a number of reasons. As we enter this new era of health care, young people will be the first generation of mHealth users. Indeed, it is already apparent that young people are 'prolific users of apps on smartphones, and apps related to diet/fitness/weight management account for half of all apps on the healthcare app store and are the top ranking apps within the category' (Aitken, 2013).

The application of these debates about 'harm' to children's bodies is complex. In part, this is because debates about mHealth frustrate the possibility of simple distinctions between potentially harmful medical devices and those 'wellness and lifestyle' apps that require less 'regulation'. This would seem to broadly correspond with some of the problems of a distinction between enhancement and therapy. Miah (2013) argues that 'the distinction between therapy and enhancement becomes redundant, since preventing many illnesses will involve treating a patient *before* they are diagnosed with an illness and before they are considered to be suffering in a way that warrants medical intervention'. This tension arises, for example, in the increasing use of digital technologies to monitor and measure children and young people's weight and diets in response to the concerns about an ostensible childhood obesity epidemic. Weight loss practices typically associated with enhancement are utilised as part of the preventative strategies to safeguard against obesity.

As I argue in this chapter, this distinction perhaps fails to capture the complexity of the potential risks to children posed by mHealth technologies. There is a growing need not only to understand what takes place within these contexts, but to carefully consider the impacts of mHealth practices whereby increasingly younger children collect, monitor and share information about their bodies. Lifestyle/wellness apps may not only perform medical functions, but their use for veillance (Lupton, 2014) impels us to revisit how we understand risk and harm in complex digital landscapes of body monitoring and modification. Drawing on the case of lifestyle apps associated with weight loss and obesity, I raise a series of questions about the ethical and moral implications of what mHealth might be doing to the subjectivities and bodies of young people.

Health and fitness apps and the biomedicalisation of children's weight

The use of mHealth in the battle against obesity means that children and young people's exposure to digital health technologies might not be of their choosing, as they become increasingly embedded in the policies and practices of more formal institutions, government policies and health promotion strategies. This raises questions about the configuration of meanings through which people understand their own and others' bodies, identities and health practices. Put another way, against this digitised and socio-political backdrop, what are young people learning about how to care for their bodies and how is this impacting their subjectivities?

This requires us to examine the health imperatives that govern use of these self-tracking technologies in a process of 'participatory surveillance' (Albrechtslund, 2008). In other words, what are the power–knowledge relations (Foucault, 1977) that come to regulate young people's understanding of their bodies and subjectivities within these digital environments? More specifically, in the drive to tackle obesity, what are these apps doing in relation to 'weight stigma' in ethical, moral, political and ideological terms in contexts where popular discourses constitute size as one of the dominant criteria through which bodies are read and judged (Evans *et al.*, 2008; Van Amsterdam, 2013)? These are some of the questions that I turn to in the sections below.

There is a broad range of conceptual apparatus that might help us address these questions and, moreover, assist in stimulating new research agendas. In a recent paper with a colleague (Rich and Miah, 2014), we made the case for conceptualising what takes place online through the lens of public pedagogy. We advance a vision of education that recognises how learning – albeit about one's body and health in this case – can occur in sites and contexts beyond formal schooling:

> In advancing a public pedagogy approach to theorising digital health, it is necessary to recognise how technology is inextricable from the manner

> in which people learn about health. Furthermore, these apparatus dictate conditions of self-tracking, collection of data, and monitoring, which have a bearing on what and how people learn about their bodies and health. (Rich and Miah, 2014: 301)

Whilst the encroachment of digital surveillance into a range of everyday contexts is now well recognised, the growing use of commercialised health apps by increasingly younger people may be understood as part of a broader process of biomedicalisation of children's bodies. Whilst the many commercialised health apps are not categorised as medical devices, one might argue that they are assembled through and constitute biomedical practices. As Clarke *et al.* (2003: 63) observed, 'in the biomedicalisation era, what is perhaps most radical is the biomedicalisation of health itself. In commodity culture, health becomes another commodity and the biomedically (re)engineered body becomes a prized possession.' Biomedicalisation occurs through five central and overlapping processes: major political economic shifts; a new focus on health and risk and surveillance biomedicines; the technoscientisation of biomedicine; transformations of the production distribution and consumption of biomedical knowledges; and transformations of bodies and identities (Clarke *et al.*, 2003: 166). The implications of the mHealth-surveillance nexus goes much wider than just the implications for obesity and weight stigma, but offer an example of a broader argument about the trend towards biomedicalisation of children's bodies. Whilst there is not space to explore processes in detail, it is worth highlighting some of the potential areas of concern for future research that are briefly addressed below:

- The burden of decision-making and adherence placed on children and the anxieties that might be associated with these processes through the individualisation of risk;
- Extended boundaries and forms of surveillance through the operation of health systems on children's bodies through digital technologies;
- The masking of surveillance through processes of 'gamification' (Whitson, 2013); and
- The blurring of public and private spaces and the sharing of health information that might lead to the transformations of bodies and identities.

Through their engagement with mHealth, children learn the moral obligations of self-transformation and individual responsibility towards the management of one's own weight and health – themes now well established within the literature on the discourse of healthism (see Crawford, 1980; Evans *et al.*, 2008). The confluence of private and public spaces (Byron, 2008; Papacharissi, 2009) in the context of mHealth means that the process of working on one's body is not only a private project but increasingly a public one. Indeed, a considerable portion of young people's lives is now organised around digital systems and the sharing of personal and public information (Lyon, 2003). Within the connected spaces of social media, mHealth technologies means young people's bodies are increasingly surveilled and monitored.

iHealth: surveillance and the individualisation of risk

While many of the technologies described in this chapter are 'new', they exist within health assemblages that connect with discourses involved in the configuration of weight. Their integration into healthcare systems evokes questions raised elsewhere (Mol, 2008) about what health 'care' is and how it should be practised. While these might be novel technologies, they are formed through complex interrelationships that have a particular socio-cultural history. In part, the context for their emergence is connected to the biomedical focus on obesity as a health crisis, often reduced to lifestyle issues, such as diet and physical activity. Central to this neoliberal health discourse is the idea that fatness is the result of an individual's lifestyle and an issue of choice and responsibility for individuals (Halse, 2009). This neoliberal perspective dominates current public and scholarly debate about weight, fatness and health (Rich *et al*., 2010; Solovay and Rothblum, 2009).

Many health and fitness apps, therefore, feature a variety of functions, such as self-tracking, goals, diet and physical activity advice, social media connections and reward systems. Users learn how to look after themselves via the disciplining regularity of the device's presence and regular notifications to maintain their good behaviour, a trend that has been depicted in the popular press as 'nag technology'. Devices such as wristbands and apps build a profile of the user's lifestyle, including calories consumed, activities undertaken and number of steps walked during the day. For example, the app CARROT Fit – '7 minutes in hell workout and weight tracker' – utilises this surveillant approach:

> CARROT is a sadistic AI construct with one goal: to transform your flabby carcass into Grade A specimen of the human race. She will do whatever it takes– including threatening, inspiring, ridiculing, and bribing you – to make this happen … you will get fit – or else.
> This diabolical interval workout can be completed anywhere, at any time, so you have no excuse not to be in fighting shape when the Robopocalypse begins.
>
> *Lose weight in style*
> Are you ready to have so much fun tracking your weight that you'll actually look forward to hopping on your scale? All you have to do is punch in your current weight, then sit back and let CARROT pass judgement upon you.
>
> *Claim your reward*
> If you work out and slough off those extra pounds, CARROT will reward you with fabulous prizes like app upgrades, cat facts, and permission to watch your friend eat a bag of potato chips.
>
> *Track your awesomeness*
> Because math is hard CARROT will do all the number-crunching for you. See how your weight loss is coming along on a pretty graph, view your workouts on a calendar, and check your BMI.

> Hello, chubby Human! Fitness overlord CARROT here with phase II of my plan to science your lazy carcass into a form more consistent with what celebrity magazines say you should look like. (CARROT Fit, 2014)

The language used in such promotions could have significant implications for subjectivity and embodiment in ways that might further impact on the conditions within which the stigmatisation of fat flourishes. Whilst engagement with apps might be a voluntary practice, it also involves a form of 'participatory surveillance' (Albrechtslund, 2008), involving self-surveillance and modification. Using self-tracking devices for monitoring and management of one's weight constitutes what Foucault (1988) terms technologies of the self. In other words, the tracking and monitoring of users' bodies, diet, weight, physical activity and other behaviours can be conceptualised as a form of governance of fat.

The data that one collects on one's body, activities or behaviours can then be shared with others through social media. In this way, mHealth does not simply respond to a vision of health but can also be considered to be characteristic of a 'confessional society' (Bauman, 2007). Conceptualising this through a public pedagogy approach, it becomes clear that with their accompanying processes of surveillance and evaluation, these technologies imply certain expectations of control, which are to be *learned*, but also are publicly displayed for evaluation by others. In the era of mobile health, then, these encounters with our bodies, weight and health have become more public-facing, social experiences.

A further characteristic of these apps and their pedagogical functions is the connectivity through social media, which produces forms of 'lateral surveillance, or peer-to-peer monitoring, understood as the use of surveillance tools by individuals, rather than by agents of institutions public or private, to keep track of one another' (Andrejevic, 2005). For example, the calorie counter and diet tracker app by MyFitnessPal has a social feature to 'connect with friends and easily track and motivate each other' (MyFitnessPal, 2015). The confluence of private and public spaces (Byron, 2008; Papacharissi, 2009) and the commercialisation of personal data raise ethical concerns about young people's privacy and the use of the data that are collected from these devices. In terms of risks, children's engagement with weight-related apps can lead to an intrusion of commercial health into their personal spaces. For example, through the sharing of third party data, users may be targeted by companies promoting weight-loss products, positioning their bodies as a 'coveted commodity' (Ibrahim, 2010: 123).

The use of such devices aligns with the etiology of obesity as often reported through an individualistic framework (Puhl and Heuer, 2010). Such a framework fails to convey the uncertainty, complexities and ambiguities of the relationship between weight and health (Gard and Wright, 2005). One such example of this type of app targeted at young people is Eat and move-o-matic: Children see food choices on one side of the screen and activity choices on the other. As they pick a food, the number of calories will be shown alongside an activity that will consume that same amount of calories. Weight is, thus, reduced to the simple matter of energy in, energy out and a result of the 'choices' one makes. The moralisation and individualisation of risk, thus, place increasing responsibility on people to make the 'appropriate' health choices. With their accompanying processes of surveillance and evaluation, these technologies imply expectations of control, which are to be *learned* by children through these technologies. In this vein, the educative force in the management of bodies through mHealth is revealed.

Through these public pedagogies, the knowledge that is derived through these apps is predominantly through quantification and the reduction of complex health issues to body data. These processes contribute to a 'new body ontology … that redefines bodies in terms of, or even as, information' (Van der Ploeg, 2003: 64). These technologies 'capture' complex flows of body information and 'reassemble' (Haggerty and Ericson, 2000) them into individualised and simple readings of health. Furthermore, as Lupton (2014: 7) argues, 'the quantification of self through these technologies is portrayed as contributing to their objective neutrality, supposedly removed from the subject actions of humans' (see also Ruckenstein, 2014). Digital solutions, such as these, contribute to the discourse that weight is a matter of personal responsibility that can be controlled by the individual; a simple matter of overeating and exercise.

The implications of this relationality of power–knowledge have long been established in the literature, where there are strong connections between assumed levels of personal responsibility for health conditions and high levels of stigmatisation (Puhl and Heurer, 2010; Weiner *et al.*, 1988). As Carels *et al.* (2009) suggest, 'While the etiology of weight stigma is complex, research suggests that it is often greater among individuals who embrace certain etiological views of obesity or ideological views of the world'. The logic of self-tracking and self-care is commensurable with the etiological perspectives of individual control of health: 'This focus on control and responsibility in relation to body size categorizations magnifies the stigmatization and discrimination of fat subjects compared to other marked positions' (Van Amsterdam, 2013: 164). These mHealth lifestyle apps are presented, in part, through broader discourses of culpability, responsibility and even military metaphors, as helping the individual to take responsibility and join 'the war on obesity' (Monaghan, 2008). The user of the app is positioned both as a subject who is 'at risk' and to be managed through data feedback and as an individual who is to be held accountable within a neoliberal reading of selfhood. Exercise and weight loss are, therefore, mobilised as moral practices of the disciplined self through these digital technologies.

Gamification of mHealth

Commercial apps specifically targeted at children and young people often feature 'gamification' (Whitson, 2013), the combination of the quantification of self with creative and game play scenarios. Part of its appeal lies in introducing playful dimensions into health apps designed to help young people *learn* about healthy lifestyles and actively encourage the reporting of exercise habits, diet and weight.

The 'game' play may involve features such as reward systems or motivational tools. Such platforms present further risks when data reported may be publicly linked through social media and sharing this information with 'friends' online.

These processes can work to mask or, at the very least, legitimise surveillance of young peoples' bodies, not confined to formal institutions but increasingly dispersed and encroaching into the private and digitised spaces of youth culture. Risk factors are presented in game play scenarios and techniques of self-surveillance offered as solutions, quite literally, the gamification of what Armstrong (1995) calls 'surveillance medicine'. Furthermore, many prescribe exercise in the broader context of the battle against obesity, encouraging users to measure their physical activity and become active subjects. The explicit link between these apps and the broader discourses of health, particularly obesity, are evidenced through their integration into educational contexts and health policies. For example, in the USA, the Let's Move! campaign was established as 'a comprehensive initiative, launched by the First Lady, dedicated to solving the challenge of childhood obesity within a generation, so that children born today will grow up healthier and able to pursue their dream' (Let's Move!, n.d.). In 2010, the campaign's 'apps for healthy kids competition' challenged software developers, game designers and students to develop fun and engaging online or mobile games and tools to encourage 9- to 12-year-olds to be more physically active and develop better dietary habits. One of the tools, 'The online tool snack neutralizer', allows users to select a food and evaluate the consequences with required physical activity to balance the caloric intake.

The surveillance of young people's bodies is, thus, valorised through broader obesity discourses and health policies. Through these game play environments, users learn not only about 'healthy' activities but of what and whose bodies may be valued, given the status and meeting the expectations of particular body pedagogies (Evans *et al.*, 2008). As Lupton (2014) suggests, 'the use of these types of digital devices in schools conforms to the biopedagogical ethos of HPE.'

A further risk is that within mHealth landscapes, there is the potential for nurturing disaffected relationships with the body. An example of this is a mobile app that required users to carry out plastic surgical interventions to an avatar: 'The game … rated for children 9 and older, walked players through the graphic steps of liposuction that must be performed on an "unfortunate girl" to make her "slim and beautiful"' (Bell, 2014). The alarming forms of body modification encouraged through game play environments, such as this, represent fatness as 'matter out of place' (Douglas, 1966), to be modified not only through changes in lifestyle but through more extreme forms of human enhancement, such as surgery. Moreover, these applications depict particular bodies and subjects as marginal, different or even problematic and abject. Here, young people are not only learning about whether their own bodies meet the norm, but undertaking practices of surveillance and modification of prostheticised bodies in cyberspace (see Miah and Rich, 2008). This particular app was only removed after a protest campaign was initiated on Twitter by Eveydaysexism group.

This example returns us to the opening questions about whether current regulatory frameworks adequately capture the complexities of risks associated with 'lifestyle' apps. This is a pressing issue, given the extensive literature revealing that young people's and children's relationships with their bodies are often troubled (Birbeck and Drummond, 2005; Burrows *et al*., 2002; Evans *et al*., 2008). To date, there is a paucity of evidence of how young people respond to mHealth, including how they might resist or resent the processes of surveillance on their bodies and potentially 'spontaneous' spaces and places for play. To this end, there is a need for more nuanced and contextualised understanding of how young people discover, select, adopt, share, employ and reject the mHealth technologies.

Conclusion: weight stigma and the future of mHealth

It is important to acknowledge at this juncture that there are many benefits to mHealth, for example, in terms of novel patient engagement. However, the intention of this chapter, albeit modestly, was to explore some of the potential ramifications of the rise of mHealth in socio-cultural contexts where currently weight stigma is pervasive and damaging (Bombak, 2014). Many of these technologies encourage young people to think about weight in terms of an outcome of individual behaviours that must prompt them to place their bodies under regular surveillance. Yet, this presumption has a strong relationship with the increase in weight stigma. The reduction of weight, health and the body to 'body data' through mHealth technologies, in the context of a neoliberal governance and logic of choice, could lead to an emphasis on self-responsibility for increasingly younger children. Physical activity and weight loss are seen to be simply a matter of individual choice in the quest to regulate bodies to normalised ideals.

This understanding of health ignores the power relations that affect different individuals and identities, including those whose weight may come to be stigmatised as outside the norm. Moreover, it overlooks the complexity of health and the inter-relationships that come to constitute health and within which health practices and choices are made possible (Mol, 2008). These discourses of personal responsibility 'not only position individuals as blameworthy, but moralize and decontextualize health inequalities by glossing over the social and structural contexts that come to bear upon this' (Rich, 2011: 16). There is little space within these systems to address the material, affective and discursive basis of health. What is missing in these representations of the body are people's everyday lives, embodied experiences and social contexts.

In terms of stigma, one might ask how embodied experiences are being produced through these technologies and the implications for the subjectivity of children and young people. What if there are no improvements in the aspects of their health or bodies being measured? Suppose a child or young person follows a particular weight loss programme and regularly monitors or measures their weight but do not actually achieve the target weight. What might this do to their subjectivities, particularly when visualisation techniques are used? Are they left feeling stigmatised, morally failing within systems of meanings of 'both the marked (disadvantaged) and the unmarked (privileged) positions' (Van Amsterdam, 2013: 156). What if one does not feel the way one is expected to, as portrayed in the normalised imagery accompanying the promotion of these apps (healthy, happy and in control)? What is the effect on one's subjectivity if one fails to achieve the ideals of these apps? What of those individuals who choose not to engage with these practices of self-surveillance and resist them?

Questions of this kind require a move beyond narrow conceptualisations of mHealth technologies as simply tools to 'improve' children's bodies and towards a more nuanced approach through which young people's subjective experiences are placed in their social, material, family, geographical and cultural contexts. In this chapter, I have made reference to a public pedagogy approach to conceptualising how and what young people might be learning about health through mHealth technologies. However, if we are to understand the implications of these technologies more fully, future research would benefit from an engagement with a range of disciplines examining the social, political and cultural aspects of mHealth. While certainly not exhaustive of all the theories of digital society, future multidisciplinary approaches could draw from a range of contemporary theories of 'veillance' (Lupton, 2013), embodiment, governance, human–computer relations and digital sociology (Lupton, 2014).

Note

1 (Gard, 2014; Lupton, 2014; Rich and Miah, 2014). Gard (2014), for example, highlights the potential implications of the rise of digital health and physical education (ePHE).

References

Aitken, M. (2013) 'Patient apps for improved healthcare: from novelty to mainstream', Institute for Healthcare Informatics. Available online at www.imshealth.com/en/thought-leadership/ims-institute/reports/patient-apps-for-improved-healthcare (accessed 06.01.16)

Albrechtslund, A. (2008) 'Online social networking as participatory surveillance', *First Monday*, 13(3). Available online at http://firstmonday.org/article/view/2142/1949 (accessed 01.06.16)

Andrejevic, M. (2005) 'The work of watching one another: lateral surveillance, risk, and governance', *Surveillance & Society*, 2(4): 479–97.

Armstrong, D. (1995) 'The rise of surveillance medicine', *Sociology of Health and Illness*, 17(3): 393–404.

Bauman, Z. (2007) *Consuming life*. Cambridge: Polity.

Bell, K. (2014) 'App store pulls "Barbie" plastic surgery app following backlash'. Available online at http://mashable.com/2014/01/14/barbie-plastic-surgery-app/ (accessed 27.03.2016).

Birbeck, D. and M. Drummond (2005) 'Interviewing, and listening to the voices of, very young children on body image and perceptions of self', *Early Child Development and Care*, 176: 579–96.

Bombak, A. E. (2014) 'The contribution of applied social sciences to obesity stigma: related public health approaches', *Journal of Obesity*. Available online at http://dx.doi.org/10.1155/2014/267286 (accessed 01.06.16).

Boxall, A. (2014) '2014 is the year of health and fitness apps, says Google'. Available online at www.digitaltrends.com/mobile/google-play-store-2014-most-downloaded-apps/ (accessed 11.12.2014).

Burrows, L., J. Wright and J. Jungersen-Smith (2002) '"Measure your belly": New Zealand children's constructions of health and fitness', *Journal of Teaching in Physical Education*, 22(1): 29–38.

Byron, T. (2008) *Safer children in a digital world: the report of the Byron Review*. Nottingham, UK: Department for Children, Schools and Families. Available online at http://webarchive.nationalarchives.gov.uk/20120106161038/https://www.education.gov.uk/publications/standard/publicationDetail/Page1/DCSF-00334-2008 (accessed 23.5.16)

Carels, R., K. Young, C. Wott, J. Harper, A. Gumble, M. Wagner Hobbs and A. M. Clayton (2009). 'Internalized weight stigma and its ideological correlates among weight loss treatment seeking adults', *Eating and Weight Disorders: EWD*, 14(2–3): e92–e97.

CARROT Fit (2014) Available online at https://itunes.apple.com/gb/app/carrot-fit-7-minute-workout/id769155678?mt=8 (accessed 27.03.2016).

Clarke, A. E., J. K. Shim, L. Mamo, J. R. Fosket and J. R. Fishman (2003) 'Biomedicalization: technoscientific transformations of health, illness, and U.S. biomedicine', *American Sociological Review*, 68(2): 161–94.

Crawford, R. (1980) 'Healthism and the medicalisation of everyday life', *International Journal of Health Sciences*, 10(3): 365–89.

Douglas, M. (1966) *Purity and danger*. London: Routledge.

European Commission (2014) Digital Health and Care Alliance (DHACA) *EU mHealth green paper: members' responses*. Available online at http://digitalhealthandcare.org.uk/wp-content/uploads/2014/12/DHACA-Members-EU-mHealth-Green-Paper-response-Final.pdf (accessed 06.01.16).

Evans, J., E. Rich, B. Davies and R. Allwood (2008) *Education, disordered eating and obesity discourse: fat fabrications*. London: Routledge.

Foucault, M. (1977) *Discipline and punish: the birth of the prison*, trans. A. Sheridan, London: Penguin.

Foucault, M. (1988) 'Technologies of the self', in L. H. Martin, H. Gutman and P. H. Hutton (eds.), *Technologies of the self: a seminar with Michel Foucault*. Cambridge, MA: MIT Press.

Fox, S. and M. Duggan (2013). *Health online. Pew Research Internet Project*. Washington, DC: Pew Research Centre.

Gard, M. (2014) 'eHPE: a history of the future', *Sport, Education and Society*, 19(6): 827–45.

Gard, M. and J. Wright (2005) *The obesity epidemic*. London: Routledge.

Grand View Research Inc (2015) mHealth Market Analysis By Service (Monitoring Services, Diagnosis Services, System Strengthening), By Participants (Mobile Operators, Device Vendors, Content Players, Healthcare Providers) Segment Forecasts To 2020. ISBN Code: 978-1-68038-076-7

Haggerty K. D. and R. V. Ericson (2000) 'The surveillant assemblage', *British Journal of Sociology*, 51(4): 605–22.

Halse, C. (2009) 'Bio-citizenship: virtue discourses and the birth of the bio-citizen', in J. Wright and V. Harwood (eds.), *Biopolitics and the 'obesity epidemic': governing bodies*. New York: Routledge.

Ibrahim, Y. (2010) 'The wired body and event construction: mobile technologies and the technological gaze', in P. Kalantzis-Cope and K. Gherab-Martin (eds.), *Emerging digital spaces in contemporary society*. Houndmills, UK: Palgrave Macmillan.

Leapfrog (2014) 'Leapband fit made fun!' Available online at www.leapfrog.com/en-gb/products/leapband (accessed 15.11.2014).

'Let's move!' (n.d.) Available online at www.letsmove.gov/learn-facts/epidemic-childhood-obesity (accessed 27.03.2016).

Lupton, D. (2012) 'M-health and health promotion: the digital cyborg and surveillance society', *Social Theory and Health*, 10: 229–44.

Lupton, D. (2013) 'The digitally engaged patient: self-monitoring and self-care in the digital health era', *Social Theory and Health*, 11: 257–70.

Lupton, D. (2014) *Digital sociology*. London: Routledge.

Lyon, D. (ed.) (2003) *Surveillance as social sorting: privacy, risk, and automated discrimination*. New York: Routledge.

Mager, A. (2012) 'Search engines matter: from educating users towards engaging with online health information practices', *Policy and Internet*, 4(2): 1–21.

Miah, A. (2013) 'Justifying human enhancement: the accumulation of biocultural capital', in M. More and N. Vita-More (eds.), *The transhumanist reader: classical and contemporary essays on the science, technology, and philosophy of the human future*. Oxford: Wiley-Blackwell.

Miah, A. and E. Rich (2008) *The medicalization of cyberspace*. New York: Routledge.

Mol, A. (2008) *The logic of care: health and the problem of patient choice*. London: Routledge.

Monaghan, L. (2008) *Men and the war on obesity: a sociological study*. Oxon and New York: Routledge.

Mort, M., C. Roberts and B. Callén (2013) 'Ageing with telecare: care or coercion in austerity?', *Sociology of Health and Illness*, 35(6): 799–812.

MyFitnessPal (2015) 'Calorie counter and diet tracker by MyFitnessPal' application. Available online at https://itunes.apple.com/au/app/calorie-counter-diet-tracker/id341232718?mt=8 (accessed 27.03.2016).

NHS (2014) Health Apps Library. Available online at http://apps.nhs.uk/ (accessed 18.01.2015).

NHS England (2014) Five Year Forward View, Available Online at www.england.nhs.uk/wp-content/uploads/2014/10/5yfv-web.pdf (accessed 24.2.2015).

Papacharissi, Z. (2009) 'The virtual geographies of social networks: a comparative analysis of Facebook, LinkedIn and A Small World', *New Media and Society*, 11 (1/2): 199–220.

Powell, A. C., A. B. Landman and D. W. Bates (2014) 'In search of a few good apps', *Journal of the American Medical Association*, 311(18): 1851–2.

Puhl, R. M. and C. A. Heuer (2010) 'Obesity stigma: important considerations for public health', *American Journal of Public Health*, 100(6): 1019–28.

Rich, E. (2011) '"I see her being obesed!": public pedagogy, reality media and the obesity crisis', *Health: An Interdisciplinary Journal for the Social Study of Health, Illness and Medicine*, 15(1): 3–21.

Rich, E. and A. Miah (2014) 'Understanding digital health as public pedagogy: a critical framework', *Societies*, 4(2): 296–315.

Rich, E., L. Monaghan and L. Aphramor (eds) (2010) *Debating obesity: critical perspectives*. Basingstoke, UK: Palgrave Macmillan.

Ruckenstein, M. (2014) 'Visualized and interacted life: personal analytics and engagements with data doubles', *Societies*, 2: 68–84.

Smarr, L. (2012) 'Quantifying your body: a how-to guide from a systems biology perspective', *Biotechnology Journal*, 7(8): 980–91.

Solovay, S. and E. Rothblum (2009) 'Introduction', in E. Rothblum and S. Solovay (eds.), *The Fat Studies Reader*. New York: New York University Press.

Swan, M. (2012) 'Health 2050: the realization of personalized medicine through crowdsourcing, the quantified self, and the participatory biocitizen', *Journal of Personalized Medicine*, 2(4): 93–118.

Van Amsterdam, N. (2013) 'Big fat inequalities, thin privilege: an intersectional perspective on 'body size', *European Journal of Women's Studies*, 20(2): 155–69.
Van der Ploeg, I. (2003) 'Biometrics and the body as information: normative issues in the socio technical coding of the body', in D. Lyon (ed.), *Surveillance as social sorting: privacy, risk, and automated discrimination*. New York: Routledge.
Weiner, B., R. P. Perry and J. Magnusson (1988) 'An attributional analysis of reaction to stigmas', *Journal of Personality and Social Psychology*, 55(5): 738–48.
Whitson, J. (2013) 'Gaming the quantified self', *Surveillance and Society*, 11(1/2): 163–76.
WHO (2011) 'mHealth — new horizons for health through mobile technologies', *Global observatory for ehealth*. Switzerland: World Health Organization.

Part III

Social lives and virtual worlds

11 Spy kids too

Encounters with surveillance through games and play

Tonya Rooney

As modes of surveillance become more digitised, it will be difficult for children to escape or resist the network of data-capture that pervades the spaces they inhabit. They will also have to make decisions about the opportunities they are presented with to 'look into' the lives of others. In this context, it is important to explore how children come to understand the practice of surveillance and what it means to be both the watched and the watcher. How might children respond to the social, privacy and ethical implications of these new spaces and relations? Focusing on childhood play, this chapter takes up these issues by looking at the ways that particular games open up spaces where children can grapple with issues such as power, exposure, secrecy and deception.

The aim of this analysis is to bring a new perspective as to why children's understanding of surveillance practice should not be underestimated. From a very young age, children experiment and play with multiple ways of hiding and seeking, and through this gain insight into how actions can be used to exert control over others and what it means to negotiate spaces that are rich with shifting and dynamic relations with others. The tendency of children to inhabit play spaces that lie at the edge of, or outside, the surveillance gaze is also noted, and it is shown how these spaces offer a place from which children are able to resist and subvert the workings of surveillance that may be imposed on them. Drawing on an analysis of some common childhood games, this chapter shows how children are afforded important opportunities to explore the complex and relational elements of notions such as power and control. It is suggested that this not only provides a basis from which they can bring meaning to the potential of new surveillance technologies, but that through this, they develop an ethical awareness and sense of responsibility of how to live in and respond to social spaces where surveillance potential is ever-present.

There is a growing body of research on children and surveillance, in this collection and elsewhere (for example, see Monahan and Torres, 2010; Rooney, 2012; Taylor, 2013), showing how pervasive the use of technology for surveillance purposes has become in children's everyday lives. This may involve a combination of watching, listening or observing, generally for the purposes of monitoring, discipline and control. Technologies, when used for the purpose of surveillance, are targeted to influence or control the object of the surveillance in a purposeful and systematic way (Lyon, 2001; Monahan, 2006). It would be tempting, therefore, to simplify the relationship between children and surveillance technologies by characterising children as passive, powerless and vulnerable objects of the surveillance gaze. While it may be the case that children are often watched over or controlled by others, whether for legitimate safety reasons or other more intrusive interventions, it does not necessarily follow that children are indifferent to the effects of control and observation that arise, or that children cannot bring their own ways of knowing to the experience.

This chapter contributes to an understanding of how children engage with new surveillance practices and aims to show that children are far from passive in respect to the structures of discipline and control that surveillance brings to children's spaces. As noted by Marx and Steeves (2010), children's engagement with surveillance as both 'watcher and watched' is complex. For example, a child may be playing with peers online and then find themselves recruited by a gaming company to act as a secret informer to report other children who break the rules. At the same time, a child may be able to resist surveillance imposed by a parent or school by using his/her technological knowledge to circumvent an email-monitoring system. These examples illustrate the ways that children are already engaged in surveillance of, by and for others in a way that is 'multi-faceted' with implications for children that are not yet adequately understood (Marx and Steeves, 2010: 225).

The concept of play provides an effective framework to examine aspects of surveillance practice, as shown through previous studies on online gaming and social media (for example, Hope, 2005; Whitson, 2013). In this chapter, children's play acts as a site for uncovering the ways children come to engage with and bring meaning to surveillance practice, with an emphasis on early play experiences. In exploring how children come to understand and test out the power and potential of the inter-subjective gaze, this chapter looks at 'hiding' games, such as peek-a-boo in the first years and the enduring game of hide-and-seek, and also at the way children 'conceal' themselves in dress-ups and disguises. Following on from this, the implications of contemporary play spaces, where technology and virtual encounters (such as via social media and online gaming) offer new forms of play and experimentation, are considered.

The overall contention here is that children, through play, engage with and bring their own meanings to societal surveillance in a context where they are already immersed in, and far from oblivious to, the effects of power-relations and the ethical responsibilities these can give rise to. As surveillance technologies become increasingly embedded in children's play environments, and if (as some suggest) the boundaries between 'play' and 'real' surveillance practice are becoming increasingly blurred in new digital play spaces, then it is important to consider how children can continue to find spaces to explore and test out what it is like to be in secret places, watch others unobserved, perhaps even to be 'caught out' and to see/feel the impact on others.

Children's social and political life is seen here as emerging from intersubjective encounters, which they both shape and are shaped by, as they explore and negotiate the world around them. The focus here is not on the extent to which children are recognised as gaining some form of autonomy through their play experiences (c.f. *Nolan et al.*, 2011) that leads to a more 'adult' state of knowledge about surveillance practice. Rather, the emphasis is on exploring how children from an early age are already navigating everyday relations in ways that are rich with meaning-making about the surveillance experiences they engage with. This draws on Prout's discussion on the relationship between children and technology, where he argues for a more open-ended and non-teleological approach to thinking about the ways that:

> technology is formed from, and in turn intermingles with, the biological and social world. In order to understand this it is important to move away from the idea of a determinant process in which one entity, biological, social or technological drives this process. (Prout, 2005: 141)

Looking at the meaning children bring to and derive from their encounters with others as something that is continually being re-made, makes it possible to also see the effects of those actions in shaping and negotiating meaning within the field of power in which these actions are situated (for example, Taylor, 2007). In analysing specific childhood games, I am therefore interested in what these bring to children's engagement with what it means to watch and be watched within a dynamic and complex set of relations and the spaces around them.

In the discussion below, it will become clear how, on the one hand, play can provide a site of transformation and negotiation through which children can build and enact meaning in a way that allows them to come to 'know' what it is that surveillance does. At the same time, surveillance itself brings the potential to threaten the possibilities within children's play experiences by depriving them of the more private and creative spaces needed for experimental and playful encounters with others. I return briefly to the implications of this second point at the end of the chapter.

The transformative potential of children's play

Given the universal tendency for children across cultures and times to engage in play, it seems likely that something important is going on when children are playing (Engel, 2005; Huizinga, 1950). While there is ongoing debate about what 'play' can tell us about children and childhood, here I highlight the transformative role of play to illustrate the connections between a child's play experience and the way children come to understand and engage with the world around them. Huizinga (1950) identified a number of key features of play. Foremost, play is a voluntary activity and, therefore, an activity cannot be considered 'play' if it has arisen from an order to play. Play is also considered totally and intensely absorbing and is enacted within the boundaries of certain limits, rules and order (Huizinga, 1950). While discussion on the nature of children's play has expanded considerably beyond Huizinga's work in recent years (for example, Brooker *et al.*, 2014), there nonetheless remains an often intangible quality to play activity, perhaps best understood through the way that play can accommodate the co-existence of freedom and order, fun and seriousness, clarity and uncertainty, and at the same time perhaps even 'make sense' out of what may appear to others as nonsensical.

In looking at the inter-relationships that emerge in children's play, some have noted the opportunity play provides to engage with the environment, often infusing physical objects, such as sticks and stones, with meaning and possibility beyond what they 'really are' (Jones, 2000). A number of theorists have also analysed the relationship between a child's play world and the 'real' world. Sutton-Smith (1997), for example, described imaginative play as belonging to the 'unreal', in contrast with the 'real' world. Yet, these two spheres need not be seen as entirely distinct. One way to explain this relationship is to consider Ricoeur's (1991) work on the imagination, where he argues that imagination transforms and expands on the real world, rather than simply referring to an 'image' or a 'copy' of that world. In this view, the imagined is more than simply a representation or reproduction of the real world. It is both creative and productive, and opens up a range of possibilities beyond what exists in the real world. This influence is not only one way (Ricoeur, 1991: 134) and, applied to children's play, this would suggest that a child's experience of the 'actual world' is both different and expanded after the child has engaged in imaginative play. It is this productive interaction of meaning across these fluid and often inseparable spheres that highlights the transformative potential of children's play. Notions, such as power, privacy, secrecy, trickery, domination, conflict and deception, can all be given a space for interpretation, action and experimentation in the relative safety of the play sphere, in a way that then intermingles with and becomes part of how the child brings meaning to these in everyday life.

The importance of play does not just relate to the activity itself but to the spaces that permit children the freedom to explore and be absorbed in the act of play. Of particular relevance here is the extent to which children require some sense of privacy or secrecy in which to explore and express themselves in and through play activities. It has been observed that 'children play differently when they do not feel they are being observed' (Opie and Opie, cited in Nolan and McBride, 2013). One of the benefits of privacy is the way it provides a space where there is a 'reprieve from scrutiny and public judgement' (Morris, 2000: 148). As Morris suggests (2000: 333), this space of non-judgement provides an opportunity to behave 'differently, perhaps deviantly'. Whether the behaviour is trivial or daring, what matters is the fact that it is not being judged or analysed. This provides an opportunity to test out and to explore different ways of behaving. Aitken (2001) draws on Morris's formulation of privacy to show that children's play spaces may begin to disappear as children are subject to increasing forms of control, supervision and surveillance. He argues that there are many instances where privacy is a condition of play, and, if children's play spaces are subject to increasing surveillance, then there is likely to be a loss of opportunity for different ways of being and behaving (Aitken, 2001). This is not to suggest that we should view children's play spaces as somehow separate from the world around them, as the interconnections are multiple and fluid, but rather to highlight why it is important for children to have spaces for play that allow for creative experimentation and exploration.

The value of children having spaces away from the adult gaze has been recognised in other ways too. Jones talks of the importance of children being able to create spaces for their own self-expression; that is, 'to spatialize their lives according to their own rather than adult agendas' (Jones, 2000: 30). Moore (2014: 9) shows the importance of 'secret spaces' for young children's well-being – spaces that provide time alone to 'make meanings of their world' or 'a quiet place for reverie and to be able to silently observe without being seen'. The children in Roe's (2007) study talk of the importance of having places to play that adults do not know about and how a messy landscape, where the grass is tall enough to hide in, is a sure sign that adults have not been there for a while. And Bonnett (2014) has highlighted the value of the spaces children create 'in between and around the adult world'. In reflecting on his childhood, he notes '(g)iven half a chance, children create their own nooks in the leftover places of the adult map. We weren't interested in the fields beyond because what we wanted were hidden places that would be bypassed by the adult world' (Bonnett, 2014: 293). A common feature across all these studies is that children seek out space and time to be left alone where they can create their own worlds and meanings. This reiterates the significance of having some privacy in play spaces, where this is understood as providing a reprieve from scrutiny or judgement.

In the discussion below, we can see how children inhabit play spaces and draw on the safety and freedom these afford to explore the possibilities within an intersubjective gaze. This includes what it means to look at or covertly follow another without being seen, at times pushing the boundaries to explore the edges of social acceptance and to understand the impact of one's actions on another.

Children's games: hiding and seeking

One reason for focusing on classic games, such as peek-a-boo and hide-and-seek, is that these games are found in one form or another across diverse geographical and cultural settings. Thus, the games can provide insights into children's play experience in a way that has some applicability across different communities. While it is not suggested that the snapshot of experience analysed here can be generalised too widely, it is noted that there are often similarities in the nature of these games across history, cultures, geographies and social contexts, allowing for some common understanding, although local conventions and adaptions remain significant in more deeply illuminating experiences at the individual level. In a cross-cultural study of peek-a-boo across 17 different countries, for example, it was noted that while it is not possible to make conclusions as to just how widespread this game is, it is possible to observe similarities in the way the game is played:

> Although we cannot conclude on the basis of the available data that mother–infant hiding games are universal across cultures, the striking similarities among the peekaboo routines … suggests that wherever such games *are* found, they will share common structural features. (Fernald and O'Neill, 1993: 268)

Similarly, Opie and Opie's (1969) study of childhood games, based in the United Kingdom, traced multiple versions of hide-and-seek back to the 1600s; and another study conducted in 1930 in the United States found that hide-and-seek was one of the top three games played by children in the 6- to 12-year age group (Foster, 1930). This brief sample, as well as more recent studies, such as the one by Barritt *et al.* (1983) discussed below, attest to the timeless and classic appeal of this particular genre of childhood games that involves some combination of hiding and seeking.

The emphasis here is on considering how these games might afford children a playful opportunity to explore the power-relations and tensions that can be associated with hiding from others, looking at others from a position of hiding, looking for others and being found. Of interest is how these games provide children with a site of affective awareness of what it 'feels like' to be the watcher and the watched, as children explore and engage with the complexity of hiding and seeking, and the potential of these actions to empower, disempower and use information or advantage against others.

Barritt *et al.* (1983) describe a game of peek-a-boo where a young child is caught gazing at a stranger and, on realising he/she has been seen, ducks away and then, cautiously at first, returns to look again. This plays out a number of times, leading to increasing hilarity and delight. In this encounter, the child is not the only one who has the experience of being seen, as the child has also 'caught' the stranger in his/her gaze (Barritt *et al.*, 1983). This encounter is an example of play where 'others slip to the periphery of concern, and both players become unaware of them in their concentration on their presence for one another' (Barritt *et al.*, 1983: 144). The transformative nature of this event lies in the expanded sense of self-awareness and identity that the child (and perhaps the adult, too) emerges with once the connection is broken.

The significance of hiding is not only in what one sees or observes of others but also in what it reveals to and about the self. According to Gibson (2014: 59), to 'hide' is to 'position one's body at a place that is concealed at the points of observation of other observers'. In playing peek-a-boo or hide-and-seek, children are practising what it means to be hidden or unhidden from the point of view of other observers. Importantly though, even when a 'hiding place' affords concealment from other observers, it does not conceal one from oneself (Gibson, 2014). In this sense, hiding (and looking at others) can reveal meaning about the self as well as the others being observed. There are insights into the power dimensions associated with looking that are evident here as well. Kind (2013) reflects on how the act of looking tends to give more power to the person who is doing the looking than to the person being looked at. That is, the object of the gaze is often seen as passive in this relationship. Yet, consistent with Kind's (2013) observations, and as the game of peek-a-boo illustrates, such power relations are not always so straightforward. Here, both child and adult are 'caught' in a playful exchange that defies definition along a simple active/passive polarity of power. This reveals an early engagement with the tensions, resistances and blurred boundaries that may arise within the power of an inter-subjective gaze.

A final point to note is that in playing peek-a-boo, it is not important whether the body is hidden completely. As Barritt *et al.* (1983: 151) suggest, even without the act of complete hiding, the game creates a social dialogue that 'differentiates between looking and being looked at'. What the child learns about looking – how one can look in different ways and the ways others can look – gives the child a growing sense of how they are positioned in the world. The game becomes a demonstration to the child of their power in relation to others and a sense of control they can test out in the safety of a space where they know the adult they are playing with will not really go away (Barritt *et al.*, 1983).

Hide-and-seek is another enduring childhood game that affords opportunities to position and view oneself and others from multiple angles. The children's narratives reported by Barritt *et al.* (1983) show how the game provides a rich opportunity to experience what it is like to hide, to observe without being seen, to know that one is being sought or to not always be sure whether one has been seen. As Opie and Opie (1969: 203) observe:

> few people can feel more tense than the young player as he sets out alone to search for his companions, seeing no one, where a minute before was a mob, yet knowing that every bush and tree may be a mask for a pair of eyes.

This highlights the affective dimension of the experience, as affirmed through the children's accounts reported by Barritt *et al.* (1983), which observed the excitement of sitting still with 'your heart beating so loudly you can hear it in your hiding place' or when hiding with someone else makes a kind of 'solidarity' possible, a 'certain trust'. The experience is not always joyful; one child describes the feeling of being seeker as an 'uncertain feeling that everyone can see me, but I am not able to see them', whereas others describe the anticipation of playing at night time as being afraid or 'terrified', but nonetheless willing or daring themselves through the experience. There is also the 'painful' sense of desertion that comes with someone not coming to find you (Barritt *et al.*, 1983: 147–54). The way children experience this game is, therefore, felt in the body and through the complex, sometimes uncertain, tensions and feelings that surface during the play activity.

From the above, it is possible to see how playing hide-and-seek provides children with both conscious and unconscious ways of coming to understand what it is to be immersed in a world of encounter and sensation (Ellis *et al.*, 2013; Gregg and Seigworth, 2010). It also reveals the body's capacity to both affect and be affected in complex ways through encounters with the world and others. The children's descriptions reflect a clear grappling with the ways their actions are deeply interconnected with the actions and reactions of others. For example, a child who is deserted or left 'unfound' in a game may not fully grasp what has happened, but even an unsettling sensation and momentary confusion can be enough to draw the child's attention to the nature of power and neglect arising from the experience. Playing hide-and-seek, therefore, provides a rich site for a child in coming to explore and experience not only their own responses but also their capacity to affect others and to be/become aware of inter-subjective responsibility this gives rise to.

The emotional and playful potential afforded by both hide-and-seek and peek-a-boo reveals the complexity of different forms of hiding and observing. The tension or thrill that arises in a game of hide-and-seek from the uncertainty as to whether one is being viewed or not is, in part, about being immersed in a series of fluid and shifting patterns of control in the relations between self and others and the affordances of the play spaces. The power associated with hiding and choosing whether or not to reveal oneself can be felt by the child through the responses he/she elicits from others. These types of games therefore bring self-awareness, including an awareness of how one's body is situated in the world, as well as an understanding of others (Barritt *et al.*, 1983; Gibson, 2014). They reveal some of what it means to look at oneself through the eyes of another when the anonymity of aloneness is shattered by the look of another (Barritt *et al.*, 1983). As Barritt *et al.* (1983: 156) observe, 'the essence of the game is to catch with your eyes. To know you are caught is to see yourself being seen, and eye contact is a tension filled event'.

In engaging in these games, children are, therefore, far from passive but are continually making decisions and negotiating the complex relations in and with the spaces around them; for example, the children in Barritt *et al.* (1983) study reveal how they are constantly scanning the places around them as they decide where to hide, whether they will be seen and/or who will they be able to see. The children may look or react, be affected, try to empathise with the position of others in the game and reflect on what responses their own actions might lead to. Whether through shared laughter, fear of rejection, camaraderie, exhilaration or pure relief, in these games children are continually grappling with the rich social and ethical dilemmas that inter-personal acts of concealment and exposure give rise to.

The two games discussed above are just some of the ways that children engage with strategies of hiding and seeking in play. Others, not analysed in detail here, include the way that children play in 'spy roles' that involve secret code writing, spying and disguises that go with this (Travis and Hindley, 2013). Costumes and dress-ups more generally also provide ways for children to explore what it means to take on alternative personas or another identity. In dressing up, children 'conceal' themselves in a different way from simply hiding. Or, as the character in a classic children's tale *Harriet the Spy* observes, if you are a spy, the best disguise may be none at all: 'If you wear spy clothes everyone knows you are a spy so what have you gained? No, you have to look like everyone else, then you'll get by and no one will suspect you' (Fitzhugh, 1964).

Disguises and role play, therefore, also open other opportunities for the child to navigate the boundaries of identity, self and what it is to be another. It is interesting to reflect on these forms of play in the context of modern surveillance practice. Surveillance relies heavily on each individual having a single, 'official', continuing and verifiable identity across all aspects of his/her life. In this context, it is possible to see role playing and dressing up as both subversive and experimental. It refuses the singularity of selfhood as a fixed and non-malleable entity imposed by others. When children have the opportunity and the inclination to play in disguise, to 'become another', they understand and simultaneously reveal to us how 'identity' need not be fixed or attached to a single name or label that can be used by others to exert power over our choices.

This brief exploration into children's games shows how themes of hiding and being hidden can feature in number of different ways. Whether this involves a game of hide and seek, or playing at 'being spy', dressing up or simply gazing at the world from a hidden position up a tree, children seek out vantage points to observe and bring meaning to their place in the world. Experimenting with private or interrupted moments of reverie, being seen and seeing others, means children come to know and attend to what it is like to be watched and the many different ways in which this might happen. Children know this not because they have been told by adults or because there is a single knowable narrative about surveillance practice they can learn, but rather because they are situated in play spaces that are filled with immediate encounters of watching, being watched and having to negotiate one's way around the complex social and ethical dimensions that such relations give rise to.

Emerging play spaces: future considerations

Children's contemporary play spaces provide new sites for engaging with themes of hiding and exposure. I briefly consider here some of the tensions and opportunities that arise as online technologies expand the potential for both surveillance and play in children's lives. A key tension in this discussion is that while online spaces add a new and innovative dimension to children's play, there are also concerns that this comes with increased surveillance over the play activities. Given the significance of private and secret spaces for play discussed earlier, this could alter the potential of these spaces to support rich and experimental forms of play.

While there is little doubt that digital play environments afford new opportunities for large-scale data surveillance of children's play activity, the question of how deeply this impacts on children's freedom to play and their opportunity to experiment with the multiple gazes that lie within these spaces remains more complex. The extent to which children and young people are able to circumvent, 'play with' or resist the surveillance gaze has been raised elsewhere (Hope, 2005; Koskela, 2004; Regan and Steeves, 2010; Rooney, 2012). Whitson and Simon (2014: 312) also draw on the notion of play as a lens through which to question the claims of those who construct 'surveillance imaginaries' of subjects as completely controlled and knowable. As Whitson and Simon point out, while these processes of control can be applied at the macro level through comprehensive data collection, monitoring and tracking, they do not take into account the fact that players may not be as 'knowable' as these data collection practices imply. That is, players, 'more often than not, tend to be more unruly than the rules of their game would pretend them to be' (Whitson and Simon, 2014: 313). One playful affordance of online spaces is that being 'watcher' can become an empowering and liberating reversal of roles. As Koskela (2004) notes, webcams and mobile technologies provide ways for individuals to make themselves visible to others, not at the whim of external forces but as a playful form of self-representation and a liberation from the 'need to hide'.

Despite these messy, unruly and liberating features of children's online play, there remains a risk that as these play spaces become saturated with a surveillance presence, children will have less chance to explore the tensions and complexities around identity, privacy and what it means to watch and be watched. For example, if a child is required to register with his/her 'real' identity to play an online game, or if the information a child shares in a game is designed primarily to fulfil a marketing need (Marx and Steeves, 2010), then the peculiar order and rules of the 'play' sphere have become dictated by what lies outside and the spaces for exploration and testing out of ideas may be diminished.

One important factor to take into account is that children's play environments are never really exclusively 'online', as this play is still connected to, interwoven with and increasingly inseparable from children's local, embodied and often highly social context. As an example, Nolan and McBride (2013) remind us that when children are playing online, they are often situated in an 'in-room' gaming environment, a space co-located with friends or family with whom the children interact with while also playing. These are 'flexible and familiar spaces that are often repurposed and organised by children' (Nolan and McBride, 2013: 11). Therefore, if we understand digital play environments as part of an extension of the wider situated context of children's social interactions and play encounters, then we can also see how these spaces may continue to afford children multiple opportunities to navigate and negotiate issues relating to identity, control and decisions on how and when to interact with virtual others.

Wide-scale surveillance brings to children's play spaces the potential to more readily control, monitor and dictate the conditions for play. Despite or in spite of these developments, there are a number of reasons to be optimistic that children will continue to find and claim spaces for play; spaces that lie at the margins or that are perhaps 'visible yet hidden' from adults who remain unaware of the constructed meanings that prevail or move through the space (for example, Moore, 2014).

The first reason lies with children themselves. Jones reminds us how children are 'play opportunists' who have a 'remarkable capacity for responding to shifting, unexpected, often fleeting opportunities for expression' (Jones, 2000: 41). Further, '(s)et against these rather pessimistic agencies of control is the seemingly irrepressible capacity in children to transform and possess the materials and spaces with which, and in which they find themselves' (Cloke and Jones, 2005).

Even in digital play environments, it has been observed that the attraction to children of digital play is not (as often thought) just in the 'game' features provided by the technology but rather that the engagement 'resides within the player's lived and embodied sociocultural identity and her own situated contexts for playing a game' (Nolan and McBride, 2013: 4). The second reason for optimism lies in the over-stated totality of the surveillance gaze that, contrary to the impression often created, can only ever provide a partial view. Even when performing at optimum levels, the reality is that surveillance devices can only still offer a particular perspective of a child's activities. That is:

> In order for something to be made observable at all, other things – certain fields that are ambiguously linked to observation and organise it in a certain way – drop out of the same observation. In brief, the paradox emerges that by means of producing something (an observation), we unwillingly also produce its opposite (concealing). (Katti, 2002: 53)

In exposing the false sense of 'completeness' portrayed by an all-seeing gaze, it is therefore possible to open up important sites of playful resistance that may be occupied by children seeking hidden spaces to play. The final reason for optimism noted here is the nature of the changing contemporary play space itself. While there are many instances where online companies, such as Facebook and Google, try to insist on individuals using their 'real' identity, there is an equally greater proliferation of websites that allow alternative identities, such as avatars, and in this way provide forms of 'concealment' or hiding within which children can experiment and play.

The potential opportunities and limitations of online play are still unfolding. Virtual spaces are still mostly built and designed by adults; that is, they are generally 'grown up creations: manicured spaces with very strict rules and a limited number of options' (Bonnett, 2014: 296). They are also subject to large-scale data collection practices, such as those imposed by governments or used by marketing companies. Nonetheless, it would appear that even within this changing landscape, there are spaces where children find some degree of privacy from the adult world to explore, bring meaning to and engage with the complexities of the world around them. As long as there are spaces that lie outside the field of vision of an adult gaze, then children will find sites for play, exploration and resistance. The way children play with surveillance themes or exploit weaknesses in the technology itself will further open up ways to understand and resist the motivations behind surveillance practices. In this way, children's play is likely to continue to offer pathways of resistance to larger-scale forms of surveillance that might otherwise limit or oppress playful inter-subjective encounters.

Conclusion

This discussion shows how one of the most powerful ways that children come to understand the potential complexities of a surveillance gaze is through the encounters of hiding and seeking that take place within everyday childhood games. Far from being passive subjects of an 'all-knowing' gaze, children from an early age are shown to be actively engaged with the meanings illuminated by playful perspectives of what it is to be both watcher and watched. Of particular significance are the spaces that lie outside, or at the fringes of, the adult gaze, as it is here that children create their own worlds and meanings. Ironically perhaps, it is in the spaces outside the surveillance gaze that children may be able to best grapple with the complex social and ethical dimensions that they are likely to encounter in a society where the surveillance gaze is becoming more pervasive.

References

Aitken, S. (2001) *Geographies of young people: the morally contested spaces of identity*. London: Routledge.

Barritt, L., T. Beekman, H. Bleeker and K. Mulderij (1983) 'The world through children's eyes: hide and seek and peekaboo', *Phenomenology + Pedagogy*, 1(2): 140–61.

Bonnett, A. (2014). *Off the map: lost spaces, invisible cities, forgotten islands, feral places, and what they tell us about the world*. London: Aurum Press.

Brooker, L., M. Blaise and S. Edwards (eds.) (2014) *SAGE handbook of play and learning in early childhood*. London: Sage Publications.

Cloke, P. and O. Jones (2005) '"Unclaimed territory": childhood and disordered space(s)', *Social and Cultural Geography*, 6(3): 311–33.

Ellis, D., I. Tucker and D. Harper (2013) 'The affective atmospheres of surveillance', *Theory and Psychology*, 23(6): 716–31.

Engel, S. (2005) *Real kids: creating meaning in everyday life*. Cambridge, MA: Harvard University Press.

Fernald, A. and D. O'Neill (1993) 'Peekaboo across cultures: how mothers and infants play with voices, faces and expressions', in K. MacDonald (ed.), *Parent-child play: descriptions and implications*. New York: State University of New York Press.

Fitzhugh, L. (1964) *Harriet the spy*. New York: Harper and Row.

Foster, J. (1930) 'Play activities of children in the first six grades', *Child Development*, 1(3): 248–54.

Gibson, J. J. (2014) 'The theory of affordances', in J. J. Gieseking and W. Mangold (eds.), *The people, place, and space reade*. New York and London: Routledge.

Gregg, M. and G. Seigworth (eds.) (2010) *The affect theory reader*. Durham, NC: Duke University Press.

Hope, A. (2005) 'Panopticism, play and the resistance of surveillance: case studies of the observation of student Internet use in UK schools', *British Journal of Sociology*, 26(3): 359–73.

Huizinga, J. (1950) *Homo Ludens: a study of the play element in culture*. Boston: Becon Press.

Jones, O. (2000) 'Melting geography: purity, disorder, childhood and space', in S. Holloway and G. Valentine (eds.), *Children's geographies: playing, living and learning*. London and New York: Routledge.

Katti, C. (2002) '"Systematically" observing surveillance: paradoxes of observation according to Niklas Luhmann's systems theory', in T. Y. Levin and U. Frohne (eds.), *CTRL[SPACE]: rhetorics of surveillance from Bentham to Big Brother*. Cambridge, MA: MIT Press.

Kind, S. (2013) 'Lively entanglements: the doings, movements and enactments of photography', *Global Studies of Childhood*, 3(4): 427–41.

Koskela, H. (2004) 'Webcams, TV shows and mobile phones: empowering exhibitionism', *Surveillance and Society*, 2(2/3): 199–215.

Lyon, D. (2001) *Surveillance society: monitoring everyday life*. Buckingham: Open University Press.

Marx, G. T. and V. Steeves (2010) 'From the beginning: children as subjects and agents of surveillance', *Surveillance and Society*, 7(3/4): 192–230.

Monahan, T. (ed.) (2006) *Surveillance and security: technological politics and power in everyday life*. New York: Routledge.

Monahan, T. and R. D. Torres (eds.) (2010) *Schools under surveillance: cultures of control in public education*. New Brunswick, NJ: Rutgers University Press.

Moore, D. (2014) '"The teacher doesn't know what it is, but she knows where we are": young children's secret places in early childhood outdoor environments', *International Journal of Play*, 4(1): 20–31.

Morris, D. (2000) 'Privacy, privation and perversity: toward new representations of the personal', *Signs*, 25(2): 323–52.

Nolan, J. and M. McBride (2013) 'Beyond gamification: reconceptualizing game-based learning in early childhood environments', *Information, Communication and Society*, 17(15): 594–608.

Nolan, J., K. Raynes-Goldie and M. McBride (2011) 'The stranger danger: exploring surveillance, autonomy, and privacy in children's use of social media', *Canadian Children: Journal of the Canadian Association for Young Children*, 36: 24–32.

Opie, I. and P. Opie (1969) *Children's games in street and playground* (2013 ed.). Edinburgh: Floris Books.

Prout, A. (2005) *The future of childhood: towards the interdisciplinary study of children*. London and New York: Routledge.

Regan, P. and V. Steeves (2010) 'Kids r us: online social networking and the potential for empowerment', *Surveillance and Society*, 8(2): 151–65.

Ricoeur, P. (1991) 'The function of fiction in shaping reality', in M. J. Valdes (ed.), *A Ricoeur reader: reflection and imagination*. Brighton: Harvester/Wheatsheaf.

Roe, M. (2007) 'Feeling "secrety": children's views on involvement in landscape decisions', *Environmental Education Research*, 13(4): 467–85.

Rooney, T. (2012) 'Childhood spaces in a changing world: exploring the intersection between children and new surveillance technologies', *Global Studies of Childhood*, 2(4): 331–42.

Sutton-Smith, B. (1997) *The ambiguity of play*. Cambridge, MA: Harvard University Press.

Taylor, A. (2007) 'Playing with difference: the cultural politics of childhood belonging', *International Journal of Diversity in Organisations, Communities and Nations*, 7(3): 143–9.

Taylor, E. (2013) *Surveillance schools: security, disipline and control in contemporary education*. Basingstoke, UK: Palgrave Macmillan.

Travis, F. and J. Hindley (2013) *The knowhow book of spycraft*. London: Usborne Books.

Whitson, J. (2013) 'Gaming and the quantified self', *Surveillance and Society*, 11(1/2): 163–76.

Whitson, J. and B. Simon (2014) 'Game studies meets surveillance studies at the edge of digital culture: an introduction to a special issue on surveillance, games and play', *Surveillance and Society*, 12(3): 309–19.

12 World of Spycraft

Video games, gamification and surveillance creep

Andrew Hope

Under the playful headline 'World of Spycraft', it was reported in December 2013 that the United States National Security Agency (NSA) and its United Kingdom counterpart were potentially conducting extensive covert surveillance in online gaming domains, such as *World of Warcraft* (WoW), *Second Life* and *Xbox Live* (*New York Times*, 2013). According to government papers released by former NSA contractor Edward Snowden, such activity was undertaken in response to the fear that terrorist or criminal organisations could use the games to communicate secretly, recruit members, move money and plot attacks. As Whitson and Simon (2014: 311) argue, the revelations in these documents clearly indicate 'that there is an imagination of possibilities for digital games in the context of the surveillance state apparatus'.

In the subsequent public discussion, there was an outcry among online gamers about the government's invasion of privacy, but little mention of the extensive information routinely gathered, stored and utilised by the gaming companies. Nor was it emphasised that participants within video games were already engaged in extensive 'spying' through gaming community management, peer surveillance and player-produced texts. While recognising that the aforementioned NSA activities should not be lightly dismissed, this chapter explores the extent to which networked video games and digital gamification result in the growth of surveillance, suggesting that the 'world of spycraft' is not merely a state enterprise.

In neoliberal societies, the use of surveillance technologies has grown exponentially. Children are socialised into accepting and even welcoming market-driven monitoring into almost every aspect of their everyday lives. Using the notion of surveillance creep (Marx, 1988), this chapter explores how children's use of gamified devices and video games has increasingly become embroiled in practices of almost relentless monitoring. After providing a brief background to gamification and video game surveillance, the focus of the chapter shifts to the concept of surveillance creep. Three threads emerge from this discussion, which partly explain the growing encroachment of surveillance practices into video gaming: the notions of responsibilisation, desensitisation and marketisation. Ultimately, it is concluded that surveillance creep is a process deeply intertwined with political, economic and social pressures, which nevertheless offers the hope of resistance.

Importantly, it might be asked whether surveillance in gamespace matters. Networked games often involve role-playing and experimentation, meaning that what is being monitored might be children's identity play (Turkle, 1995). Moreover, the data gathered may be seen as more frivolous than that collected by government bodies. Ultimately, as Whitson (2013: 173) suggests, although consumer-monitoring devices may foster the creation of neoliberal, responsibilised citizens, individuals can always exit the game at any point. Yet, there is something disconcerting about the manner in which surveillance creep through online gaming contributes to ever expanding 'big data'. Networked video games are complicit in 'collecting and collating massive databases of seemingly trivial data in the hopes of inferring hidden patterns and correlations in human behaviour that then can be used to profile subjects, predict their actions, and to act upon them accordingly' (Whitson and Simon, 2014: 313). Whitson (2013) infers that gamified surveillance is not necessarily 'bad' or 'evil'. Rather, such judgements are dependent on the manner in which they intrude into everyday lives and how the data collected are utilised. Nevertheless, responsibilisation through online play is occurring, people are becoming desensitised to everyday monitoring practices and corporate surveillance is smuggled into seductive participatory gaming experiences.

Surveillance, video games and gamification

In late modernity, the term 'surveillance' is commonly used to denote the monitoring of behaviour, activities and information for the purpose of informing, influencing and managing individuals or groups (Lyon, 2007). Surveillance 'both enables and constrains, involves care and control' (Lyon, 2001: 3). Yet, it can also play a key role in young people's identity formation, while offering new opportunities for entertainment. In the latter category, amusement is to be found in watching people, engaging in a 'skilled' performance for others to observe and discussing the activities seen. Indeed, these three elements form a key part of many children's game-playing experiences. Consider the blocky freeform building game Minecraft in which children can play together online, post messages on forums and watch YouTube videos of others gaming. Peer surveillance and feedback is a central element of its entertainment appeal.

Yet, monitoring video game player behaviour is not merely concerned with pleasure. As Canossa (2014: 433) notes, since the installation of Computer Space, the first commercially sold coin-operated video game, designers have 'spent considerable time watching people play, [and] the practice of observing players has become a cornerstone of game development'. From the late 1990s, sophisticated game telemetry started to emerge, entailing the automatic, remote gathering of video game play data. Such data-gathering processes expanded exponentially thereafter. Thus, as O'Donnell (2014: 350) notes:

> [G]ames cannot help but surveil the user … they increasingly store data in a variety of locations. … A player's in-game avatar can be customized on a mobile device, the character's inventory managed from a website and the

game played on a console or personal computer. Each of these interactions inherently involves the monitoring and storage of information about the player.

Such surveillance is undertaken to improve the gaming experience and increase corporate revenue, with the latter concern often taking precedence (Canossa, 2014: 435). Ultimately, 'video gaming is informatics …[a]s such, video games are synonymous with the forms of technology driving the burgeoning information age and the changing forms of social life and political control it engenders' (Welsh, 2007: 1). Video games are an intrinsic part of the surveillance society.

While video games are inherently intertwined with surveillance activities, the rationale for undertaking such monitoring can be complex, multi-faceted and situational. This analysis becomes more complicated when considering what constitutes a video game. In simple terms, it is an electronic game played by manipulating images produced by a computer program on a display. Yet, such a broad definition creates difficulties, particularly as social media and networking sites increasingly incorporate 'game elements' into their products. In recent years, the emergence of 'gamification' has raised further questions concerning conceptual boundaries. As Deterding *et al.* (2011: 11) observe 'the boundary between game and artifact with game elements can often be blurry. … To complicate matters, this boundary is empirical, subjective and social'. Moreover, as new regimes of self-care and monitoring have proliferated as a result of the gamified Quantified Self (QS) movement, any analysis of the surveillance of children's networked gaming activities would be inadequate if it did not include such broader digital elements of their lives.

Although the practice of gamification has a long history (for example, rewards for good school grades and merit badges in youth organisations), it wasn't until 2010 that the term became widely adopted. While it is often defined as the use of game design components (such as points, badges and leaderboards) in non-game contexts, it nevertheless remains a contested term within the game industry and game studies. This partly reflects a view that rewards should not be seen as the same as game mechanics. Deterding *et al.* (2011: 10) note that gamification is used by industry in one of two ways: either to reference 'the increasing adoption, institutionalization and ubiquity of (video) games in everyday life' or, more specifically, as motivational technology 'to make other, non-game products and services more enjoyable and engaging as well'. Focusing on the second element of this definition, Burke (2014) suggests that it should be seen as the use of game mechanics and design to digitally engage and motivate people to achieve their goals.

Such a conceptualisation raises two points. First, Burke (2014) argues that in contemporary society, gamification should be used to refer solely to digital engagement, utilising technologies such as computers, smartphones, wearable monitors and other digital devices. He asserts that a definition that includes non-digital gamification misses the defining feature of this current trend. Second, Burke's (2014) definition allows for the possibility that video games themselves can be gamified. This is a highly contentious point and one that is seen by many to undermine the value of the concept itself. After all, pursuing this argument to its logical conclusion, it could be argued that everything in modern life could be perceived as a 'game' (Wark, 2007). Nevertheless, Burke's (2014) notion of gamification usefully encourages an exploration of digital games and gamification, without raising distracting questions as to where definitional boundaries between the two should lie.

Surveillance creep

Gary Marx (1988) coined the term 'surveillance creep' in his classic work *Undercover: Police Surveillance in America*. In this book, he noted that '[a]s powerful new surveillance tactics are developed, the range of their legitimate and illegitimate use is likely to spread. … There is the danger of an almost imperceptible surveillance creep' (Marx, 1988: 2). While this term could describe the general encroachment of monitoring practices in everyday life, it has been used more specifically to refer to situations where surveillance technologies introduced for a particular purpose are subsequently utilised for an entirely different end. For example, closed circuit television cameras were legally authorised in certain public spaces in the UK to counter terrorism; yet, were also used by local authorities to regulate people putting their garbage out for collection on the wrong day, littering, public urination, dog fouling, the posting of flyers and anti-social driving (Haggerty, 2012: 241).

Although not strictly synonymous, surveillance creep is often closely associated with Winner's (1977) notion of 'function creep', that is, the gradual expansion of the use of a particular technology beyond the purpose for which it was originally intended. Thus, social games, such as Candy Crush Saga, use gaming data in a more sophisticated way, not only to gather data to improve game play but also to sell targeted products, such as in-game purchases (Vie, 2014). In this context, surveillance creep occurs as companies use existing game telemetry not merely to improve their product but also to engage in new forms of marketing. Such 'creeping' helps to partly explain why monitoring technologies and related practices have spread to almost every corner of children's lives.

Marx (1988: 3) also suggests that '[t]he new forms of social control tend to be subtle, invisible, scattered, and involuntary. They are often not defined as surveillance, and many people … are barely conscious of them … these conditions represent the normal order of things'. This hints that surveillance creep may, upon occasion, be a covert process with people failing to recognise that monitoring technologies are even being utilised. Consequently, it might be asked whether gamers even realise that their online play is being monitored and, if so, whether they are aware of the true extent of such surveillance. Reflecting on such furtive undercurrents, Graham and Wood (2007: 220) infer that there is often little political and economic discussion around the widening use of surveillance devices once installed, with systems integration presented as necessary and inevitable.

Barnard-Wills (2012a) draws attention to a further element of surveillance creep, namely, its potential to be eerie and disturbing. Highlighting the possible emotional impact of surveillance that contravenes social conventions and norms, he asserts that 'changes to the way that social networks work can come across as potentially creepy when they reveal the amount of information that a network has, leverages the information in new, often unexpected ways or increases the amount of information it collects' (Barnard-Wills, 2012a). Of course, surveillance creep need not be sinister or alarming, and in situations where it is covert, no psychological response would be expected. Yet, as surveillance technologies permeate even mundane aspects of everyday lives, it would be wise to consider that such encroachment might have an emotional cost.

In exploring surveillance creep in video gaming, questions arise regarding why and how such processes occur. A detailed analysis would need to examine economic pressures, legal permissions and processes of commodification, to name just a few factors (see Hope, 2015a). Out of this complex tapestry, it is possible to identify key elements, emerging threads worthy of further consideration. In this context, the impact of responsibilisation, desensitisation and marketisation in the burgeoning of video game surveillance will be briefly considered. Whilst these concepts will not provide an exhaustive explanation of surveillance creep in online gaming, it is asserted that they will cast some light on the socio-economic forces at play, offering insights that can be used to explore similar processes in other areas of everyday life.

Responsibilisation, e-safety and health

Surveillance often occurs on gaming sites aimed at younger children to protect them from possible online dangers. In such cases, moderators paid by the gaming companies are often used. Indeed, Merrifield *et al.* (2007) estimated that almost three-quarters of Club Penguin staff were employed in this capacity. Gamers are also persuaded to police behaviour and take responsibility not just for their own actions but those of others as well. In this context, responsibilisation emerges as a key element of video game surveillance creep, wherein children are increasingly encouraged to police 'inappropriate' online play from a growing litany of supposed misdemeanours.

The theoretical roots of responsibilisation can be found in the work of Foucault (1994) on governmentality, Cohen's (1985) consideration of the diffusion of discipline and Rose and Millar's (1992) examination of the operation of the neoliberal state. It is used to describe strategies that attempt to shift certain liabilities away from the state through encouraging individuals to see social risks, such as ill health, crime, poverty and unemployment, as issues of self-care rather than purely the responsibility of the state. Thus, Barnard-Wills suggests (2012b: 247) that through e-safety initiatives, the government seeks to make both children and their parents responsible for appropriate online conduct. Children become co-opted into surveillance work through responsibilisation. This can engender surveillance creep as existing technologies are used to facilitate new ways of watching.

Codes of conduct on gaming sites can be seen as attempts to encourage self-policing, while placing the impetus upon children to play an active role in protecting themselves online. Moreover, online e-safety policies may seek to encourage children to report incidents of inappropriate use (Hope, 2015b), encouraging peer surveillance. Club Penguin does this explicitly through encouraging children to become 'secret agents' who can undertake secret missions and '[r]eport any players that are using bad language, being mean, cheating, or breaking any of the other rules' (Club Penguin, 2009). This is not to reject that surveillance undertaken by players and 'game master' volunteers in Massively Multiplayer Online Games (MMOGs), such as WoW, Eve and Tibia, 'can be empowering and playful' (Kerr *et al.*, 2014: 332) but rather to highlight that surveillance creep may be occurring. Online play becomes networked spying. Drawing on Barnard-Wills's (2012a) insights, it might be asked whether there is something inherently 'creepy' in encouraging children, however playfully, to become 'secret agents'. Such a practice might appear to be an imaginatively labelled e-safety strategy, but given the relentless creep of surveillance, it could also be an early step to a lifetime of informing on people.

Parents are also subjected to responsibilisation. Under increasing pressure to observe their children's online activities, a failure to do so leaves them open to accusations of being poor guardians. Hence, it is common for gaming websites aimed at younger children to include statements encouraging parental surveillance in their consent forms, such as 'we encourage you to monitor and supervise your child's Internet activities during his or her exploration of our site' (Neopets, n.d.). Furthermore, some gaming websites allow parents to set up a separate account so that they can monitor and control the online activities of their offspring. Such online surveillance is potentially open-ended and could grow exponentially. Monitoring might start simply with parents checking that their children's gaming friends are 'suitable'; next, they might read their children's private messages; before long, they might be lurking online, watching real-time interactions. Whilst this might be a somewhat sensationalist description of possible events, it hints at how surveillance protocols introduced so that parents can safeguard children might be subsequently misused to spy upon mundane online gaming activities.

One of the most recent trends in the responsibilisation of children's play is the use of gamified high-tech sensors to monitor exercise and food intake. For example, LeapBand is a wearable activity tracker aimed at 4- to 7-year-olds, which gives commands, such as 'wiggle like a worm' or 'pop like popcorn'. Through completing these tasks, children accrue points that can be used to unlock new content. Such self-surveillance is not only encouraged at home. Some US school districts are giving students pedometers to ensure that they meet their gym class's physical activity requirement (Associated Press, 2014). These types of gamification encourage self-surveillance, enrolling individuals into self-governance through combining aspirations and entertainment. Thus, gamification technologies operate under the umbrella of play while 'providing feedback on how to better care for one's self' (Whitson, 2013: 167). Responsibilisation through the use of game incentives and pleasure is seen as effective in shaping desirable behaviours. Yet, such devices also mean that student physical activity can be monitored outside of schools. Linked to other digital devices, they can provide information about the wanderings of students. The creep of surveillance reaches far beyond school grounds.

It is not only activity trackers that have helped to extend gamified responsibilisation. Game applications, such as the Nintendo Wii Fit and Microsoft's Xbox Fitness, capture real-life movements, seeking to record and visualise 'health measures', such as heart rate, calories burned and body mass index. Although children might be merely eager to play video games, the monitoring capacity of such devices can be seen as socialising individuals into new modes of self-policing, while 'normalising' certain measures of the 'healthy body'. Surveillance of the body sneaks into video game play.

Desensitisation, datafication and the viewer society

In simple terms, desensitisation is the process whereby someone becomes less affected by something. While it is not the same as being unaware, which describes ignorance of a situation, it is possible for desensitisation to ultimately foster a certain degree of ignorance on a subject. This distinction may be important when trying to distinguish whether people are desensitised to surveillance creep in video games or merely unaware of it; nevertheless, the outcome might be the same.

The fascination of the masses with a host of 'reality television' programmes and 'fly on the wall' documentaries partly explain why people are surveillance tolerant. The cultural significance of surveillance as play is illustrated in video games, such as Watch Dogs, the Splinter Cell series and the Grand Theft Auto franchise, where missions within the games necessitate player characters engaging in monitoring activities. At the same time that individuals are becoming less sensitised to the intrusion of surveillance practices into their everyday lives, the amount of data gathered through online play is growing. This surveillance creep is a consequence of expansive game metrics as well as licences enabling the gaming companies to engage in extensive data gathering and use.

Game telemetry is an important part of the online surveillance process. Consider the location-based mobile game (LBMG) Ingress that uses players' geospatial coordinates and social networking to facilitate cooperative play in subduing an invasion of 'alien matter'. Digital devices, GPS, social media and Google Glass are utilised not only to track physical and online encounters but also to record observations and communicative output. Hence, players must submit to datafication of their movements in public and private spaces. This opens up new modes of governing the mobile playing subject. As Hulsey and Reeves (2014: 389) suggest, through the game mechanics, an LBMG 'encourages players to actively participate in a surveillance community while also normalizing data mining and surveillance as a valid exchange for the privilege of play'. Gamers are not only increasingly desensitised to surveillance but also offer ever more detailed personal information so that they can play. Location-based games, such as Ingress, Botfighters, Mogi and Foursquare, result in conspicuous mobility (Wilson, 2012), as players are encouraged to share their location online. Such willing engagement in surveillance practices is not just a result of desensitisation but also reflects that '[i]n and outside of the video game world, pervasive datafication is becoming a necessary condition of digital sociability' (Hulsey and Reeves, 2014: 396). In this situation, surveillance creep may offer the promise of accumulating cultural capital.

Almost as significant as video game metrics in the surveillance of children's online play is commercial organisation's right to gather, store and analyse the data produced. Companies' legal capacities to engage in such activities are often enshrined in end-user licence agreements. These almost always contain a clause permitting the gathering of user data (Canossa, 2014: 435). Thus, Xbox Live Terms of Use (Microsoft, 2014) includes the conditions that 'Microsoft parties may use, track, store, copy, distribute, broadcast, transmit, publicly display and perform, and reproduce' an extensive range of game-related data, including scores, 'your game play sessions', 'your presence', time spent playing, 'statistics' and '*other usage information*'. The final catch-all covers any game-related use omitted from the lengthy list. To leave players in no doubt, it is affirmed that '[w]e may use these permissions without notice or compensation to you of any kind' (Microsoft, 2014). The majority of online gamers unquestioningly accept such terms, often without reading them. Agreeing to such extensive surveillance is a price to be paid for playing the games. Ultimately, without sympathetic laws, surveillance creep might still occur, but it would be difficult to defend from subsequent legal action.

Marketisation and corporate surveillance

For Foucault (2008: 132), neoliberalism involves 'permanent vigilance, activity, and intervention', as behaviour becomes increasingly defined and regulated through marketisation. This is manifested in the 'roll-back' of the traditional state and the 'roll-out' of competition. Thus, under neoliberalism, 'forms of surveillance and regulation that are designed to inject market principles of competition into all spheres of social and cultural life' (Gane, 2012: 625) become rife. In this context, networked video games and gamification are not just technologies that normalise increasingly invasive surveillance practices but also ways of facilitating the permeation of market principles into everyday life.

In a neoliberal society where the market penetrates all aspects of life, gamers routinely exchange their personal data for consumer perks, such as recommendations, discounts and rewards (Hulsey and Reeves, 2014). For example, information generated by the Nike+ gamified running program is used to target marketing of related products. Long-term data about health, recreational activities, purchasing histories and relationships enable companies to ensnare more consumers through nuanced, specialised targeting of their sales pitch. Furthermore, LBMGs, like Ingress, not only allow for players' activities to be monitored but can also redirect individuals through targeted commercial spaces. Sending hungry players to restaurants may help boost food sales, while generating extra income for the gaming company through commissions. Surveillance creep can be profitable as the data gathered is used in new ways.

Such practices not only encourage individuals to consume more but also seek to increasingly commodify children's online activities. Gamers are also manipulated to privilege behaviours that conform to the needs of neoliberal capitalism:

> [S]ocial networking sites – like Club Penguin, Webkinz and Neopets – are modeled on a system of commerce that includes stores, a service industry, job opportunities and currency (including a banking system, a stock market and daily inflation reports, in the case of Neopets) … they encourage children to believe that the objective of play and social interaction is to acquire consumer goods. (Steeves, 2012: 357)

Thus, within such games, children are not merely encouraged to engage in surveillance, of themselves, their consumer opportunities and a faux economic system but are also socialised into monitoring practices that are central to the neoliberal economies. This could be labelled as commercial function creep. Through online play, young people learn to engage in new surveillance opportunities that adapt to the current needs of the market.

As control is devolved from the state to the market, corporations collect greater amounts of consumer data so that they can more effectively develop and market their products. Indeed, the technologies used for corporate surveillance are increasingly sophisticated and their use grows as operating costs fall. Kerr *et al.* (2014) describe how, in the MMOG Tibia, volunteers who monitored and punished rule violations were replaced by monitoring software. Thus, automatic tools of hierarchical surveillance are increasingly introduced, undermining processes of participatory surveillance, disempowering gaming communities. Consequently, the nature of surveillance changes, through processes of relentless, automatic, embedded data-gathering processes, online gaming starts to morph into something that appears increasingly like a panspectron. DeLanda coined the term 'panspectron' in his consideration of a surveillance system that the NSA was constructing towards the end of the twentieth century. He describes a network that utilises a 'multiplicity of sensors' to 'feed into its computers all the information that can be gathered' that is 'then processed through a series of filters' (DeLanda, 1991: 206). At the heart of the panspectron model lies the possibility of ubiquitous surveillance: 'The Panspectron does not merely select certain bodies and certain (visual) data about them. Rather, it compiles information about all at the same time, using computers to select the segments of data relevant to its surveillance tasks' (DeLanda, 1991: 206).

While it is an exaggeration to assert that surveillance of online gaming can be seen as a contemporary panspectron, the concept is still useful in drawing attention to the extensive range of data gathered, which then await whatever interrogations are subsequently deemed appropriate. It points the way towards mass datafication and the ever-present promise (or threat) of data interrogation. Whereas individuals might object when governments pursue such strategies, corporate surveillance appears to offer a soft form of coercion. As Hulsey and Reeves (2014: 397) observe, 'unabashed corporate surveillance is smuggled into seductive forms of participatory play'. Consumers exchange access to their personal data for the 'gift of play'. Indeed, it could be argued that the panspectron might be the endgame of surveillance creep.

Conclusion

Advanced metrics embedded in networked video games and gamified devices have extended the reach of surveillance technologies further into the spaces that children play. It has been argued that increased responsibilisation, desensitisation and marketisation have facilitated processes of surveillance creep. It is on such foundations that a 'world of spycraft' could be built. The abrasive, coercive surveillance of the state partly gives way to the soft, seductive persuasion of corporate monitoring. Online gaming domains offer possibly the most accommodating of spaces in which to start harvesting children's growing data profiles. Much of the information gathered might have no immediate, evident use, but this is a long game. Persistent mundane datafication hints at the colonisation of the future, the suggestion of data interrogation to come.

If such thoughts seem depressing, it is important to remember that there always exists the possibility of resistance (Foucault, 1978). After all, play is a type of 'free activity', inspiring improvisation both within and beyond rule-governed behaviour (Schechner, 1994: 21). It can involve the inventive dissembling of social boundaries, confusing distinctions between real and unreal, creating possibilities of being. Thus, as Turner (1983: 233) notes, '[p]layfulness is a volatile sometimes explosive essence'. Monitoring children's online play may be far from a simple technological endeavour. Indeed, such acts of surveillance might create spaces within which children can develop strategies to resist invasive observation. Responsibilisation, desensitisation and marketisation within networked gaming might ultimately be rejected, as playful resistance becomes the new game. It could be imagined that in the 'world of spycraft', acting becomes the norm, secrets are jealously guarded and everyone practises espionage.

References

Associated Press (2014) 'Marshalltown, Iowa, school district to give students pedometers', 17 Feb. Available online at www.omaha.com/news/marshalltown-iowa-school-district-to-give-students-pedometers/article_658d4a45-7906-5790-8567-9b0ca0565506.html (accessed 19.09.2014).

Barnard-Wills, D. (2012a) 'Epistemology of creep', *Surveillance and Identity*. Available online at http://surveillantidentity.blogspot.com.au/2012/05/epistemology-of-creep.html (accessed 19.02.2015).

Barnard-Wills, D. (2012b) 'E-safety education: young people, surveillance and responsibility', *Criminology and Criminal Justice*, 12(3): 239–55.

Burke, B. (2014) *Gamify: how gamification motivates people to do extraordinary things*. Brookline, MA: Bibliomotion.

Canossa, A. (2014) 'Reporting from the snooping trenches: changes in attitudes and perceptions towards behavior tracking in digital games', *Surveillance and Society*, 12(3): 433–6.

Club Penguin (2009) 'Factual information spy handbook'. Available online at http://archives.clubpenguinwiki.info/swf.cpcheats.info/catalogues/old_2009/fish.swf (accessed 29.10.2014).

Cohen, S. (1985) *Visions of social control*. Cambridge: Polity Press.

DeLanda, M. (1991) *War in the age of intelligent machines*. New York: Zone.

Deterding, S., D. Dixon, R. Khaled and L. Nacke (2011) 'From game design elements to gamefulness: defining gamification', *Proceedings from MindTrek '11*. Tampere: ACM.

Foucault, M. (1978) *The history of sexuality, vol. 1: an introduction*. Harmondsworth: Penguin.

Foucault, M. (1994) 'Governmentality', in *Power: essential works of Foucault 1954–1984*, ed. J. Faubion. London: Penguin.

Foucault, M. (2008) *The birth of biopolitics: lectures at the Collège de France, 1978–1979*. Basingstoke, UK: Palgrave Macmillan.

Gane, N. (2012) 'The governmentalities of neoliberalism: panopticism, post-panopticism and beyond', *Sociological Review*, 60(4): 611–34.

Graham, S. and D. Wood (2007) 'Digitizing surveillance: categorization, space, inequality', in S. Hier and J. Greenberg (eds), *The surveillance studies reader*. Maidenhead, UK: Open University Press.

Haggerty, D. (2012) 'Surveillance, crime and the police', in D. Lyon, K. D. Haggerty and K. Ball (eds), *The international handbook of surveillance studies*. London: Routledge.

Hope, A. (2015a) 'Governmentality and the "selling" of school surveillance devices', *Sociological Review*, 63(4): 840–57.

Hope, A. (2015b) 'Schoolchildren, governmentality and national e-safety policy discourse', *Discourse: Studies in the Cultural Politics of Education*, 36(4): 343–53.

Hulsey, N. and J. Reeves (2014) 'The gift that keeps on giving: Google, Ingress, and the gift of surveillance', *Surveillance and Society*, 12(3): 389–400.

Kerr, A., S. De Paoli and M. Keatinge (2014) 'Surveillant assemblages of governance in massively multiplayer online games: a comparative analysis', *Surveillance and Society*, 12(3): 320–36.

Lyon, D. (2001) *Surveillance society: monitoring everyday life*. Buckingham: Open University Press.

Lyon, D. (2007) *Surveillance studies: an overview*. Cambridge: Polity Press.

Marx, G. (1988) *Undercover: police surveillance in America*. Berkeley: University of California Press.

Merrifield, L., M. Males and C. Flanagan (2007) 'Safety first?', *Atlantic Monthly*, 300(3): 17.

Microsoft (2014) '*Xbox.com terms of use*'. Available online at www.xbox.com/en-CA/Legal/LiveTOU (accessed 29.10.2014).

Neopets (n.d.) 'Parental consent form'. Available online at www.neopets.com/coppa/consentform.phtml (accessed 29.10.2014).

New York Times (2013) 'World of Spycraft?', 9 Sept. Available online at http://takingnote.blogs.nytimes.com/2013/12/09/world-of-spycraft/?_r=0 (accessed 29.10.2014).

O'Donnell, C. (2014) 'Getting played: gamification, bullshit, and the rise of algorithmic surveillance', *Surveillance and Society*, 12(3): 349–59.

Rose, N. and P. Miller (1992) 'Political power beyond the state: problematics of government', *British Journal of Sociology*, 43(2): 173–205.

Schechner, R. (1994) 'Ritual and performance', in T. Ingold (ed.), *Companion encyclopedia of anthropology*. London: Routledge.

Steeves, V. (2012) 'Hide and seek: surveillance of young people on the Internet', in D. Lyon, K. D. Haggerty and K. Ball (eds), *The international handbook of surveillance studies*. London: Routledge.

Turkle, S. (1995) *Life on the screen: identity in the age of the Internet*. New York: Simon & Schuster.

Turner, V. (1983) 'Body, brain and culture', *Zygon*, 18(3): 221–46.

Vie, S. (2014) 'Casual surveillance: why we should pay attention to Candy Crush Saga and other casual games', *First Person Scholar*. Available online at www.firstpersonscholar.com/casual-surveillance/ (accessed 19.02.2015).

Wark, M. (2007) *Gamer theory*. Cambridge, MA: Harvard University Press.

Welsh, T. (2007) 'Review of gaming: essays on algorithmic culture', Resource Center for Cyberculture Studies. Available online at http://rccs.usfca.edu/bookinfo.asp%3FReviewID=474&BookID=364.html (accessed 19.05.2016).

Whitson, J. R. (2013) 'Gaming the quantified self', *Surveillance and Society*, 11(1/2): 163–76.

Whitson, J. R. and B. Simon (2014) 'Editorial: game studies meets surveillance studies at the edge of digital culture: an introduction to a special issue on surveillance, games and play', *Surveillance and Society*, 12(3): 309–19.

Wilson, M. (2012) 'Location-based services, conspicuous mobility, and the location-aware future', *Geoforum*, 43(6): 1266–75.

Winner, L. (1977) *Autonomous technology: technics-out-of-control as a theme in political thought*. Cambridge, MA: MIT Press.

13 Terra Cognita

Surveillance of young people's favourite websites

Valerie Steeves

In 1999, when MediaSmart's Young Canadians in a Wired World Project was initiated,[1] marketers were found to be among the first sector to take notice of the children who were beginning to flock to the Internet. Online branded playgrounds seamlessly blended commercial content into advergames; product spokes-characters like Toucan Sam, the cartoon mascot for Kellogg's Fruit Loops cereal, sought to build relationships between children and products; and quizzes and other forms of interactive media encouraged them to divulge personal information in exchange for opportunities to win contests or points (Center for Media Education, 1996; United States, 1998). Many of the children and parents we spoke to at the time saw this as a positive aspect of their online lives. From their perspective, these activities were not just fun; the sites that belonged to corporations they 'knew' were trustworthy, and the brands they encountered online were 'friends' with whom they could safely interact (Media Awareness Network, 2004: 13).

Although concerns about the potentially deceptive nature of commercial practices targeting young people had been raised as early as 1996 (Center for Media Education, 1996), legislators in North America and Europe largely saw the profusion of children's sites through the lens of economic growth. They accordingly sought to balance concerns about commercialisation with the needs of the emerging online marketplace through the enactment of privacy laws (Steeves, 2015a). These laws typically required transparency and/or consent mechanisms to enable children (and their parents) to make informed decisions about the information they chose to disclose to the corporations that owned the sites they visited (Grimes, 2008; Steeves, 2015a, 2015b).

Since those early days of the net, websites have developed increasingly sophisticated methods to collect vast amounts of data about young people as they chat, surf and play online. The goal is to deepen children's relationships with commercial products through the use of micro-targeted 'one-on-one' marketing and communications strategies that create a cognitive, emotional and behavioural relationship between the child and the brand (Montgomery, 2015). However, after privacy legislation was put in place to protect children, policymakers – who are increasingly focused on the two 'Cs' of children's online exposure to offensive *content* and *contact* with potentially dangerous strangers (Steeves and Bailey, 2013) – largely lost interest in what Cairns calls 'the third "C": *commercialism*' (Nairn, 2008: 240 emphasis added).

A growing number of academics have called for a reinvigorated debate on the effect of commercial surveillance in children's networked spaces (Buckleitner, 2008; Grimes, 2008, 2015; Grimes and Shade, 2005; Hasebrink *et al.*, 2008; Montgomery, 2007, 2015; Nairn, 2008; Steeves, 2006, 2007). This chapter contributes to that debate by providing a snapshot of surveillance practices used on popular websites. It also presents quantitative findings on young people's attitudes towards this surveillance. I argue that contrary to popular conceptions, many young people are both increasingly sceptical about commercial surveillance and dissatisfied with the kinds of privacy protections that were intended to protect them from commercial manipulation. Moreover, the ubiquity of commercial collection on the sites they inhabit strongly suggests that current regulations do little to restrict surveillance but instead legitimise the rampant commodification of their online communications. Accordingly, I call for more nuanced and critical regulatory interventions that can better insulate children from marketplace logics and push back against the ongoing commodification of the networked spaces in which they play, learn and mature.

Methodology

In 2013, as part of Phase III of the Young Canadians in a Wired World Project, 5,436 young people aged 9–17 years in schools across Canada were surveyed. Participants were recruited through school boards and schools and both parental consent and the child's assent were obtained. Approximately one-third (1,721) of the surveys were completed on paper and the remaining two-thirds (3,715) were completed electronically. Statistical analysis was conducted by Directions Research, Inc.[2] Among other things, participants were asked to identify their five favourite sites on the Internet, resulting in a list of more than 3,000 individual sites. The sites on this list were ranked according to the percentage of participants who included them on their favourite five, and a list of the top 50 sites was generated. Content analysis was then used to identify the presence, length and complexity of privacy policies, and the number of trackers and other forms of surveillance on each site.

The top 50: an overview

Although there is a great deal of diversity in the 3,000 sites participants listed in total, the top 50 list is made up of specific types of sites (see Table 13.1). Gaming sites are the most prevalent (21 sites), followed by social media (13 sites), sports and entertainment (8 sites), informational tools (4 sites), online stores (3 sites) and free email services (2 sites). Slightly more than half (27) of the sites are intended for a general adult audience; the remaining 23 sites specifically target young people. All of the 50 sites on the list collect personal and non-personal information, and 48 of them – with the exception of Wikipedia (no. 10) and Animal Jam (which is operated by the National Geographic Society) – use that information to generate profit.

Table 13.1 Top 50 sites by order of popularity

1. youtube.com	18. addictinggames.com*	35. bitstrips.com
2. facebook.com	19. clubpenguin.com*	36. coolmath4kids.com*
3. google.com	20. pubtropica.com*	37. kijiji.ca
4. twitter.com	21. moshimonsters.com*	38. fantage.com*
5. tumblr.com	22. reddit.com	39. nba.com
6. instagram.com	23. andkon.com*	40. ytv.com*
7. minecraft.net*	24. roblox.com*	41. agame.com*
8. miniclip.com*	25. yahoo.com	42. sumdog.com*
9. hotmail.com	26. skype.com	43. tsn.com
10. wikipedia.com	27. family.ca*	44. ask.fm
11. y8.com*	28. nhl.com	45. armorgames.com*
12. google.ca	29. coolmath-games.com*	46. wattpad.com
13. netflix.com	30. kizi.com*	47. 9gag.com
14. gmail.com	31. pornhub.com	48. itunes.com
15. pinterest.com	32. girlsgogames.com*	49. weheartit.com
16. friv.com*	33. ebay.com	50. moviestarplanet.com*
17. webkinz.com*	34. animaljam.com*	

*Children's site.

After YouTube, which is the most popular site across all age groups, social media dominate the top 10 favourites (nos. 2, 4, 5 and 6). This preference for social media is particularly pronounced among participants aged 13–17 years; it is notable that teenaged girls selected social media sites for five of the top seven slots. Although younger respondents (aged 9–12 years) tend to prefer gaming sites, Facebook (no. 4 for boys and no. 2 for girls) and Twitter (no. 10 for boys and no. 7 for girls) both make their top 10 lists, even though the sites expressly forbid children under 13 years of age from participating. In addition, three of the five gaming sites on the top 10 list for young girls (nos. 4, 5 and 8) incorporate elements of social media into their design.

This preference for social media is also reflected in the finding that children's use of social media tends to start young and grows across age groups. Thirty per cent of the 11-year-olds we surveyed reported that they have created their own social media pages where they post their own comments or photos. By the age of 12 years, the percentage of children posting content on their own sites doubles to 60 per cent, and from the age of 13 to17 years, it increases from 76 to 90 per cent. Young people who use social media also tend to do so fairly frequently; half (49 per cent) of the oldest participants are on social media on a daily basis, and more than half of all age groups (approximately 55 per cent) use social media once a week or more. Accordingly, a large number of teens are disclosing personal information on social media as a matter of course.

Social media has clearly increased the amount of digital information young people reveal as they go about their daily lives. But its growing popularity has also changed the kinds of online surveillance young people experience. In 2005,[3] when half of the top 10 were gaming sites (Steeves, 2005), information was typically collected in the background as children surfed the sites and played the games available to them. Since many of the sites did not require registration to play, there was an element of (restricted) anonymity for the children who frequented them. In contrast, social media in general is predicated upon express disclosure on the part of site users who often identify themselves by their real names.[4] Although information about the links they click, the content they 'like' and with whom they communicate continues to be collected in the background, that information is used in combination with the information they voluntarily disclose to create highly detailed, individualised profiles which are, in turn, used to shape their interactions (Montgomery, 2015).

The kind of voluntary disclosure common on social media is also becoming more prevalent on other types of platforms. Most notably, a number of the gaming sites on the list now incorporate chat functions so players can talk to each other as they play. Even though pseudonyms may be used, the information collected from their conversations is linked to an IP address and helps to build individual profiles of unique players. Moreover, a number of sites encourage users to log in using their Facebook or Google Plus accounts, which often enables site owners to link their online behaviours with their real names and locations. Accordingly, the space for anonymous online play enjoyed in 2005 has largely been replaced with an expectation that users will publicly perform a singular and 'real' identity that is often linked to their name, their physical location and their physical appearance as portrayed in photos.

The collection of children's information in 2013 is also significantly shaped by the fact that *more* young people now tend to congregate on the *same* sites and that many of these same sites are owned by a small number of large high-tech companies. Again, the contrast with the 2005 list is striking, as none of the sites of the top 10 list in 2005 attracted the votes of more than one-fifth of the respondents and there was no concentration of corporate ownership. For example, the no. 1 site in 2005 (Addicting Games) was selected by only 18 per cent of respondents, and more than half of the sites on the 2005 list attracted the support of less than 5 per cent of respondents (Steeves, 2005). By way of contrast, a remarkable 75 per cent of respondents in 2013 voted for top site YouTube, and the next three most popular sites each garnered the support of one quarter or more of respondents. Even the no. 10 site on the 2013 list was selected by 10 per cent of respondents.

In addition, although all of the 10 top sites in 2005 were owned by corporations, eight out of 10 were relatively small companies whose main business was tied to online gaming or music. The large corporations on the list included YTV, a television station targeting youth, and Candystand, an advergaming site created by Nabisco, Inc. to market its candy products. This differs sharply from the picture in 2013, when two corporations, in particular, dominated the top 10: Google (which also owns YouTube) and Facebook (which also owns Instagram). Other high-tech giants, including Twitter, Yahoo (which owns Tumblr) and Microsoft (which owns Hotmail), also made the 2013 top 10.

This concentration of ownership in a small number of large tech corporations is a significant factor in young people's experiences of surveillance. Although the commercialisation of young people's online environment has been taking place for some time (Davies, 2010), the commercial agenda behind children's favourite sites – i.e. disclosure of personal and/or non-personal information in exchange for free access to content – is more deeply entrenched when the major players, like Google and Facebook, operate integrated information-collection systems across the sites they own as well as the sites owned by their (largely unnamed) corporate partners and use the information they collect for marketing purposes. As Montgomery notes (2015: 773–4), 'The entire digital media enterprise has been structured to facilitate and maximize user interaction with brand promotion and marketing, and to enable continuous monitoring and analysis of all these interactions in real time'.

Certainly, advertising is ubiquitous on the top 50 sites: 49 are populated by advertisements (the exception is no. 10, Wikipedia), ranging from ads for site products/services and traditional ads for third parties, to 'pre-roll' ads on videos, sponsored content, product placement and advergames. But the real goal is less to advertise and more to blend marketing messages into the social environment in a seamless and natural way (Calvert, 2008). Instagram summarises it well on their Sponsored Photos and Videos page: 'Our aim is to make any advertisements you see feel as natural to Instagram as the photos and videos many of you already enjoy …'.

The naturalisation of commercial content in children's play and social interaction is also normalised through games and other activities that present commerce as a form of play/entertainment (Chung and Grimes, 2005; Nansen *et al.*, 2012). This is key to understanding how commercial surveillance shapes young people's online experiences because the information corporations collect is used to encourage certain kinds of identities that are consistent with commercial messaging. For example, sites on the top 50 list, like Webkinz and Club Penguin, encourage children to earn points to buy things for their virtual pets. Girlsgogames.com contains a series of Shopaholic Games, where players go on shopping sprees for dresses, shoes, make-up, jewellery and fast food in glamorous locales like Paris, Milan and Hawaii. Weheartit reinforces shopping as entertainment through the 'Swag tag', where young people can post photos of their latest purchases.

Even Animal Jam, operated by the non-profit National Geographic Society, greets new users with a treasure box, which one of the animals points out by saying, 'Hey look, free stuff!', and then encourages the child to purchase new clothes and items for their virtual house. They are then asked, 'What would you like to do next?' and given four options (in the following order): go to your den (a virtual home they can decorate with virtual purchases); shop for new clothes; play games; and go on an adventure. Even as they play or go on an adventure, they are greeted with ads, such as this one, encouraging them to upgrade their den: 'Introducing the BEACH HOUSE, the incredible NEW DEN filled with huge ROOMS, great VIEWS, and your own PRIVATE BEACH!! Pick up your own BEACH HOUSE in the Diamond Shop today!' As Grimes (2015: 129) notes, the

> type of play afforded is noteworthy in both its limited scope and its close alignment with consumerist values. … In the process, economic priorities not only come to shape and constrain the field of play, but also impose a particular, deeply ideological, vision of what children's play looks like.

Regulatory compliance

As noted above, the current regulatory regime is built upon an uneasy compromise that sought to encourage online commerce through the commodification of user data while still providing some protection for children's privacy. Although early concerns raised by the US-based Center for Media Education focused on the impact of deceptive trade practices that disguised market research labs as children's playgrounds, the US legislative debate was quickly overtaken by data-protection discourses that reduced the issues to informational control (Steeves, 2015b). The US model accordingly focused on mechanisms that would promote informed parental consent for children under 13 years to any collection and use of a child's personal information. In keeping with other data protection laws, information collectors were required to be transparent about their information practices and provide access so individuals could see and correct the data collected from them. But the crux of the regime rested on the requirement that websites seeking to collect personal information from children under 13 years of age were required to first obtain permission from their parents. Children aged 13 years and older, on the other hand, could consent on their own behalf.

Although Canada, Europe and Australia have typically relied on general data-protection legislation to regulate sites aimed at children, the reach of the US model is evidenced by the ways in which non-US sites have adopted US standards. This is most clearly reflected in the fact that the de facto age of consent for many non-US sites is 13, even though domestic laws regarding the ability of mature minors to consent on their own behalf mandate a different age.[5] This dominance of the US approach is, at least partly based on the popularity of US sites among non-US children. In the Canadian context, for example, more than half of the top 50 favourites (32) are owned by US-owned corporations.[6] Only seven are Canadian,[7] and the remaining ten sites are owned by corporations in the United Kingdom, the Netherlands, Luxembourg, Switzerland, Hong Kong and Sweden.[8]

On the positive side, all of these jurisdictions have data-protection laws in place that require corporations to make their information practices transparent and provide children (and/or their parents) with certain rights to control their information. And, at first blush, the regulatory regime appears to be working. All 50 sites had a privacy policy posted on the site and 46 could be located with a single click from the site's home page. The vast majority (92 per cent) were easy to find: The links on 12 sites were highly visible and particularly easy to find and the links on 34 sites were clearly visible to a user interested in learning about the site's information practices and willing to scroll down to the bottom of the page.[9] Only four were hard to find because of nondescript icons (friv.com and kizi.com) or because the user was required to click on a general link to 'FAQ' (andkon.com) or 'More' (ytv.com) before finding a link to 'Privacy Policy'. Interestingly, all four of the hard-to-find links were on sites specifically targeting children.

The length of the privacy policies varied significantly from 54 words on andkon.com to 7,250 words on Skype. On average, policies on children's sites are approximately 60 per cent as long as policies on adult sites

(2,044 and 3,468 words, respectively). However, the language in four-fifths of both children and adult policies was not highly accessible (i.e. written in short sentences, without technical terms) and policies on children's sites were slightly more likely – 35 per cent compared to 30 per cent of adult sites – to be written in inaccessible ways (i.e. long, compound sentences, undefined legal and technical terms). For example, the privacy policy on Miniclip (a gaming site for youth) states:

> Miniclip may disclose information to third parties in special cases, such as (1) when we have reason to believe that disclosing this information is necessary to identify, contact or bring legal action against someone who may be causing injury to or interference with Miniclip's property, visitors, or anyone else who could be harmed by such activities or to comply with the law, applicable regulations, governmental and quasi-governmental requests, court orders or subpoenas; (2) our agents, outside vendors or service providers to perform functions on our behalf (e.g., analyzing data, providing marketing assistance, providing customer service, processing orders, etc.); (3) when the information is provided to help complete a transaction for you; (4) if the disclosure is done as part of a purchase, transfer or sale of services or assets (e.g., in the event that substantially all of our assets are acquired by another party, customer information may be one of the transferred assets); or (5) as otherwise described in this Privacy Policy.

The length and inaccessibility of the policies may pose barriers to children who are attempting to learn what happens to their information on these sites. It is noteworthy that 68 per cent of our survey respondents mistakenly agreed with the statement, 'If a website has a privacy policy, that means it will not share my personal information with others.' A similar percentage (65 per cent) report that no one has ever explained a policy to them, which suggests that they are often struggling with policies without assistance from adults. But even students who have had a policy explained to them may need additional support, as they are *more* likely to agree with the above statement (70.3 per cent) than those who have not had an explanation (66.7 per cent).

Part of the confusion may also stem from the ways in which the policies talk about privacy. Many contain statements that they value user privacy in spite of broad collection, use and disclosure practices. Bitstrips is typical: 'At Bitstrips, we respect the privacy of our users. … By using the Service, you consent to our collection and use of personal data as outlined therein.' Others use empowering language and/or collapse privacy concerns into security and safety. For example, Google's privacy policy states:

> We know security and privacy are important to you – and they are important to us, too. We make it a priority to provide strong security and give you confidence that your information is safe and accessible when you need it. We're constantly working to ensure strong security, protect your privacy, and make

> Google even more effective and efficient for you. We spend hundreds of millions of dollars every year on security, and employ world-renowned experts in data security to keep your information safe. We also built easy-to-use privacy and security tools like Google Dashboard, 2-step verification and Ads Settings. So when it comes to the information you share with Google, you're in control.

Social media sites, in particular, tend to valorise 'sharing' and 'control'. For example, Facebook's privacy policy starts with the statement that, 'We give you the power to share as part of our mission to make the world more open and connected', and continues, 'You're in charge. We're here to help you get the experience you want.' Twitter's policy has a similar tone: 'Our Services are primarily designed to help you share information with the world. Most of the information you provide us through the Twitter Services is information you are asking us to make public.' However, it then goes on to list items that the site considers public, moving quickly from 'the messages you tweet' (clearly intended by the user to be distributed) to other information that is not so easily understood as 'public', including:

> the metadata provided with Tweets, such as when you Tweeted and the client application you used to Tweet; the language, country, and time zone associated with your account; and the lists you create, people you follow, Tweets you mark as favorites or Retweet, and many other bits of information that result from your use of the Twitter Services.

In this way, any conflict between the social value of privacy to the user and the commercial value of disclosure to the corporation collapses. If there is a privacy issue, it is generally seen as the responsibility of the user or his or her parents. Twitter concludes the above paragraph by telling users, 'When you share information or content like photos, videos, and links via the Services, you should think carefully about what you are making public.' Kizi tells its users that it collects 'non-personal information', such as IP address and click-through data, and suggests, 'For the protection of your privacy, we ask that you avoid sending us any and all personally identifiable information.' MovieStarPlanet states, 'we strongly encourage parents and guardians to take an active role in promoting online safety.' Animal Jam advises, 'Parents, you can take steps to protect your kids too. To learn more about how to protect your child online, read the helpful information provided by the [Federal Trade Commission].'

Accordingly, the regulatory framework provides for some level of transparency, but the length, wording and tone of policies may make it difficult for young people to fully understand the extent to which information about them is collected and commodified, and place the burden of limiting surveillance on them and/or their parents. Moreover, the adult sites on the top 50 list typically sidestep any additional protections that may be afforded for children by posting blanket prohibitions telling young people they are not to use their services. The majority

(20 out of 27) include a provision that children under 13 years are simply not allowed to access their services. Skype restricts users to those who are old enough to participate under the laws of the user's country of residence. The remaining sites are e-stores that either: restrict users to those 18 years and over (Netflix, Porn Hub, eBay); require children under 16 years to have their parents access their services (Kijiji); or sell merchandise to children under 13 years only through a shared family account (iTunes). The exception is again Wikipedia: It does not impose age restrictions, but it is also a non-profit site that does not commodify users' information.

Although the practical impact of these clauses is questionable, given that these sites all appear on the list of young people's favourites, they provide evidence to support a legal defence should any of these corporations be faced with lawsuits or other processes seeking to hold them accountable for their collection and use of children's information. As Nansen *et al.* (2012: 1222) concluded:

> the architectures of participation … are shaped not solely for the benefit of participants … just as much for the benefit of the digital object itself and for its value to owners. Web 2.0 is not just a user or social model, but also a technical and business model.

But perhaps the most important test of the value of the current framework is whether or not it limits surveillance in the first place. Our analysis indicates that commercial collection on these sites is rampant: 48 of them used trackers to continually collect the data users drop as they chat, play and entertain themselves.[10] The number of trackers per site ranged from 1 to 15, with an average of 5. Moreover, of the 40 sites that have privacy settings, only 6 were set to private by default.[11] The remaining sites were either set to public (16) or contained a mixture of public and private defaults (24). This suggests that the regulatory framework acts less to protect young people's privacy and more to legitimise the commercial collection and use of their data by providing a veneer of privacy protections that do little to nothing to limit commercial surveillance.

Surveillance and control of young people's communications

The near-ubiquitous presence of acceptable-use policies or 'community standards' on young people's favourite sites (found on 42 of the top 50 sites) also reshapes the kinds of surveillance they experience. These policies set out strict behavioural guidelines that are almost always defined and imposed by the corporation (only Wikipedia relies on norms and solutions negotiated by members of the Wiki community). On the majority of sites (78 per cent), users are expected to both comply with guidelines and monitor other users to ensure their compliance. The removal of non-compliant content is at the discretion of the site owners – Tumblr is the only site that even contacts the user accused of misbehaviour before taking action – and active moderation is common, especially on children's sites.

These practices not only normalise corporate surveillance, which takes on a protective function, but extend the surveillant gaze of the corporation by enlisting users as informants. Club Penguin has made this explicit, through the creation of its Penguin Spy Agency (PSA). Children who sign up to work for PSA are told that '*your duty* (as an agent) is to report any penguin that says bad words, asks or reveals personal information or is rude, mean or breaks any of the other rules.' This kind of peer surveillance reshapes the online environment to encourage conformity to corporate and commercial values (Marx and Steeves, 2010).

Chat among young children is also subjected to particularly tight controls on Webkinz, Club Penguin, Poptropica, Roblox and Animal Jam. All five sites enable parents to limit their children's communications to stock words and phrases and threaten to remove privileges from those who disobey the rules. The language is often quasi-criminal, as in the notice to parents posted in the Parents Area on Webkinz:

> Breaking any of the Rules may lead to one's account being silenced or banned from KinzChat PLUS for a period of time, or permanently, depending on the severity of the offense. For serious or repeat offenses one's account may also be banned permanently from the website.

However, the surveillant gaze behind the enforcement of these rules is legitimised by positioning the corporate site owner as a guardian of the young person's safety. The corporation is no longer a threat to privacy but is actively monitoring the child and ready to take action to keep her safe – from others or from herself. As Roblox states, the site has:

> a team of moderators who are constantly keeping an eye on discussion forums, fielding abuse reports from members, and screening uploaded content. These moderators follow our policies in regard to swearing and obscenities, messages and content of a sexual or violent nature, and any sort of aggressive or threatening communication … [an] infringing member is immediately suspended or permanently expelled.

From this perspective, the potential harm is not a loss of privacy vis-à-vis the corporation, but the possible harms of publicity: The child may be approached by malicious strangers or ill-intentioned peers; or the child may act badly in public as a result of his or her own poor judgement (Steeves and Bailey, 2013). Surveillance is presented as the solution and the commercial nature of corporate surveillance accordingly recedes from view.

Conclusion

Given the ubiquity of constant monitoring on our respondents' favourite websites, one might assume that young people are comfortable with commercial surveillance. However, the qualitative research that preceded our Phase II survey suggested that many young people are either ambivalent about corporate surveillance or see it as a 'creepy' form of 'stalking' (Steeves, 2012). To test this, we asked our survey respondents who *should* be able to see what they post on social media. Less than one-fifth (17 per cent) reported that the company that owns the site should be able to see their content, and only 5 per cent thought marketing companies that want to advertise to them should have access to their posts. The numbers are even lower when it comes to website/app companies or marketers tracking their location (4 per cent and 1 per cent, respectively).

This raises serious questions about young people's comfort with the current regulatory framework and its attempts to 'balance' online commerce and privacy. It is remarkable that 72 per cent of respondents reported that they did not like it when companies use their personal information to advertise to them,[12] and three quarters indicated that they want more control over what companies do with the photos and information they post online. This desire for control is understandable given the fact that many young people:

> spend very large amounts of time online, and in many ways, conduct their friendships through social networks, largely unaware of the level and intensity of scrutiny that takes place. … Yet, precisely at the times in their lives when they are forging their own identities, navigating their social worlds, and developing their abilities to form and sustain lasting relationships, their personal and social interactions are increasingly shaped and facilitated by the force of the digital marketplace (Montgomery, 2015: 775, 777).

Further research is needed to gauge the extent to which this surveillance constrains healthy child development (Nairn, 2008), but we must also begin to grapple with the political-economic factors at play (Grimes, 2015; Monahan, 2004). Now that children's digital culture is increasingly shaped by corporate interests (Nansen *et al.*, 2012), policymakers should revisit basic questions about commercialisation, question the use of networked technologies that operate as 'significant vectors for market infiltration' (Bartow, 2014: 36) and interrogate the ways that the networked spaces inhabited by children intensify their experience of surveillance, privilege a commercial model based on the rampant corporate collection of their information and 'constrain conceptions of the possible' (Bartow, 2014: 36).

Notes

1 MediaSmart's Young Canadians in a Wired World Project tracks young people's use of and perspectives on networked technologies. The Project has collected qualitative data from children aged 11–17 years and parents of children aged 11–17 years and quantitative data from more than 5,000 children aged 9–17 years, in three phases (2000–1, 2004–5 and 2012–13). Qualitative data were collected from teachers in Phase III, and a follow-up quantitative survey was completed by over 4,000 teachers in 2015. Full reports on each phase of the project can be found at http://mediasmarts.ca/research-policy.

2 For full details, see Steeves (2014: 42–50).

3 Respondents to the 2005 survey listed their top three, not their top five sites.

4 'Facebook users provide their real names and information, and we need your help to keep it that way' (www.facebook.com/legal/terms).
5 See, for example, Miniclip (based in Switzerland), Y8.com (based in Hong Kong), Webkinz and YTV (based in Canada) and Girlsgogames and Agame (based in The Netherlands).
6 This includes four companies that were purchased by US firms: Skype (which originated in Estonia); ask.fm (which originated in Latvia); Weheartit (which originated in Brazil); and Minecraft (which originated in Sweden).
7 Webkinz, Family.ca, YTV, NHL, Bitstrips, TSN and Wattpad.
8 Based on a whois search: Friv.com, Poptropica, Moshimonsters, Sumdog are based in the UK; Girlsgogames and Agame in The Netherlands; Pornhub in Luxembourg; Miniclip in Switzerland; Y8 in Hong Kong; and MovieStarPlanet in Sweden. There is no information on andkon, indicating where the site owner is located, and whois has no locational information for the URL registrant.
9 Very visible links were clearly labelled 'Privacy' or 'Privacy Policy' in regular or large-sized font and typically were easily found at the bottom of the home page without scrolling. Visible links were labelled 'Privacy' in small-sized font. Although they were also typically located at the bottom of the page, the user was required to scroll down through a significant amount of content.
10 Data was collected in October 2014 using Ghostery, an app that identifies over 2,000 trackers, including cookies, tags, web bugs, pixels, widgets and beacons. The number of trackers on sites can fluctuate. All sites of the top 50 list, except Wikipedia and friv.com, used at least one tracker.
11 There are twice as many children's sites with private defaults (4), as adult sites (2).
12 Girls are more likely than boys to report this (78 per cent of girls compared to 66 per cent of boys).

References

Bartow, S. M. (2014) 'Teaching with social media: disrupting present day public education', *Educational Studies*, 50(1): 36–64.

Buckleitner, W. (2008) *Like taking candy from a baby: how young children interact with online environments*. Flemington, NJ: Media Tech Foundation.

Calvert, S. L. (2008) 'Children as consumers: advertising and marketing', *Future of Children*, 18(1): 205–34.

Center for Media Education (1996) *The web of deception*. Washington, DC: Center for Media Education.

Chung, G. and S. M. Grimes (2005) 'Data mining the kids: surveillance and market research strategies in children's online games', *Canadian Journal of Communication*, 30(4): 527–48.

Davies, M. M. (2010) *Children, media and culture*. New York: McGraw Hill Open University Press.

Grimes, S. M. (2008) 'Researching the researchers: market researchers, child subjects and the problem of "informed" consent', *International Journal of Internet Research Ethics*, 1(1): 66–91.

Grimes, S. M. (2015) 'Playing by the market rules: promotional priorities and commercialization in children's virtual worlds', *Journal of Consumer Culture*, 15(1): 110–34.

Grimes, S. M. and L. R. Shade (2005) 'Neopian economics of play: children's cyberpets and online communities as immersive advertising in Neopets.com', *International Journal of Media and Cultural Politics*, 1(2): 181–98.

Hasebrink, U., S. Livingstone and L. Haddon (2008) *Comparing children's online opportunities and risks across Europe: cross-national comparisons for EU kids online*. London: EU Kids Online (Deliverable D3.2).

Marx, G. and V. Steeves (2010) 'From the beginning: children as subjects and agents of surveillance', *Surveillance and Society*, 7(3): 6–45.

Media Awareness Network (2004) *Young Canadians in a wired world, phase II: focus groups*. Ottawa: Media Awareness Network.

Monahan, T. (2004) 'Just another tool? Pedagogy and the commodifcation of education', *Urban Review*, 36: 271–92.

Montgomery, K. (2007) *Generation digital: politics, commerce, and childhood in the age of the Internet*. Cambridge, MA: MIT Press.

Montgomery, K. (2015) 'Youth and surveillance in the facebook era: policy interventions and social implications', *Telecom Policy*, 39(9): 771–86.

Nairn, A. (2008) '"*It does my head in … buy it, buy it, buy it!*" The commercialisation of children's websites', *Young Consumers*, 9(4): 239–53.

Nansen, B., K. Chakraborty, L. Gibbs, F. Vetere and C. Macdougall (2012) 'You do the math: mathletics and the play of online learning', *New Media and Society*, 14(7): 1216–35.

Steeves, V. (2005) *Young Canadians in a wired world, phase ii: trends and recommendations*. Ottawa: Media Awareness Network.

Steeves, V. (2006) 'It's not child's play: the online invasion of children's privacy', *University of Ottawa Law and Technology Journal*, 3(1): 169–88.

Steeves, V. (2007) 'The watched child: surveillance in three online playgrounds', in T. Collins, R. Grondin, V. Pinero *et al.* (eds.), *Proceedings of the International Conference on the Rights of the Child*. Montreal: Wilson Lafleur.

Steeves, V. (2012) *Young Canadians in a wired world, phase III: talking to youth and parents about life online*. Ottawa: MediaSmarts.

Steeves, V. (2014) *Young Canadians in a wired world, phase III: online privacy, online publicity*. Ottawa: MediaSmarts.

Steeves, V. (2015a) 'Now you see me: privacy, technology and autonomy in the digital age', in G. DiGiacomo (ed.), *Human rights*. Toronto: University of Toronto Press.

Steeves, V. (2015b) 'Privacy, sociality and the failure of regulation: lessons learned from young Canadians' online experiences', in B. Roessler and D. Mokrosinska (eds.), *Social dimensions of privacy: an anthology*. Cambridge: Cambridge University Press.

Steeves, V. and J. Bailey (2013) 'Will the real digital girl please stand up?', in H. Koskela and J. M. Wise (eds.), *New visualities, new technologies: the new ecstasy of communication*. Farnham, UK: Ashgate.

United States Federal Trade Commission (1998) *Privacy online: a report to Congress*. Washington, DC: Federal Trade Commission.

14 Rise of pre-emptive surveillance

Unintended social and ethical consequences

Rosamunde Van Brakel[1]

Several authors (Beck, 1992; Feeley and Simon, 1992; Garland, 2001; Rose, 1998), in their own ways and with different nuances and emphases, have argued that a 'risk society' or a culture of control emerged at the end of the twentieth century. At the same time, there have been huge developments in information technologies, leading to what some term the 'surveillance society' (Wood, 2006). One of the results of these parallel developments is the emergence of the so-called pre-emptive or pre-crime turn in criminal justice (Donkin, 2014; Wall, 2010; Zedner, 2007). Inspired by Lyon's (2001) definition of surveillance, pre-emptive surveillance can be defined as the systematic or targeted collection and processing of data of entities, which are used to make predictions about future harm on the basis of profiles, with the main goal of intervening before harm is done.

This chapter sets out to provide a socio-technical exploration of some of the main unintended social and ethical consequences of the implementation of pre-emptive surveillance practices in England and Wales in relation to children and youth. I focus on a case study from the RYOGENS (Reducing Youth Offending Generic Electronic National Solution) database and seek to (1) problematise the use of technological predictions from predictive interventions to big data approaches in relation to juvenile justice and social care; and (2) offer a more applied and empirical approach in comparison to somewhat disparate and broad theories in the area. I do so by bridging across surveillance studies, risk society and pre-emptive policy interventions in the broader sphere of criminal and social justice discourses. The chapter first explores the emergence of pre-emptive surveillance of children in England and, more specifically, the emergence of the RYOGENS database, before providing an overview of the main social and ethical consequences related to this database and pre-emptive surveillance in general.

'Pre-emptive turn'

There has been little discussion of how visions of a pre-crime society, or the pre-emptive turn, are intertwined with the emergence of the surveillance society. Although several authors refer to surveillance (Garland, 2001; Zedner, 2010), the role of technology and (technological) agency has largely been ignored.

Moreover, the pre-crime society is explained in terms of uncertainty (Zedner, 2007). This chapter presents the converse argument that pre-emptive surveillance is not about controlling or taming uncertainty; instead, pre-emption 'becomes a new (old) superstition, a courting of fates and furies in an attempt at one and the same time to know a determined future and to be able to reshape that determination in a god-like fashion' (Elmer and Opel, 2008: 21). It can be seen as the imaginary of surveillant control, which is:

> a fantastic dream of seeing everything capable of being seen, recording every fact capable of being recorded, and accomplishing these things, whenever and wherever possible, prior to the event itself ... it circulates as an effective mechanism in the technical evolution of control in postindustrial societies. (Bogard, 1996: 4–5)

It is about controlling not the present but the future.

In the pre-emptive surveillance logic, authorities can punish or intervene pre-emptively because they (think they) *know* the future and believe their prediction is always true (Bigo, 2010). The result is an unfettered and uncritical belief in the predictive powers of statistics and/or technology, which fails to recognise its limitations (Van Brakel and De Hert, 2011). This mind-set can be recognised in several criminal justice domains, including anti-terrorism strategies, policing and probation, as well as in youth justice and crime prevention in the form of early intervention strategies (Case and Haines, 2013; McCullough and Pickering, 2009; Van Brakel and De Hert, 2011; Zedner, 2007).

The Emergence of 'pre-emptive logic' and the surveillance of children in England

According to Muncie and Goldson (2006), the most significant developments in the last decades in youth justice have been: the targeting of the non-criminal as well as the criminal within formal systems of justice; the persistent punitive incarceration of children, despite a 'new' rhetoric of youth-crime prevention, restoration and social inclusion; and finally, a concern with 'what works'. This rhetoric can be traced back to the Audit Commission's (1996) *Misspent Youth* report, in which the slogan 'tough on crime, tough on causes of crime' made its entrance. The report was empirically underpinned by the seminal longitudinal Cambridge Study of Delinquent Development (West and Farrington, 1973), which claimed to identify risk factors that increase the probability of offending and concluded that criminality can be prevented by implementing measures designed to counteract them. This is what Case and Haines (2008) have called the 'Risk Factor Prevention Paradigm'.

Ten years after the *Misspent Youth* report, former prime minister Tony Blair asserted that there is 'a very clear body of evidence that you can predict reasonably accurately the kids and the families that are going to be difficult in the future'.

It was clear to him that government policy should be directed at early intervention 'pre-birth, even'. He also stated, in a clear illustration of pre-emptive logic:

> If we are not prepared to predict and intervene far more early then there are children that are going to grow up in families that we know perfectly well are completely dysfunctional and the kids a few years down the line are going to be a menace to society and actually a threat to themselves. (Blair, 2006)

In parallel to this development in youth justice, child protection policy saw significant changes. The way in which information was shared between agencies and the provision of services for children in need became a high-profile issue in England following the death in 2000 of Victoria Climbié, a 9-year-old girl who died as a result of abuse and neglect, and similar cases. Several agencies involved knew the child was being abused, but no one took up the responsibility to intervene when the child was in danger. The public inquiry into the child's death indicated that causes for this could be found in the chronic shortage of skilled staff and funding and bad coordination between the agencies involved (Laming, 2003).

The new Children Act of 2004 addressed this problem.[2] It emphasised even more strongly than its 1989 predecessor that there should be improved coordination between agencies involved in child protection and crime prevention (for further discussion, see Parton, 2008). So, while the Climbié case was not the direct driver, it served as a trigger to give an extra push to certain policy proposals (see Keymolen and Broeders, 2013, for similar developments in the Netherlands).

The new Children Act had two main goals. The first was to improve data sharing between agencies, so that local authorities could have easy access to information about the children in their area, what services they are in contact with and the contact details of the professionals involved. The main method suggested for doing this is the application of databases. The second goal was to identify and keep track of those at risk from abuse, neglect, school exclusion, offending and social exclusion and intervene before it is too late. In other words, the aim was to predict which children will become criminals or victims in the future. As a result of this new policy and developments in e-government, in 2002, a pilot project emerged, which claimed it could address some of the issues associated with a lack of inter-agency communication and data sharing. This signalled the birth of the RYOGENS database.

RYOGENS and its successor ShareCare are prime examples of the 'electronic turn' in children's services (both child protection and youth justice) instigated by the Labour government (Garrett, 2009). The ideas that crime runs in certain families and that anti-social behaviour in childhood is a predictor of later criminality underpinned Labour's policy and continued to be apparent in the subsequent government's discourse (Cameron, 2011). Although the coalition government that came into power in 2010 criticised Labour's deployment of surveillance technologies, a very similar discourse can be seen in the new social justice strategy it proposed in 2012 (Department for Work and Pensions, 2012). Meanwhile, new initiatives are emerging to explore the application of 'big data' solutions in this area. For instance, London's council, in partnership with a technology firm Xantura, is developing a predictive risk model for young children to help social workers intervene early when they are in danger of being harmed and predict and identify potential and emerging troubled families (Xantura, n.d.).

Ryogens

RYOGENS started out in 2003 as a national project funded by the Office of the Deputy Prime Minister (ODPM), as part of the e-Government program of the British government to enable all local authority services by 2005.[3] The consulting firm Deloitte was appointed to design and implement the program, Esprit to build the technical solution and Attenda to provide the external hosting services to the RYOGENS partners. Warwickshire operated as Lead Authority from May 2003, originally with Tower Hamlets and Lewisham, which later withdrew. Coventry, West Berkshire, and Redcar and Cleveland joined as second wave authorities (Youth Offending Service, 2005).

After pilot phases, an evaluation was conducted by the University of Oxford (Hill *et al.*, 2004). The evaluation was quite positive; among the findings were that practitioners overwhelmingly felt that there was a need for something like RYOGENS and considered it an important step towards delivering both improved information sharing between agencies and the early identification of young people at risk. After funding ceased in 2005, the project migrated from the ODPM to Esprit Ltd and was renamed ShareCare, with a broader scope focusing on vulnerable children in general.[4] The initial authorities using RYOGENS continued using the ShareCare tool, which was later taken over by OLM Group (OLM Group, 2012). The following provides an overview of the first incarnation of the RYOGENS database.

RYOGENS is an online database in which professionals from agencies, like Education, Police, Health Services, Social Services, the Youth Offending Team and Housing Services, can enter their concerns about a child or youth that they feel is at risk. After the professional has filled in personal details about the child, he/she can choose from a list of 40 factors (see Table 14.1) that they think characterises the child or youth. When concerns develop about a child and reach a certain threshold, the system generates an alert, which is sent to the RYOGENS management function.

The factors are based on the Youth Justice Board's ONSET form, together with the Department of Health's Assessment Framework for children in need and their families.[5] These two tools provide risk factors that have been identified in children who are in trouble. Specifying which risk factors apply to the child or youth in question is intended to enable prediction of whether the child is likely to become at risk of committing a crime (Anderson *et al.*, 2006, 2009). The ultimate goal is to reduce crime and anti-social behaviour by providing better support to children at risk and their families, through improving youth justice practices and overcoming poor communication and coordination between the disparate agencies involved.

Table 14.1 RYOGENS factors — Checkbox list designed to identify risk factors

Child: mental health	Absent from home	Child: substance abuse	Frequently moving house
Child: physical health	Involvement in crime/antisocial behaviour	Non-constructive leisure/easily bored	Caring for relatives at home
Child: sexual health	Denies involvement in crime/antisocial behaviour	No other agency support	Lack of family support
Child: mental well-being	Self-harm	Parent: physical health	Domestic conflict/ violence
Missed medical appointment	Dangerous behaviour	Parent: mental health	Family and/or peers involved in crime/ antisocial behaviour
Not registered with healthcare professional	Has harmed others	Parenting difficulties	Living in high-crime area
Bad behaviour in school	Has intent to harm others	Parental lack of awareness of child's needs	Animal cruelty
Exclusion from school	Suffering actual harm	Parent: substance misuse	Substance availability
Learning difficulties	Perpetrator of bullying/harassment	Lack of facilities/ equipment	Social isolation
Poor school attendance/truanting	Victim of bullying/ harassment	Financial and/or housing difficulties	Negative home influence on education

Social and ethical issues

The implementation of the RYOGENS database and similar case-management software has been subjected to little critical reflection or consideration of what social and ethical issues might emerge as a result. Previous research exploring the unintended consequences of such developments is of two types. The first includes policy reports and publications that focus on the human rights consequences of the use of databases in government policy (Anderson *et al.*, 2006, 2009; Dowty, 2008; Dowty and Korff, 2009). These publications have a clear focus on the use of the technology and the privacy and data protection risks accompanying it. The second type mainly focuses on questioning the effectiveness of risk assessment and the 'electronic turn' in children's services and youth justice (Case and Haines, 2013; Garrett, 2009; Warner and Sharland, 2010). The former pays little attention to issues surrounding effectiveness and social consequences, while the latter pays little to the consequences of the use of these technologies, such as risks to privacy or other ethical questions. This section, therefore, aims to provide a more holistic overview of some of the main social and ethical issues, taking both technology and methodology seriously and highlighting some previously overlooked issues.

Privacy and Dignity

Privacy means the right to protect actions and thoughts that persons want to keep to themselves and it is closely related to intimacy (Dratwa, 2014). It is not an absolute right and, especially in the case of children, it needs to be balanced with the child's interest. For example, in cases of child abuse, it is sometimes necessary to override privacy for the safety of the child. However, as Munro (2006) argues:

> the new policy extends this level of intrusion into families that are not even suspected of abusing their children, and to all concerns about children's development. It will also over-stretch scarce resources, damage parents' confidence and divert services from focusing on real cases of abuse.

Children need their own space, both literally and figuratively, to realise their capabilities and be able to flourish as human beings. Dignity means respect for the need to have one's own space and one's secrets (Dratwa, 2014). Before implementing such technologies, policymakers must consider the potential impacts. There are many questions that need addressing before the roll-out of data-gathering technologies (Rooney, 2010). How does the use of these technologies contribute to flourishing, well-being and the future of the child and to their life chances? More specifically, how will the retention of data affect their employment opportunities or their sense of well-being if they become stigmatised as a potential criminal? How does this affect the identity and self-image of these children? How might these technologies change the way children conduct their day-to-day activities, build relationships with others and come to an understanding of who they are and the world they live in? Dowty (2008: 120) makes an especially important observation that it 'is meaningless to tell a child that they have independence of thought and the private space to discover who they are, if we are habitually demonstrating through our actions that this is simply not true'. Privacy is important for a child's development as the gradual evolution of 'the capacity to be alone' is essential to imagination, play and the 'symbol-making' at the heart of the creative process and essential to the development of an authentic self (Dowty, 2008, citing Winnicott, 1971).

Trust

The information that is collected about children in such databases is often sensitive and usually that which the children in question mostly would want to keep private. Information that previously would only have been accessible to a social worker with whom the child had built up a rapport is now entered into a centralised database without a clear sense of exactly who will be able to access the information now and in the future. Data retention is a problem because for children to be able to grow, there needs to be room for forgiveness and forgetfulness (Warnick, 2007). For social workers, gaining trust is the starting point of being able to work with vulnerable children; so, the fact that private information is now entered into a system that is beyond the control of that individual or agency can have a serious impact on trust relations between social worker and child.

This process could affect the level of trust that children place in government agencies in the future. For example, recent empirical research by Brayne (2014) found that individuals who have been stopped by the police, arrested, convicted or incarcerated are less likely to interact with institutions, including medical, financial, labour market and educational institutions, than their counterparts who have had no contact with the criminal justice system (CJS). As CJS contact is disproportionately distributed, the study suggests that avoidance is a potential mechanism through which the CJS contributes to social sorting and increased marginalisation. One could hypothesise that people who had been in contact with these kinds of data collection systems as a child had a negative experience, felt that their privacy was violated and/or felt stigmatised will try and avoid other institutions that use similar data collection mechanisms. In a 'big data' society where data collection is increasingly necessary to obtain rights, this will contribute to social exclusion of already marginalised social groups (Lerman, 2013), raising questions of justice and fairness.

Justice and fairness

Pre-emptive methodologies, such as RYOGENS, give rise to serious issues of justice. Individuals or groups may be stigmatised and discriminated against, based on simple prejudices of the professionals, faulty statistical methods or problems with the methodology. The risk that certain children will be systematically and disproportionately targeted as potential criminals is high, and the resulting stigma is almost impossible to 'shake off', potentially leading to a self-fulfilling prophecy (Jussim *et al.*, 2003) whereby the stigmatised child begins to engage in crime having internalised it as a fait accompli.

Such stigmatisation has very serious consequences for flourishing and well-being in later life and the life chances of these children (see, for example, Farrington *et al.*, 1978; Goffman, 1963/1990). Hence, it also contributes to normalisation processes and chilling effects (Raab and Goold, 2011; Wood and Webster, 2009). On the one hand, people might conform to certain habits or codes not because they want to or truly embrace them but because they do not want to be stigmatised as potential criminals; on the other hand, people might not speak out when witnessing injustice because they are afraid. Sorting people into categories of normal, abnormal, potential criminal, potential victim, and so on creates a climate of fear and distrust in which social cohesion deteriorates (Gandy, 1993; Lyon, 2003). Further, the increased aggregation of data from all areas of our lives in the context of big data, in combination with all other surveillance technologies, will increase both normalisation and chilling effects.

Transparency and accountability

It is important to distinguish between transparency of the work conducted through ICT systems and the transparency of the technology in general. Often, transparency is suggested as the key to solve the issues of privacy, data protection and other fundamental rights that are generated by new data collection systems. Social work ICT systems provide more transparency and, in turn, more accountability, since they provide a service trail relating to each child. When something goes wrong, it is easier to establish why and how. By entering information into standardised forms, work becomes more transparent and predictable and classification and processing of data becomes easier. However, the forms are also tools of control and surveillance, as Franko Aas (2005: 153) points out:

> They are the tools that enable a shift of discretion and power from professionals to administrators … Managerial control in contemporary … systems is based on limiting the access of certain groups to introduce alternative types of knowledge and language that do not correspond with closed-ended formats and classifications.

Paradoxically, increasing transparency by using ICT systems brings new risks to the privacy and safety of the children concerned. Databases, such as RYOGENS, have the potential to be interlinked with other systems, creating new ways in which to correlate and assemble information, creating profiles of individuals in a way previously impossible. It is not clear how the resulting 'data-doubles' (Poster, 1990) are governed nor who develops the code underlying definitions of risk and to what end. Thus, the systems become less transparent again, with consequences for accountability. Furthermore, power relations are not straightforward, top-down and panoptic, but diffuse; this has consequences for safety and justice in the sense that accountability, too, is diffused (Haggerty and Ericson, 2000; Rose, 2000). It becomes increasingly unclear who is responsible. Hence, the policy of improving data sharing and overcoming communication problems may actually exacerbate issues of transparency and accountability.

Efficacy of pre-emptive surveillance databases

The predictive utility and accuracy of the applied risk factors have been assumed and largely imputed from previous risk-factor research, such as West and Farrington's (1973) study, rather than established via evaluation of the actual tool. The existing evaluations of the ONSET tool have demonstrated a developmental bias and imputation of efficacy that have created a self-serving evidence-base for its use (Case and Haines, 2013) and, therefore, also for RYOGENS, which is based on the ONSET risk factors. The main issue here is that the major correlations of offending behaviour by young people, which was identified by risk-factor research, are neither sufficient for predicting nor indicating that the onset of exposure to risk factors predates the onset of offending. In addition, previous risk-factor research is characterised by numerous methodological flaws, such as over-simplification, imputation, determinism, psychosocial bias and a scant evidence base. As a consequence, ShareCare, which is based on RYOGENS, which is based on ONSET, which is based on ASSET, has 'updated, broadened and further engrained the misapplication of risk factor research within the youth justice process' (Case and Haines, 2013: 296).

These methodological problems mean that the number of false positives and false negatives will be high. On the one hand, there is the danger that children who are being abused or at risk of committing crimes are being ignored because they do not show the 'typical' risk factors, whereas on the other hand, there is the risk that parents are inappropriately scrutinised for potential child abuse and children for criminal behaviour. Apart from the false positives/negatives, the true positives also pose a problem. You can never test empirically what did not occur, so the system can be declared effective at diverting criminal activity, despite never knowing whether a crime would have indeed taken place without intervention.

In evidence to the House of Commons Home Affairs Committees (House of Commons, 2008), the UK Information Commissioner stated:

> Technology can take you a long way but it is not going to be 100% effective. When we raised concerns about profiling we raised concerns about social sorting. It is to signal the risks involved without the human intervention. Machines can do a lot to gather and to help you inform your decisions but without the human intervention I think there are grave dangers.

Simon Wessely's evidence to the same committee explained: 'The problem is that it is incredibly inaccurate. It is okay for a large group of people and so you can make predictions about large samples in populations, but when it comes to the individual, it is incredibly inaccurate'. Similarly, Carol Dezateux pointed out that 'just because certain factors are associated with an increased likelihood of a behaviour, it does not mean that just because they are present in an individual that they are behaving in this way' (House of Commons, 2008: 89–90).

Apart from the methodological flaws explained above, errors can also result from technological problems, human error and resistance. Technological failings include glitches, bugs and malfunctions, design (user-friendliness, errors in design) of the software, software not being updated or problems with hardware (system crashes). Unintended human error includes was incorrectly input by practitioners, problems with inputting information and wrong information unintentionally provided by children and parents. Purposeful resistance can lead to deliberately entering incorrect information or children and parents intentionally providing the wrong information. These issues can lead to false accusations, wrong conclusions and interventions and discrimination. Existing evidence about child protection and social work points to the fact that the main problems lie in how social work practice is organised, working conditions and lack of expertise and budget – they will not be solved by technology (Anderson *et al.*, 2006; Munro, 2011).

Finally, although RYOGENS and similar systems were introduced to improve communication between agencies, according to practitioners, it has had no positive effect. In fact, according to some who participated in this research, it can actually reduce communication. Whereas prior to the implementation of RYOGENS, practitioners might have communicated by phone or email, now they presume that all information is in the system and does not need to be discussed further.

Conclusion

This chapter has shown how pre-emptive surveillance has emerged in England, focusing specifically on one manifestation, the RYOGENS database, to highlight some of the main social and ethical consequences that have accompanied this development. This more holistic overview of the possible unintended consequences reveals that these technologies are problematic for several reasons, including, in summary: (1) current regulation and policy do not provide safeguards to protect children from the impacts of being stigmatised as potential criminals or parents being falsely accused of abusing their children or to prevent discrimination; (2) the impact of these technologies, in combination with the whole array of surveillance technologies children are exposed to (see Chapter 1; Steeves and Jones, 2010), on child development and children's trust in government and public services urgently needs more attention; (3) the impact of technological issues on the effectiveness of the assessment is rarely taken into account and there is too much belief by policymakers that the technology works. To conclude, information technology should be seen as one of several tools for modern management, not as the solution to the problem (Anderson *et al.*, 2009); (4) the evidence base of risk-factor research needs critical assessment; and (5) despite all the criticism so far, new technologies are being developed and considered for implementation, such as the mentioned predictive analytics software, to identify troubled families without taking into account any of the existing research and evidence on this (Anderson *et al.*, 2006, 2009; Case and Haines, 2013; Munro, 2011). Overall, the investment in developing, implementing and managing new pre-emptive technologies takes money away from funding other resources, such as extra staff, training and improving practices.

In summary, I argue that the enthusiasm for being able to predict the future needs to be tempered by thorough critical evaluation of the evidence. Policymakers should adopt a much more critical stance towards these new technologies, as well as to the promises of risk-factor research. Furthermore, decades of criminological research informs us that potential labelling effects and stigmatisation are very hard to escape and so, the generation of risk profiles from these databases are potentially impeding the life chances of the most vulnerable in our society. The methods upon which they are based are ethically dubious and, as yet, there is no published evidence to suggest that systems, such as RYOGENS, are actually effective in what they set out to do.

Notes

1 I would like to thank Emmeline Taylor, Tonya Rooney, an anonymous reviewer and Paul De Hert for their comments and constructive feedback on a previous version of this chapter.
2 The Children Act implemented the main proposals outlined in the Green Paper, *Every Child Matters*, published by the Department for Children Families and Education in September 2003.
3 The information provided on RYOGENS comes from the RYOGENS website, www.ryogens.org.uk, shortly after its launch. The website was later taken offline, but parts can still be consulted via a web archive: web.archive.org/web/20060110181231/http://www.localegovnp.org/default.asp?sID=1107187790130.
4 The majority of practitioners who were interviewed in the context of the PhD research on RYOGENS and ShareCare was less enthusiastic and sceptical that communication had improved as a result of using the system.
5 The ONSET framework is almost entirely based on ASSET (a profiling tool used to assess offenders and prepare pre-sentence reports for the courts). The tool lists a number of factors that suggest whether a young person is likely to become involved in crime. The risk factors used in these tools are based on West and Farrington (1973).

References

Anderson, R., L. Brown, R. Clayton, T. Dowty, D. Korff and E. Munro (2006) *Children's databases safety and privacy: a report for the Information Commissioner*. Sandy: Foundation for Information Policy Research. Available online at www.fipr.org/childrens_databases.pdf (accessed 15.02.2015).

Anderson, R., I. Brown, T. Dowty, P. Inglesant, W. Heath and A. Sasse (2009) *The database state*. York: Joseph Rowntree Reform Trust. Available online at www.jrrt.org.uk/sites/jrrt.org.uk/files/documents/database-state.pdf (accessed 15.02.2015).

Audit Commission (1996) *Misspent youth … young people and crime*. London: Audit Commission for Local Authorities and the National Health Service in England and Wales. Available online at:http://archive.audit-commission.gov.uk/auditcommission/subwebs/publications/studies/studyPDF/1172.pdf (accessed 15.02.2015).

Beck, U. (1992) *Risk society: towards a new modernity*. London: Sage.

Bigo, D. (2010) 'The future perfect of (iin)security (p8): pre-crime strategy, proactivity, preemption, prevention, precaution, profiling, prediction, and privacy'. *Interdisciplines*. Available online at http://archive-org.com/page/3765529/2014-02-22/http://www.interdisciplines.org/paper.php?paperID=342 (accessed 12.11.2014).

Blair, T. (2006) 'Interview with BBC on social exclusion', 31 Aug. [Full text no longer available; previously online at www.pm.gov.uk/output/Page10023.asp. More information available online at http://news.bbc.co.uk/2/hi/uk_politics/5301824.stm (accessed 12.11.2014).

Bogard, W. (1996) *The simulation of surveillance: hypercontrol in telematic societies*. Cambridge: Cambridge University Press.

Brayne, S. (2014) 'Surveillance and system avoidance: criminal justice contact and institutional attachment', *American Sociological Review*, 79(3): 367–91.

Cameron, D. (2011) 'Troubled families speech', 15 Dec. Available online at www.gov.uk/government/speeches/troubled-families-speech (accessed 12.11.2014).

Case, S. and K. Haines (2008) 'The rhetoric and reality of the "risk factor prevention paradigm" approach to preventing and reducing youth offending', *Youth Justice*, 8(1): 5–20.

Case, S. and K. Haines (2013) *Understanding youth offending: risk factor research, policy and practice*. London: Routledge.

Department for Work and Pensions (2012) *Social justice: transforming lives: policy paper*. London: Social Justice and Disadvantaged Groups Division Department for Work and Pensions. Available online at www.gov.uk/government/uploads/system/uploads/attachment_data/file/49515/social-justice-transforming-lives.pdf (accessed 12.11.2014).

Donkin, S. (2014) *Preventing terrorism and controlling risk: a comparative analysis of control orders in the UK and Australia*. Dordrecht: Springer.

Dowty, T. (2008) 'Overlooking children: an experiment with consequences', *Identity in the Information Society*, 1(1): 109–21.

Dowty, T. and D. Korff (2009) *Protecting the virtual child: the law and children's consent to sharing personal data*. London: Action on Rights for Children. Available online at http://medconfidential.org/wp-content/uploads/2013/03/Protecting-the-virtual-child.pdf (accessed 12.02.2015).

Dratwa, J. (ed.) (2014) 'Ethics of surveillance and security technologies', Opinion no. 28 of the European Group on Ethics in Science and New Technologies. Available online at http://ec.europa.eu/bepa/european-group-ethics/docs/publications/ege_opinion_28_ethics_security_surveillance_technologies.pdf (accessed 04.12.2014).

Elmer, G. and A. Opel (2008) *Preempting dissent: the politics of an inevitable future*. Winnipeg: Arbeiter Ring Publishing.

Farrington, D. P., S. G. Osborn and D. J. West (1978) 'The persistence of labelling effects', *British Journal of Criminology*, 18(3): 277–84.

Feeley, M. M. and J. Simon (1992) 'The new penology: notes on the emerging strategy of corrections and its implications', *Criminology*, 30(4): 449–74.

Franko Aas, K. (2005) 'The ad and the form: punitiveness and technological culture', in J. Pratt, D. Brown, M. Brown *et al.* (eds.), *The new punitiveness: trends, theories, perspectives*. Cullompton: Willan.

Gandy, O. H. (1993) *The panoptic sort: a political economy of personal information*. Boulder, CO: Westview Press.

Garland, D. (2001) *the culture of control: crime and social order in contemporary society*. Chicago: University of Chicago Press.

Garrett, P. M. (2009) *"Transforming" children's services: social work, neoliberalism and the "modern" world*. Maidenhead: McGraw Hill Open University Press.

Goffman, E. (1963/1990) *Stigma: notes on the management of spoiled identity*. London: Penguin Books.

Haggerty, K. D. and R. V. Ericson (2000) 'The surveillant assemblage', *British Journal of Sociology*, 51(4): 605–22.

Hill, R., S. Jones, C. Roberts and K. Baker (2004) *An evaluation of the early application and piloting of RYOGENS*. Oxford: Oxford University Press.

House of Commons (2008) *Home Affairs fifth report*. Available online at www.publications.parliament.uk/pa/cm200708/cmselect/cmhaff/58/5802.htm (accessed 12.02.2015).

Jussim, L., P. Palumbo, C. Chatman, S. Madon and A. Smith (2003) 'Stigma and self-fulfilling prophecies', in T. F. Heatherton, R. E. Kleck, M. R. Hebl and J. G. Hull (eds.) *The social psychology of stigma*. New York: Guildford Press.

Keymolen, E. and D. Broeders (2013) 'Innocence lost: care and control in Dutch DIGITAL YOUTH CAre', *British Journal of Social Work*, 43(1): 41 –63.

Laming, Lord (2003) *The Victoria Climbié inquiry*. Available online at www.gov.uk/government/uploads/system/uploads/attachment_data/file/273183/5730.pdf (accessed 10.02.2015).

Lerman, J. (2013) 'Big data and its exclusions', *Stanford Law Review Online* 66: 55–63.

Lyon, D. (2001) *Surveillance Society: monitoring everyday life*. Buckingham, Open University Press.

Lyon, D. (ed.) (2003) *Surveillance as social sorting: privacy, risk and automated discrimination*. London, Routledge.

McCullough, J. and S. Pickering (2009) 'Pre-crime and counter-terrorism: imagining future crime in the war on terror', *British Journal of Criminology*, 49(5): 628–45.

Muncie, J. and B. Goldson (2006) *Youth* Crime and Ju*stice*. London: Sage.

Munro, E. (2006) 'IT systems designed to protect kids will put them at risk instead', press release, 22 Nov. Available online at www.fipr.org/press/061122kids.html (accessed 04.12.2014).

Munro, E. (2011) *The Munro review of child protection final report: a child-centred system*. Available online at www.gov.uk/government/uploads/system/uploads/attachment_data/file/175391/Munro-Review.pdf (accessed 04.12.2014].

OLM Group (2012) 'OLM Group acquires Esprit', 29 May. Available online at www.olmgroup.com/systems/NewsAndEvents.aspx?id=905 (accessed 04.12.2014).

Parton, N. (2008) 'The "Change for Children" programme in England: towards the "preventative-surveillance state"', *Journal of Law and Society*, 35(1): 166–87.

Poster, M. (1990) *The mode of information: poststructuralism and social context*. Cambridge: Polity Press.

Raab, C. and B. Goold (2011) *Protecting information privacy: Equality and Human Rights Commission Research Report 69*. Available online at www.equalityhumanrights.com/sites/default/files/documents/research/rr69.pdf (accessed 15.02.2015).

Rooney, T. (2010) 'Trusting children: how do surveillance technologies alter a child's experience of trust, risk and responsibility?', *Surveillance and Society*, 7(3/4): 344–55.

Rose, N. (1998) 'Governing risky individuals: the role of psychiatry in new regimes of control', *Psychiatry, Psychology and Law*, 5(2): 177–95.

Rose, N. (2000) 'Government and control', *British Journal of Criminology*, 40: 321–39.

Steeves, V. and O. Jones (2010) 'Editorial: surveillance and children', *Surveillance and Society*, 7(3/4): 187–91.

Van Brakel, R. and P. De Hert (2011) 'Policing, surveillance and law in a pre-crime society: understanding the consequences of technology based strategies', *Journal of Police Studies*, 20(3): 163–92.

Wall, D. (2010) 'From post-crime to pre-crime: preventing tomorrow's crimes today', *Criminal Justice Matters*, 81(1): 22–3.

Warner, J. and E. Sharland (2010) 'Editorial: special issue: risk and social care', *British Journal of Social Work*, 0: 1035–45.

Warnick, B. (2007) 'Surveillance cameras in schools: an ethical analysis', *Harvard Educational Review*, 77(3): 317–43.

West, D. and D. Farrington (1973) *Who becomes delinquent?* London: Heinemann.

Wood, D. M. (ed.) (2006) *A report on the surveillance society: a report for the Information Commissioner*. Available online at www.ico.gov.uk/upload/documents/library/data_protection/practical_application/surveillance_society_full_report_2006.pdf (accessed 02.03.2015).

Wood, D. M. and W. R. Webster (2009) 'Living in surveillance societies: the normalisation of surveillance in Europe and the threat of Britain's bad example', *Journal of Contemporary European Research*, 5(2): 259–73.

Xantura (n.d.), 'Solutions: supporting troubled families'. Available online at www.xantura.com/pages/30/Supporting-families-with-complex-needs (accessed 19.12.2015).

Youth Offending Service (2005) *RYOGENS: final report. report of the chief executive and head of youth offending service, Warwickshire*. Available online at www.warwickshire.gov.uk/corporate/committe.nsf/f97183b3a13d475d80256f7000397ba1/3ff79c40c63bfda980257043002c7d71/$FILE/11%20Ryogens%20FINAL%20REPORT.am%20%5B29%20KB%5D.pdf (accessed 15.02.2015).

Zedner, L. (2007) 'Pre-crime and post-criminology?', *Theoretical Criminology*, 11(2): 261–81.

Zedner, L. (2010) 'Pre-crime and pre-punishment: a health warning', *Criminal Justice Matters*, 81(1): 24–5.

Index

For Product Safety Concerns and Information please contact our EU representative GPSR@taylorandfrancis.com
Taylor & Francis Verlag GmbH, Kaufingerstraße 24, 80331 München, Germany

www.ingramcontent.com/pod-product-compliance
Lightning Source LLC
Chambersburg PA
CBHW070419270326
41926CB00014B/2856